AUDIT COMMITTEES:

A Guide for Directors, Management, and Consultants

AUDIT COMMITTEES:

A Guide for Directors, Management, and Consultants

By
Frank M. Burke, J.D., CPA

and
Dan M. Guy, Ph.D., CPA

With Contributing Author
Kay W. Tatum, Ph.D., CPA

Foreword by The Honorable Barbara Hackman Franklin

ASPEN LAW & BUSINESS
A Division of Aspen Publishers, Inc.
Gaithersburg   New York

This publication is designed to provide accurate and authoritative information in regard to the subject matter covered. It is sold with the understanding that the publisher is not engaged in rendering legal, accounting, or other professional services. If legal advice or other professional assistance is required, the services of a competent professional person should be sought.

— From a *Declaration of Principles* jointly adopted by
a Committee of the American Bar Association and
a Committee of Publishers and Associations

Copyright © 2001 by Aspen Law & Business
A Division of Aspen Publishers, Inc.
A Wolters Kluwer Company
www.aspenpublishers.com

Permissions
Aspen Law & Business
1185 Avenue of the Americas
New York, NY 10036

Printed in the United States of America

Library of Congress Cataloging-in-Publication Data

Burke, Frank M.
    Audit committees: a guide for directors, management, and consultants /
by Frank M. Burke and Dan M. Guy; with contributing author, Kay W. Tatum;
foreword by Barbara Hackman Franklin — 1st ed.
    p. cm.
    Includes bibliographical references and index.
    ISBN 0-7355-2260-X
    1. Audit committees — United States.   I. Guy, Dan M.   II. Tatum, Kay W.
III. Title.
HF5667.15 .B87 2001
657'.458 — dc21   2001022203

About Aspen Law & Business

Aspen Law & Business is a leading publisher of authoritative treatises, practice manuals, services, and journals for attorneys, corporate and bank directors, accountants, auditors, environmental compliance professionals, financial and tax advisors, and other business professionals. Our mission is to provide practical solution-based how-to information keyed to the latest original pronouncements, as well as the latest legislative, judicial, and regulatory developments.

We offer publications in the areas of accounting and auditing; antitrust; banking and finance; bankruptcy; business and commercial law; construction law; corporate law; criminal law; environmental compliance; government and administrative law; health law; insurance law; intellectual property; international law; legal practice and litigation; matrimonial and family law; pensions, benefits, and labor; real estate law; securities; and taxation.

Our Aspen Law & Business products treating accounting and auditing and corporate governance issues include:

Accounting Irregularities and Financial Fraud
A Practical Guide to SEC Proxy and Compensation Rules
A Practical Guide to Section 16: Reporting and Compliance
Business Judgment Rule: Fiduciary Duties of Corporate Directors
Construction Accounting Deskbook
CPA's Guide to Developing Effective Business Plans
CPA's Guide to Effective Engagement Letters
CPA's Guide to E-Business
EDGAR and Electronic Filing
European Accounting Guide
Federal Government Contractor's Manual
How to Manage Your Accounting Practice
Medical Practice Management Handbook
Meetings of Stockholders
Miller Audit Procedures
Miller Compilations and Reviews
Miller GAAP Financial Statement Disclosures Manual
Miller GAAP Guide
Miller GAAP Practice Manual
Miller GAAS Guide
Miller GAAS Practice Manual
Miller Governmental GAAP Guide
Miller International Accounting Standards Guide
Miller Local Government Audits
Miller Not-for-Profit Organization Audits
Miller Not-for-Profit Reporting
Miller Single Audits

Professional's Guide to Value Pricing
Regulation of Corporate Disclosure
The Corporate Governance Advisor
Takeover Defense

ASPEN LAW & BUSINESS
A Division of Aspen Publishers, Inc.
A Wolters Kluwer Company
www.aspenpublishers.com

SUBSCRIPTION NOTICE

This Aspen Law & Business product is updated on a periodic basis with supplements to reflect important changes in the subject matter. If you purchased this product directly from Aspen Law & Business, we have already recorded your subscription for the update service.

   If, however, you purchased this product from a bookstore and wish to receive future updates and revised or related volumes billed separately with a 30-day examination review, please contact our Customer Service Department at 1-800-234-1660, or send your name, company name (if applicable), address, and the title of the product to:

ASPEN LAW & BUSINESS
A Division of Aspen Publishers, Inc.
7201 McKinney Circle
Frederick, MD 21704

SUMMARY TABLE OF CONTENTS

DETAILED TABLE OF CONTENTS

LIST OF EXHIBITS

LIST OF APPENDICES

HOW TO USE THIS BOOK

Audit Committees: A Guide for Directors, Management, and Consultants (*Guide*) is designed as a reference book. Ordinarily, most users will probably not read the *Guide* from cover to cover. However, a new audit committee member, a first-time chairperson of an audit committee, or a consultant (including, for example, an internal or external auditor) who is developing their knowledge and skill set about audit committees, should consider a cover-to-cover review of the *Guide*. That review will facilitate their use of the *Guide* as a primary reference source.

The authors, anticipating that most readers will use the *Guide* as a reference source, have designed the *Guide* with this in mind. Therefore, the *Guide* contains a detailed **table of contents** (with page numbers shown for sections within each chapter). Each chapter also has a **chapter summary** that highlights the significant points made in the chapter. The busy reader may look at the table of contents for a chapter that addresses a subject of interest and then proceed directly to the chapter summary to determine if the information he or she needs is presented in that chapter.

Page xix contains a list of the **appendices** that are included in the *Guide*. The authors have designed each appendix to be practical and easy to use. The appendices can be easily modified to fit a unique audit committee need or situation.

The *Guide* also contains a comprehensive **glossary** (starting on page 286). The glossary is designed to enable a user to quickly look up a term that he or she may have heard but is not sure of its meaning. For example, the terms "SAS 71 Review," "SAS 60 Letter," "COSO," "Material Weakness," and "Business Judgment Rule," are all defined in the glossary. The *Guide* also includes a section on **Where to Find More Information** that contains addresses, phone numbers, and web sites of key organizations, and a **List of Acronyms** for the user's quick reference. Finally, the *Guide* contains a detailed traditional **index** to enable a user to quickly locate all of the significant discussions of a defined term.

ABOUT THE AUTHORS

Frank M. Burke, J.D., CPA, lives in Dallas, Texas, where he is Managing General Partner of Burke, Mayborn Company, Ltd., a private investment firm holding interests in banking, real estate, electronics, publishing, and commercial fishing. In addition, through Burke, Mayborn Company, Ltd., he provides consulting services to companies engaged in oil and gas, equipment rental, real estate, cable television, and newspapers. Mr. Burke serves, or has served, on nine public company boards of directors and audit committees, chairing three of the audit committees. He also serves, or has served, on numerous private company and not-for-profit boards.

Prior to the creation of Burke, Mayborn Company, Ltd. in 1984, Mr. Burke was a partner in Peat, Marwick, Mitchell & Co. (now KPMG) and served as Chairman–Energy Group for Peat Marwick International, having as one of his responsibilities meeting with boards and audit committees worldwide. He also served on the board of directors of Peat, Marwick, Mitchell & Co. for six years. Over the past 30 years, Mr. Burke has written seven books and over one hundred articles on various business, financial, and tax subjects. In 1977, he drafted the terms of the original limited liability company legislation enacted in Wyoming, and in 1981 obtained the first ruling from the IRS regarding the partnership status of the Wyoming limited liability company. Mr. Burke received his BBA and MBA from Texas Tech University and his J.D. from Southern Methodist University.

Dan M. Guy, Ph.D., CPA, lives in Santa Fe, New Mexico, where he is a writer and consultant in litigation services, specializing in auditor malpractice issues. He completed an 18-year career with the American Institute of Certified Public Accountants (AICPA) in January 1998, where he was Vice President–Professional Standards and Services, having overall responsibility for, among other things, the Auditing Standards Board and international auditing matters. During his tenure at the AICPA, Dr. Guy was significantly involved in developing the authoritative standards on audit risk and materiality, fraud, illegal acts, internal control, and communication with audit committees. He is the author of ten books, including *Practitioner's Guide to GAAS, The Auditor's SAS Field Guide, The Guide to International Standards on Auditing and Related Services, The CPA's Guide to Professional Ethics,* and a widely used university textbook on auditing.

Prior to joining the AICPA as Director of Auditing Research in 1979, Dr. Guy was a professor of accounting at Texas Tech University and a visiting professor at the University of Texas at Austin. He was also in public accounting with Peat, Marwick, Mitchell & Co. (now KPMG) and Arthur Andersen. He received his Ph.D. at the University of Alabama. In 1998, he received the John J. McCloy Award for outstanding contributions to audit quality in the United States. The Public Oversight Board that monitors the SEC Practice Section of the AICPA's Division for CPA firms presented the award. In January 2001, he received the Distinguished Service in Auditing Award from the Auditing Section of the American Accounting Association.

Contributing Author

Kay W. Tatum, Ph.D., CPA is an associate professor of accounting at the University of Miami in Coral Gables, Florida. Professor Tatum earned her Ph.D. in accounting at Texas Tech University. Professor Tatum is co-author of the monograph *Developments in the Audit Methodologies of Large Accounting Firms* and articles on auditing topics that have appeared in the *Journal of Accountancy* and *The CPA Journal.*

Professor Tatum has been an active member of the AICPA and the American Accounting Association. She was a member of the AICPA's Task Force that developed SAS 84 on communications between auditors and is currently a member of the AICPA's International Auditing Standards Subcommittee. She also serves as chairperson of the Auditing Standards Committee of the Auditing Section of the American Accounting Association.

ACKNOWLEDGMENTS

We are grateful to the many individuals who contributed to *Audit Committees: A Guide for Directors, Management, and Consultants.* In particular, we express our appreciation to Ron Sinesio, Director–New Product Development, and Anita Rosepka, Managing Editor, both of Aspen Law & Business. Our appreciation also goes to Terri Guy for her research and editing contributions. To our technical editor and advisor, Linda Lach, CPA, thank you for an exceptional job.

PREFACE

Audit Committees: A Guide for Directors, Management, and Consultants (*Guide*) presents the history, responsibilities, and operation of audit committees. The *Guide* focuses primarily on publicly held companies, but we have included a short chapter on audit committees for not-for-profit and public sector entities. The *Guide* is written in a non-technical, active-voice, easy-to-read format. We write to communicate, not to impress. We consider our primary audience to be:

- Directors serving on audit committees.
- Other members of the board of directors.
- Chief executive officers, chief financial officers, and in-house legal counsels.
- Internal and external auditors.
- Outside legal counsels.
- Other consultants to audit committees.

We bring a unique combination of experience and skills to the *Guide*. One author has served as a director of a number of public, private, and not-for-profit entities, having organized, chaired, and participated as a member of a number of audit committees. In addition, he has over 30 years experience as a partner in, industry head of, and consultant to, international accounting firms and has dealt with audit committees from that perspective on many occasions. The other author recently completed an 18-year tour of duty with the American Institute of Certified Public Accountants, where he served as Vice President having responsibility for audit and attest matters. He participated in the debates and preparation of many of the documents and materials discussed in this book. The *Guide* is synergistic in that it combines real-world audit committee experience with expert knowledge of materiality, internal control, fraud and illegal acts, and the independence requirements for external and internal auditors. The *Guide* is unique in that it presents technical topics in a manner that is understandable for the reader who is not an attorney or a certified public accountant. The *Guide* also is unique in that it covers subjects that are rarely discussed, such as the process for terminating an external auditor.

Another significant feature of the *Guide* is the emphasis on the importance of regular evaluations of audit committee performance, not only as a means of possibly reducing legal liability of the board of directors, but also enhancing the credibility of the company in the eyes of third parties. It seems quite likely that the Securities and Exchange Commission (SEC) or issuers of directors and officers liability insurance will, at some point, require reviews of the activities of audit committees to determine if proper procedures are being followed. The current rash of accounting misrepresentations and fraud in public companies may accelerate consideration of this type of periodic review.

As indicated above, the *Guide* fills a "gap" in the existing literature in that it blends (1) observations based on real-world experience serving on audit committees, (2) expert knowledge of the standards of external and internal auditors, and (3) knowledge of the latest requirements from the New York Stock Exchange, National Association of Securities Dealers, American Stock Exchange, and the SEC.

The *Guide* is current as of December 31, 2000, and will be updated annually. Please help us improve the *Guide*. We welcome your comments, questions, and suggestions. Please direct your correspondence to:

Frank M. Burke, J.D., CPA   Dan M. Guy, Ph.D., CPA
Burke, Mayborn Co., Ltd.   314 Paseo de Peralta
5500 Preston Road, Suite 315   Santa Fe, New Mexico 87501
Dallas, Texas 75205   dmguy@worldnet.att.net
frankburke@inetmail.att.net

December 31, 2000

FOREWORD

Since joining my first corporate board more than two decades ago, I have witnessed dramatic changes in the business environment, corporate governance, and especially in audit committee work.

The interconnected global economy, the pace of competition, and advances in technology — these are among the forces that have created the most dynamic and exciting business environment of my career. And that dynamism has spawned the shareholder activism and regulatory attention that has focused squarely on corporate governance. The result is the biggest change for us as directors during this time: higher expectations for performance. The expectations flow from the many constituencies of public companies. Shareholders are first and foremost. They are a diverse group, with a variety of objectives, and, since more than half of U.S. households own stock, there are many more of them today. Employees, customers, communities, public officials, (including regulators), and the press are among the other constituencies. All of them are scrutinizing directors more closely and demanding that we do a better job.

The audit committee is a clear focal point of these higher expectations. When I first joined boards, it was customary to place new directors on the audit committee, "to learn about the company." Audit committees were simply not at the top of the board's pecking order. Those days are gone for good. Audit committees have clearly arrived and are now being recognized for the uniqueness of their work. The audit committee is the only board committee with the responsibility to monitor what management does — constantly. Other board committees have assignments of great consequence but the magnitude and sensitivity of their work usually ebbs and flows. This is not true of the audit committee's work, and for this reason, it is one of the more challenging committee assignments and will continue to be in the years ahead.

Directors have been rising to the challenges by becoming more independent, more vigilant, and more willing to disagree with management when necessary. We take our oversight responsibilities more seriously than even before. We expect more of each other.

But we are always looking for useful tools to enhance our performance. Dan Guy and Frank Burke have made a great contribution to the cause in their book, *Audit Committees: A Guide for Directors, Management, and Consultants.* They are an excellent team. Burke earned his stripes serving on nine boards and their audit committees and chairing three of those committees. Guy, a former Vice President–Auditing at the AICPA, was responsible for developing many of the auditing standards for which audit committees have oversight responsibility.

I am impressed with the completeness of the *Guide*. It brings together in one volume all the materials that impact the responsibilities and duties of audit committees. It is completely up to date and includes the new rules issued in the past two years by the SEC, stock exchanges, and the AICPA, as well as the new SEC rules on auditor independence issued in November 2000. The *Guide* also has the great virtue of simplifying complex technical requirements and presenting them in any easy-to-read fashion. For instance, Chapter 9, "The Audit Committees' Oversight of Internal Control," is one of the most understandable overviews on that subject I have ever read. All in all, this book is an indispensable reference book for both experienced and new audit committee members.

The enhanced importance, seriousness, and visibility of audit committee work has illuminated the need for a book like this. Burke and Guy are to be commended for giving it to us.

Barbara Hackman Franklin
December 31, 2000

Barbara Hackman Franklin, currently President and CEO of Barbara Franklin Enterprises, has served as the 29th U.S. Secretary of Commerce. She has served on the boards of 11 public companies, 4 private companies, and a variety of professional and not-for-profit entities, including Nasdaq and the AICPA. Franklin has served on 12 audit committees, chaired 4, and is the only non-CPA to receive the prestigious John J. McCloy award for outstanding contributions to audit excellence. She has been honored as Director of the Year by the National Association of Corporate Directors.

AUDIT COMMITTEES:

A Guide for Directors, Management, and Consultants

CHAPTER 1
THE NEED FOR AN AUDIT COMMITTEE

Corporations have made possible much of the industrial and commercial advancement of the past two centuries. Through corporations, individuals combine their capital and efforts to participate in large business enterprises, with their risk being limited to their capital contributions. Because of the unique legal characteristics of companies organized as corporations, no other form of entity could have been successfully used to accumulate the capital needed for today's business enterprises.

A corporation is an association of individuals, or other business entities, formed to carry on a joint enterprise having the capacity to act as an entity or person under the law. A corporation is technically an artificial person composed of natural persons or other business entities, and has interests distinguishable from the interests of its individual members. Traditionally, corporate attributes include: (1) the power to sue and be sued in the company name; (2) the power to hold, own, and convey property in the company name; (3) free transferability of company stock; (4) perpetual succession; (5) limited liability; and (6) centralization of management in a board of directors.

It is the centralization of management in a company's board of directors, and the resulting responsibilities of the board for financial and internal control matters, as discharged by the board's audit committee, that is the subject of this book — a user-friendly guide containing the needed tools to assist companies, not-for-profit organizations, and public sector entities with creating and maintaining effective audit committees. The goal of this chapter is to explain the purpose of an audit committee in relation to the board of directors.

The Board of Directors

Due to the increased emphasis on corporate accountability over the past forty years, boards of directors have been strengthened in terms of talent and objectivity, and potential conflicts of interest are more frequently recognized and dealt with in an appropriate manner. In addition, most companies have a significant number of non-management, outside, independent directors with various skills and backgrounds to assist in providing oversight of the company's activities. In fact, the typical *Fortune*-listed company has an average of 9 outside directors and 2 or 3 inside directors (with bank boards averaging 12 outsiders and 3 insiders).[1]

A board of directors has several basic responsibilities as the ultimate governance body. First, the board must provide the policies, oversight, and general direction for the company's activities. Second, the board is responsible for selecting, monitoring, and changing management of the company when appropriate. Third, the board must set the business and ethical standards of the company (usually referred to as the tone at the top). Accordingly, the board must have appropriate mechanisms in place to assure that such standards are communicated, complied with, and properly administered by the company.

The board of directors is first and foremost responsible for protecting and promoting the interests of the shareholders. A board of directors is accountable to the shareholders for the long-term successful performance of the company. As fiduciaries for the shareholders, the powers and responsibilities of a board of directors are defined under the appropriate state or federal law, the corporate charter, and the corporate bylaws.

As indicated in a publication of The Business Roundtable, a board of directors is accountable to a number of constituencies or stakeholders in addition to its shareholders.[2] For example, a board is accountable to the creditors and customers of the company and to the financial markets. Various laws also impose accountability and regulations intended to limit and control corporate action. If directors overextend their authority, their decisions are subject to reversal by the courts. In addition, directors may be held personally liable if they violate their duty of loyalty to the company.

As indicated above, over the past 40 years there has been a significant increase in initiatives intended to broaden corporate accountability. The Watergate investigation, corporate scandals, and bankruptcies of major corporations in the 1970s increased public pressure for corporate accountability. Also, the corporate world itself recognized the advantages of increased corporate accountability.[3]

More recently, during the early 1990s, a number of high-profile U.S. companies attempted to revitalize their boards of directors. Companies made structural modifications to promote director independence and improve the

---

[1] Korn/Ferry International, *26th Annual Board of Directors Study* (1999), p. 9.

[2] The Business Roundtable, *Statement on Corporate Governance* (September 1997), p. 3.

[3] See generally *The Changing Boardroom — Making Policy and Profits in an Age of Corporate Citizenship* (1982), chapters 2, 3, and 9.

board's ability to monitor management. Perhaps the most significant of these modifications occurred in late 1992 and early 1993 when the General Motors Board of Directors replaced the Chairman and Chief Executive Officer with a new Chief Executive Officer and separate non-executive Chairman. Until the General Motors action, open and obvious board action in replacing executives was rare.

In the spring of 1994, the General Motors Board issued guidelines designed to ensure effective monitoring of management by an independent board.[4] Key provisions of the GM guidelines include:

1. Independent board leadership either by a separate chairman or lead director.
2. Independent director meetings without management at least three times each year to discuss management performance and to evaluate the chief executive officer (CEO).
3. Annual formal CEO evaluation by independent directors based on objective criteria.
4. Annual formal board self-evaluation.
5. Determination by independent directors of board structures and corporate governance processes.
6. Joint determination of board agenda by both independent board leadership and the CEO with input from all board members (information regarding board agenda items to be circulated in advance).
7. Nominating committee selection of independent directors with input from independent board leadership and chief executive officers (invitations to join board issued by the board itself).[5]

The General Motors Board guidelines have attracted significant attention and have received substantial acclaim in the corporate governance field. Shortly after the adoption of the General Motors Board guidelines, the California Employees Retirement System urged other boards of public companies to follow the General Motors example.[6] While the suggestions have not been widely accepted in total, significant support has emerged for the con-

---

[4] "GM Board Adopts Formal Guidelines on Stronger Control Over Management," *The Wall Street Journal* (March 28, 1994), p. A4.

[5] General Motors Board of Directors, *GM Board of Directors Corporate Governance Guidelines on Significant Corporate Governance Issues* (January 1994, as revised in August 1995 and June 1997).

[6] "Calpers Announces Results of Governance Study," Calpers Press Release (Sacramento, California; May 31, 1995).

cepts of non-executive board chairmen, lead director, board member independence, and board self-assessment.

Accountability and the Audit Committee

One of the primary results of the emphasis on corporate accountability has been the increased attention to the audit committees (see definition at Exhibit 1-1) as guardians of financial integrity. Initially, audit committees were formed by a board of directors to fulfill part of the board's responsibilities for oversight in the area of financial reporting and related areas. Over the past fifteen years, audit committees have become more involved in the review of corporate accountability and governance, particularly as the focus on risks and controls expands to include not only financial integrity, but also compliance systems and processes needed for a company to meet legal and ethical standards. Hence, the audit committee has had a broadening agenda in recent years, *at least in some companies.*

Exhibit 1-1
Definition of Audit Committee

An audit committee is a standing committee of the board of directors that is charged with overseeing the integrity of the company's financial reporting processes. The audit committee oversight responsibility typically includes (1) internal and external financial reporting, (2) risks and controls related to financial reporting, and (3) the internal and external audit processes.

According to The Business Roundtable report, the audit committee's role is described as follows:

> The primary functions of the audit committee are generally to recommend the appointment of the public accountants and review with them their report of the financial reports of the corporation; to review the adequacy of the system of internal controls and of compliance with material policies and laws, including the corporation's code of ethics or code of conduct; and to provide a direct channel of communication to the

board of the public accountants and internal auditors and, when needed, finance officers, compliance officers, and general counsel.[7]

Given the present corporate governance environment, it is clear that the activities that audit committees perform will continue to expand, especially in being more proactive in overseeing risks and controls related to financial and non-financial information. The role and purpose of an audit committee, of course, is not a new concept, but the committee's place in the corporate governance mosaic is expanding in importance.

In recent years, federal and state legislation has imposed a number of rules and regulations on companies, intended to reach various social goals. Laws relating to equal employment, racial and sexual discrimination, environmental matters, and other programs have dramatically increased the responsibility of companies and their boards of directors. In most legislation, policies are created and implementation is left to the company and others affected by the legislation. As implementation requirements increase, the audit committee will find its role continuing to expand or other board committees will be created to meet the increased monitoring requirements.

In any event, the importance of the audit committee in overseeing financial integrity will continue to be significant. Since measurements and disclosures provided by financial information are the most commonly used benchmarking data set among profit-making entities, financial reporting is probably the most significant information for which a corporate board is responsible. Financial information is the most widely accepted measure of corporate accountability and is used to evaluate the effectiveness of a board of directors and its management group. In many cases, financial executives are pressured to manipulate or manage earnings to provide more favorable results or results more in line with forecasts and other expectations. Two recent reports indicate that at least 50 percent of public company financial executives have been pressured to tweak financial information.[8] Recent cases of financial fraud or misrepresentations, such as those involving Sunbeam, Cendant, and Waste Management, have heightened public concern about corporate accountability.[9] More than ever, a board must be certain that financial information, including net income, is being reported properly. A recent example of the serious interest of the Securities and Exchange Commission

---

[7] *The Business Roundtable,* p. 15, note 2.

[8] See "Flaky Accounting on the March?" *The Wall Street Journal* (February 5, 1999) p. A14.

[9] See "Corporate Earnings: Truth, Please," *Business Week* (October 5, 1998), p. 194.

in financial accounting abuses is the suit it filed in December 1998 against W.R. Grace & Co. for fraud, alleging that the company had diverted up to $20 million of 1991 and 1992 earnings into reserves and shifted such amounts back into earnings in weaker later years.[10] An active and informed audit committee should be the vehicle used by a board of directors to assure that financial reporting is understandable, accurate, and conveys the proper message to financial markets, shareholders, and other stakeholders, including the general public.

Assessing the Company's Support for the Audit Committee

If the company's board of directors and senior management do not understand and support the audit committee, or if they consider the committee a necessary evil, the committee cannot be the guardian or overseer of the company's financial reporting integrity. In other words, the company's culture must have the "right tone at the top." What is the appropriate tone at the top? Michael R. Young best describes the tone at the top as follows:

> It involves an unrelenting insistence upon accuracy in financial reporting. It involves an unrelenting insistence that numbers are not to be massaged. It involves an unrelenting insistence upon truthfulness as the foremost objective of the corporate enterprise. It is a tone that makes financial misreporting unthinkable.[11]

Young emphasizes that "if the audit committee is to accomplish nothing else, it should first and foremost strive to establish the right tone at the top."[12] Similar comments were made by the National Association of Corporate Directors (NACD) in its guide for audit committees. That guide indicates that: "Audit Committees should encourage a 'tone at the top' that conveys basic values of ethical integrity as well as legal compliance and

---

[10] See "Busting Up A Balance Sheet Game," *Business Week* (January 11, 1999), p. 45. Grace consented to the entry of a cease and desist order and agreed to establish a $1 million fund for educational programs about financial statements and generally accepted accounting principles. See *In the Matter of W. R. Grace & Co.*, Release No. 34-41578. AAER No. 1140 (June 30, 1999).

[11] Michael R. Young, *Accounting Irregularities and Financial Fraud* (San Diego: Harcourt Professional Publishing, 2000), p. 215.

[12] *Ibid.*, p. 214.

strong financial reporting." [13] Appendix 1 presents a list of items that an audit committee should consider in assessing senior management's understanding and support for the committee.

Here is a summary of the important concepts in this chapter:

1. The board of directors is the ultimate governance body.
2. The audit committee is a standing committee of the board of directors.
3. The audit committee's responsibility and authority cannot exceed that of the board of directors.
4. The audit committee's responsibility and authority should not exceed that which the board of directors has delegated to it.
5. The audit committee, as a check and balance on management, is the guardian of the company's financial integrity.
6. As the guardian of financial integrity, the audit committee is charged with overseeing the company's:
   - Financial reporting of internal and external information.
   - Risks and controls related to such financial information.
   - Internal and external audit processes.
7. The audit committee, as a standing committee of the board of directors, enables an oversight body to focus on financial integrity and to help companies convey the essential need for ethics and integrity in financial reporting — the tone at the top.

---

[13] Report of the NACD Blue Ribbon Committee on Audit Committees, *Audit Committees: A Practical Guide* (Washington, D.C.: National Association of Corporate Directors, 2000), p. 3.

CHAPTER 2
EARLY HISTORY OF THE AUDIT COMMITTEE
CONCEPT — 1939 TO 1987

The authors could not locate any discussion of audit committees in the legal and accounting literature of the early twentieth century. One source indicates that The Prudential Insurance Company of America has had an audit committee for over seventy-five years.[1] Presumably, banks and insurance companies were among the earliest companies to establish audit committees because of statutory requirements for audits. This chapter presents the history of the development of the audit committee concept from its documented creation in the late 1930s until 1987.

Events from 1939–1970

The concept of the audit committee is first found in published literature in the SEC investigation of McKesson & Robbins, Inc., regarding the reporting of approximately $10 million of nonexistent inventory and $9 million of overstated accounts receivable in the financial statements of a company having consolidated total assets of approximately $90 million. In 1939, in response to the McKesson & Robbins investigation, the New York Stock Exchange (NYSE) stated that it was desirable for a committee of non-officer directors to select the external auditors where practical.[2] Shortly thereafter, in 1940, the SEC issued a recommendation that outside directors nominate the external auditors and that the shareholders vote on the accounting firm nominated by the outside directors.[3] While McKesson & Robbins revolutionized thinking about the relationship between the company, its external auditor, and certain auditing techniques used, the investigation did not cause widespread adoption of the audit committee concept by corporate America.

More than twenty-five years after McKesson & Robbins, the Canadian government, through a Royal Commission Report, acknowledged, as a result of the collapse of Atlantic Acceptance Corporation Limited, the need for an

---

[1] Robert S. Kay and D. Gerald Searfoss, Eds., *Handbook of Accounting and Auditing,* 2nd Ed. (1989), p. 6-2.

[2] New York Stock Exchange, Report of the Subcommittee on Independent Audit Procedure of the Committee on Stock Lists (1939).

[3] Accounting Standard Release No. 19, Exchange Act Release No. 2707 (December 5, 1940).

audit committee to review a company's financial statements before submission to its board for approval.[4] At about the same time, an Ontario legislative committee studying corporate law recommended mandatory audit committees.[5] Thereafter, several Canadian provinces, for example, Ontario, British Columbia, and the Yukon Territory, and the Canadian federal government enacted legislation requiring that companies offering securities to the public establish and maintain audit committees.[6]

Until 1967, the audit committee concept received little attention in the United States. Shortly after recognition by the Canadian government of the need for audit committees, the Executive Committee (currently the Board of Directors) of the American Institute of Certified Public Accountants (AICPA) recommended in 1967 that public companies create audit committees made up of outside directors. The Executive Committee stated that the external auditors should communicate with the audit committee regarding ". . . any significant question having material bearing on the company's financial statements which has not been satisfactorily resolved at the management level."[7]

Events from 1971–1980

In 1972, the SEC issued a release entitled "Standing Audit Committees Composed of Outside Directors."[8] In that release, the SEC for the first time endorsed the establishment of an audit committee composed of outside directors by all public companies. The SEC urged the business and financial communities, as well as the shareholders, to support the implementation of the audit committee recommendation to assist in affording the greatest possible protection to investors who rely upon financial statements of public companies. The SEC reinforced its position several months later, urging that

---

[4] The Honorable S.H.S. Hughes, *Report of the Royal Commission Appointed to Inquire into the Failure of Atlantic Acceptance Corporation, Limited* (Toronto, 1969), Vol. 3, p. 1653.

[5] Ontario Legislative Assembly, *Interim Report of the Select Committee on Company Law* (Toronto, 1967), p. 92.

[6] Business Corporations Act, S.H. 1981, c. B-15, s. 165; Company Act, R.S.B.C. 1979, c. 59, s. 211; Canada Business Corporations Act, R.S.C. 1985, c. C-44, s. 171; Corporations Act, R.S.M. 1987, c. C-225, s. 165; Business Corporations Act, R.S.S. 1978, c. B-10, s. 165; Business Corporations Act, R.S.Y.T. 1986, c. 15, s. 173.

[7] "AICPA Executive Committee Statement on Audit Committees of Boards of Directors," 24 *J. Acct.* 10 (1967).

[8] Accounting Standard Release No. 123, Securities Act Release No. 5237 (March 23, 1972).

the external auditor's independence would be strengthened by the presence of an audit committee.[9]

In 1974, the SEC amended its rules to require a registered company to identify in its proxy statement the members of its audit committee, or state that no such committee existed.[10] This requirement, as discussed below, was expanded in 1978 to include a description of the committee's function.

The American Bar Association (ABA), in its 1975 "Corporate Director's Guidebook," stated that the audit committee is of great value to public companies, acting as a communications link between the board of directors and the external auditors.[11] In addition, the audit committee provides a mechanism for reviewing the integrity of the company's financial reporting and internal controls. The ABA has also recommended that audit committees be composed of non-management directors and be able to employ their own legal counsel, accountants, and other experts when needed. The ABA's "Guidebook" identified four prime responsibilities of the audit committee:

1. Recommend the external auditors.
2. Consult with the external auditor about the audit plan.
3. Review the audit report and management letter with the external auditor.[12]
4. Consult with the external auditor, without management being present, about the adequacy of the company's internal controls.[13]

In 1976, the SEC recommended to the Senate Banking, Housing and Urban Affairs Committee that corporations establish permanent audit committees composed of independent directors.[14] That testimony came in hearings that were addressing questionable practices of U.S. companies overseas. Those hearings eventually resulted in the enactment in 1977 of the Foreign Corrupt Practices Act (FCPA).[15] The FCPA created new responsibilities for

---

[9] Accounting Standard Release No. 126 (July 5, 1972).

[10] Accounting Standard Release No. 165, Securities Act Release No. 5550 (December 20, 1974).

[11] ABA, "Corporate Director's Guidebook," 33 *Bus. Law.,* 1595 (1975).

[12] Today management letters, which discuss weaknesses in a company's internal control, are frequently referred to as SAS No. 60 letters, reportable conditions letters, or internal control letters.

[13] ABA, 1626.

[14] *Report of the SEC on Questionable and Illegal Payments and Practices* (May 19, 1976).

[15] P.L. No. 95-213, December 19, 1977. The FCPA has often been cited as creating a competitive disadvantage for U.S. companies operating internationally. For more than 20 years, other parts of the world have gradually (and reluctantly) at least acknowledged the need for FCPA-like legislation, but progress is very slow. See, for example, "OECD Ministers Agree

companies subject to the Securities Exchange Act of 1934. As discussed in Exhibit 2-1, the FCPA, among other things, legally mandates that companies keep accurate books and records and have internal accounting controls (currently referred to as "internal controls over financial reporting") that provide reasonable or very high assurance that reliable financial statements will be produced.

Exhibit 2-1
A Summary of the Foreign Corrupt Practices Act of 1977*

The FCPA, which amends the Securities Exchange Act of 1934, has two parts: one deals with specific acts and penalties associated with certain corrupt practices such as bribery; the second, with requirements relating to internal accounting controls (for example, internal controls over financial reporting). Briefly, the first part of the FCPA, which applies to all U.S. businesses, prohibits domestic companies (including its directors, officers, employees, agents, or stockholders) from paying or offering to pay a foreign official to obtain, retain, or direct business to any person, except for payments to expedite routine government action.

The second part of the FCPA establishes a legal requirement that applies to every SEC registrant. Specifically, Section 102 of the FCPA requires every public company to:

(A) Make and keep books, records and accounts, which, in reasonable detail, accurately and fairly reflect the transactions and dispositions of the assets of the issuer; and
(B) Devise and maintain a system of internal accounting controls sufficient to provide reasonable assurances that the following four objectives are met:
    (i) transactions are executed in accordance with management's general or specific authorizations;
    (ii) transactions are recorded as necessary (a) to permit preparation of financial statements in conformity with generally accepted

---

*The FCPA was amended in 1988 to impose criminal liability for failing to comply with the internal accounting control provisions if an individual knowingly circumvents or fails to implement a system of internal accounting controls or knowingly falsifies any book, record, or account.

---

to Bar Bribery as Means for Companies to Win Business," *The Wall Street Journal* (May 27, 1997), p. A2. The 1988 amendments to the FCPA were intended to reduce the compliance burden and anti-competitive effect of the Act.

accounting principles or any other criteria applicable to such
statements, and (b) to maintain accountability for assets;
(iii) access to assets is permitted only in accordance with management's general or specific authorization; and
(iv) the recorded accountability for assets is compared with the existing assets at reasonable intervals and appropriate action is
taken with respect to any differences.

The legislative history clearly shows that the intent of Congress in pass-
ing the FCPA was to prevent, as the name of the Act implies, illegal payments to foreign officials, and that the requirement for books and records
and internal accounting controls was related to that objective. However, the
books, records, and controls requirement of the FCPA covers all transactions, not just those related to bribery of foreign officials. In fact, the SEC
enforces the FCPA in connection with deficiencies in books, records, and
controls related to domestic and foreign transactions. Interestingly, the
FCPA does not specifically refer to audit committees.

In 1977, the SEC issued several official releases indirectly reaffirming its
support for audit committees.[16] In one release, the SEC proposed that companies be required to disclose the reasons for changing their external auditor and to indicate whether the audit committee had approved that decision.

In 1977, the NYSE also adopted a policy statement requiring that each
company listed on the NYSE, as a condition of listing and continued listing,
establish no later than June 30, 1978, an audit committee composed of independent directors. According to the policy, directors should be free from any
relationship that, in the opinion of its board of directors, would interfere with
their exercise of independent judgment as committee members.[17] The NYSE
specifically provided that directors who are affiliates of the company or its
subsidiaries are not qualified for audit committee membership. Shortly thereafter, the American Stock Exchange, while not specifically requiring an audit
committee, recommended that all listed companies have such a committee.[18]

In 1978, the SEC proposed that registrants set forth the customary functions of their audit, nominating, and compensation committees and identify
nominees for the three committees.[19] After significant criticism about hav-

---

[16] See Exchange Act Release No. 13872 (August 24, 1977) and Exchange Act Release
No. 13989 (September 26, 1977).

[17] *NYSE Company Manual,* Section A2, Pt. V.

[18] "The AMEX Board Recommends Audit Committees," *The Wall Street Journal* (December 14, 1979), p.2.

[19] Exchange Act Release No. 14970 (July 17, 1978).

ing to disclose customary functions that would perhaps be unsuitable and inflexible, the amendments were modified to require only that companies state whether audit and other committees exist, identify directors serving on the committees by name, and disclose the functions actually performed by the audit committee.[20]

Also in 1978, the SEC again suggested strengthening the functions that an audit committee performs when it promulgated a rule requiring proxy statement disclosure of management advisory services (now more frequently referred to as "consulting services") provided by the company's principal external auditor. The rule required disclosure of whether the entire board, or its audit committee, had approved each service and considered the potential affect of the service on the auditor's independence.[21] This rule was supplemented in 1979 when the SEC identified factors that the audit committee should consider in determining whether to engage their external auditor to perform non-audit or consulting services.[22] The SEC rescinded the rule mandating disclosure in proxy statements of non-audit services in 1982.[23] The rescission was based in part on the establishment by the AICPA's SEC Practice Section of a membership requirement that obligated accounting firms to disclose information about their consulting services for SEC clients.[24] Nevertheless, the 1978 and 1979 SEC releases clearly indicated its views about the role of the audit committee in overseeing the independence of the external auditor. (As discussed in Chapter 4, "Additional Developments from *Treadway* to 2001," in November 2000, the SEC resurrected the requirement to disclose information about the performance of non-auditing services.)

The Audit Committee and Securities Litigation in the 1970s

During the 1970s, the SEC repeatedly recognized and emphasized the importance of independent directors and audit committees. The Commission accomplished this in a number of ways, not the least of which was in settle-

---

[20] Exchange Act Release No. 15384 (December 6, 1978).

[21] Accounting Standard Release No. 250, Securities Act Release No. 5940 (June 19, 1978).

[22] Accounting Standard Release No. 264 (June 14, 1979).

[23] Accounting Standard Release No. 304 (January 28, 1982).

[24] The principal objective of the SEC Practice Section is to improve the quality of practice by establishing membership requirements for CPA firms and to create an effective system of self-regulation. A member of the AICPA who practices with a CPA firm that audits one or more SEC clients can only practice with a firm that is a member of the SECPS.

ments of securities litigation providing for the establishment or strengthening of audit committees with independent directors and the broadening of the functions and powers of the audit committee. Three of the more significant SEC actions are discussed in the following paragraphs.

In 1974, the SEC obtained a consent injunction against Lum's, Inc. which required, among other things, that Lum's establish an audit committee to oversee the external auditor's evaluations of internal controls and to oversee other casino activities involving security and personnel.[25] The court mandated that the audit committee consist of two or more directors who were not officers or directors of the company.

In another consent injunction in 1974 against Mattel, Inc., the court ordered the company to establish an audit committee having three or four unaffiliated directors.[26] Significantly, the court also required Mattel's audit committee to perform certain duties, such as overseeing quarterly financial statements. The duties were not as extensive as those required in Killearn Properties, discussed next, but the case is significant because it is the first to set forth duties and responsibilities for an audit committee.

In 1977, as part of the injunctive relief sought by the SEC, a federal district court ordered Killearn Properties, Inc. to follow the policies and practices set forth below for its audit committee (to consist of at least three outside directors):[27]

1. Review the engagement of the external auditor, including the scope of the proposed audit, the planned audit procedures, and the fee to be charged.
2. Review with the external auditor and with the company's chief financial officer (and with other company personnel, as needed) the general policies and procedures for internal auditing, accounting, and financial controls. The audit committee members should be generally familiar with the accounting and reporting principles and practices used by the company in its financial statements.
3. Review with the external auditor, upon completion of its audit:
   a. Any report or opinion proposed to be rendered;
   b. The external auditor's perceptions of the company's financial and accounting personnel;

[25] *SEC v. Lum's, Inc.,* Fed. Sec. L. Rep. (CCH), par. 94,504 (S.D.N.Y. April 11, 1974).

[26] *SEC v. Mattel Inc.,* Fed. Sec. L. Rep. (CCH), par. 94,807 (D.D.C. Oct. 1, 1974).

[27] *SEC v. Killearn Properties, Inc.,* Fed. Sec. L. Rep. (CCH), para 96,256 (N.D. Fla. May 2, 1977).

    c. The cooperation received by the external auditor during the audit;

    d. The extent to which company resources were used to minimize time spent by the external auditor;

    e. Any significant unusual transactions;

    f. Any changes in accounting principles;

    g. All significant adjustments proposed by the external auditor; and

    h. Any recommendations that the external auditor might have, including improvement in internal controls, choice of accounting principles, or management reporting systems.

4. Inquire of the appropriate company personnel and external auditor about deviations from codes of conduct of the company and periodically review conduct policies.

5. Meet with the company's financial staff at least twice a year to review and discuss the internal accounting and auditing procedures being used and to determine whether recommendations made by the internal auditor or by the external auditor have been implemented.

6. Prepare and present a report to the company's board of directors recommending the retention or discharge of the external auditor for the coming year.

7. Direct and supervise an investigation into any matter brought to its attention within the scope of its duties (including retention of outside counsel in connection with such investigation).

In addition, the company's audit committee was directed to have the following special duties:

1. Review, either by the entire audit committee or by a designated member, all financial information, including projections, to be disseminated by the company to the media, the public, or the shareholders.

2. Review the activities of the officers and directors of the company as to dealings with the company and take any action deemed appropriate regarding such activities.

Killearn Properties, Inc. is a leading case regarding audit committees because it provides a detailed statement of responsibilities for such committees.

The SEC often sought to influence the structure, responsibilities, and functions of audit committees in enforcement actions during the 1970s. Consequently, a number of companies consented to the SEC's demands about the structure, size, and functions of their audit committees, and the characteristics of audit committee members.

Significantly, by the end of the 1970s, the SEC, as evidenced by its enforcement activities, viewed the audit committee as a very important part of corporate governance and was clearly encouraging and requiring the establishment of audit committees to further proper corporate financial reporting and governance.

Here is a summary of the important milestones from 1939 to 1987 in the development of the audit committee concept:

1939

- NYSE endorses the audit committee concept as a consequence of the SEC's McKesson & Robbins, Inc. investigation.

1940

- SEC, in the McKesson & Robbins, Inc. investigation, expresses its position on the desirability of audit committees. The SEC indicated that the committee of non-officer members should nominate the external auditor and arrange the details of the audit engagement.

1967

- AICPA recommends that all publicly held companies form audit committees of outside directors to nominate the external auditor and to discuss the auditor's work.

1972

- SEC states that all publicly held companies should establish audit committees composed of outside directors.

1974

- SEC amends proxy disclosure requirements to mandate that companies identify the names of the members of their audit committees or indicate that no such committee exists.

1977

- In *SEC v. Killearn Properties, Inc.,* a leading SEC enforcement case, the Commission provides a detailed set of tasks for an audit committee.
- NYSE adopts a listing requirement for audit committees composed entirely of independent directors; specific duties were not established. (This requirement became effective in 1978.)

- The Foreign Corrupt Practices Act is enacted to address corporate bribery and to require public companies to keep accurate books and records and to devise and maintain a system of internal accounting controls sufficient to generate reliable financial statements. (The Act was amended in 1988.)
- SEC expands its proxy rules under Schedule 14A (see 1974 above) to require disclosure of the functions performed by the audit committee. SEC also required proxy statement disclosure of consulting services provided by the external auditor and whether the board or the audit committee approved each service and considered its effect on the external auditor's independence. The requirement to disclose consulting or non-audit services was rescinded in 1982, in part, because of the establishment of membership requirements by the AICPA's SEC Practice Section mandating disclosure of information about consulting services.

CHAPTER 3
THE 1987 TREADWAY COMMISSION REPORT —
A DEFINING EVENT

Sporadic efforts to define the need for, and the duties of, an audit committee marked the period leading up to the 1980s. However, with the exception of SEC settlements, no meaningful guidelines were developed until the Report of the National Commission on Fraudulent Financial Reporting (a private-sector initiative jointly sponsored by the American Institute of CPAs, the American Accounting Association, the Financial Executives Institute, the Institute of Internal Auditors, and the National Association of Accountants, now known as the Institute of Management Accountants) was published in October 1987.[1] Better known as the Treadway Commission[2] (hereafter referred to as *Treadway*), the working group had three major objectives: (1) to determine the causes of fraudulent financial reporting, (2) to examine the external auditor's role in preventing, detecting, and reporting fraud, and (3) to identify corporate structural attributes contributing to fraudulent financial reporting.

While *Treadway* focuses on the seriousness and consequences of fraudulent financial reporting and the realistic potential for reducing the risk of fraud, the 1987 report emphasizes the importance of the audit committee in detecting and preventing fraudulent financial reporting. In fact, *Treadway* makes 11 recommendations (out of a total of 49) about audit committees. This chapter summarizes those recommendations and the good practice guidelines that *Treadway* offers for consideration.

Recommendations for Audit Committees

Treadway (which dealt only with public companies) concludes that top management must set the tone that influences the corporate environment within which financial reporting occurs. To set the proper tone, top management must identify and assess the risk factors that could lead to fraudulent financial reporting. Accordingly, all public companies should maintain inter-

---

[1] *Report of the National Commission on Fraudulent Financial Reporting* (National Commission on Fraudulent Reporting) (October 1987). The complete report is available on the Committee of Sponsoring Organizations of the Treadway Commission's web site (at www.coso.org).

[2] The chairman of the National Commission was James C. Treadway, Jr., a former Commissioner of the SEC.

nal controls to provide reasonable assurance that fraudulent financial reporting will be prevented or subject to early detection. *Treadway* specifically states that the "internal controls" required for this purpose are a broader concept than in the traditional accounting sense in that they include, for example, the internal audit function and the audit committee. In addition, all public companies should develop and enforce effective written codes of corporate conduct.

Of significant interest to observers of the development of the audit committee concept is the recommendation that all public companies, regardless of size, should be required by SEC rules to have audit committees composed entirely of independent directors. But, according to *Treadway*, the mere existence of an audit committee is not enough — the audit committee must be **informed, vigilant,** and **effective** overseers of the financial reporting process and the related internal controls. Further, *Treadway* recommends that the board of directors set forth the audit committee's duties and responsibilities in a written charter. Among other things, the audit committee should be responsible for reviewing management's evaluation of the independence of the external auditor and management's plans for engaging the external auditor to perform consulting or management advisory services.

Throughout *Treadway*, the audit committee plays an important part in the suggested process for implementing the report's 49 recommendations. *Treadway* recommends that the audit committee annually review the program that management establishes to monitor compliance with the code of corporate conduct. In addition, the audit committee should be sure that the internal audit involvement in the entire financial reporting process is appropriate and properly coordinated with the external auditor.

Treadway recommends that management advise the audit committee when it seeks a second opinion on a significant accounting issue, with an explanation of why the particular accounting treatment being reviewed was chosen. *Treadway* also recommends audit committee oversight of the quarterly financial reporting process. Finally, *Treadway* recommends that the chairman of the audit committee provide a letter describing the committee's responsibilities and activities for inclusion in the annual report to shareholders.

Because of the significantly expanded audit committee role recommended by *Treadway*, the report indicates that an audit committee must have adequate resources and authority to discharge its responsibilities. Audit committees should be allocated the necessary resources, including in-house staff and administrative support. Generally, staff support for an audit committee should come from existing employees. *Treadway* recognizes that only in the most unusual circumstances should an audit committee need a separate staff, and then not on a continuing basis. In addition, the report recommends that the audit committee should have the discretion to institute investigations of improprieties or suspected improprieties, including the standing authority to retain special legal counsel or experts.

Good Practice Guidelines for Audit Committees

One of the most important parts of *Treadway* is an appendix entitled "Good Practice Guidelines for the Audit Committee." In addition to the 11 recommendations discussed above, *Treadway* provides specific guidelines for audit committee duties and responsibilities.

The guideline duties and responsibilities were developed from (1) review of practices of a number of well-managed companies, (2) published materials from the public accounting and legal professions, (3) contracted research, and (4) presentations made to *Treadway*. In providing detailed guidelines, *Treadway* does not specifically recommend the guidelines for adoption, since the Commission recognizes that more detailed delineation of duties and responsibilities would be best tailored to fit individual company circumstances. Nevertheless, the guidelines are offered as suggestions that a company can consider in exercising judgment as to the scope of duties and responsibilities of its audit committee.

The good practice guidelines are summarized as follows:

Guidelines for General Matters

Size and Term — The audit committee should not consist of fewer than three independent directors, although it is recognized that the size of the committee may vary depending on the facts and circumstances of the company. The board of directors should determine the term for audit committee members, but terms should be arranged in such a manner as to assure continuity on the committee and to bring needed fresh perspective.

Meetings — The audit committee should meet on a regular basis and have special meetings as circumstances dictate. The committee should periodically meet in private with representatives of the internal auditor and the external auditor.

Reporting to Board — The committee should report to the full board of directors on a regular basis, perhaps after each meeting, so that the board is kept fully informed of the activities of the audit committee on a current basis.

Expand Knowledge of Company Operations — The company should provide a systematic and continuing learning process for audit committee members to increase their effectiveness. An approach to achieving this goal is to review various financial aspects of the company on a planned basis.

Company Counsel — Regular meetings should be held with the company's general counsel and outside counsel, when appropriate, to discuss legal matters affecting the company's financial statements. In a number of companies, general counsel and outside counsel routinely attend audit committee meetings.

Audit Plans — The audit committee should review the audit plans of both the internal auditor and the external auditor and be familiar with the degree of coordination of the respective plans. The committee should make inquiries about the planned audit scopes and the extent that they can be relied upon to detect frauds or weaknesses in internal controls.

Electronic Data Processing — The audit committee should discuss with the internal auditor and the external auditor the steps being taken for a review of the company's electronic data processing procedures and controls, and inquire as to the specific security programs being used to protect against computer fraud or misuse from both within and outside the company.

Other Auditors — The audit committee should inquire as to the extent that external auditors other than the principal external auditor are to be used and understand the rationale for use of other auditors. The audit committee should request that the work of all other external auditors be coordinated and reviewed by the principal external auditor.

Officers' Expenses and Perquisites — The audit committee should review the company's policies and procedures for approval of officers' expenses and perquisites, including any use of corporate assets. In addition, the committee should inquire about the results of the company's review. If appropriate, the committee should review a summary of expenses and perquisites of the period under review.

Areas Requiring Special Attention — The audit committee should instruct the external auditor and the internal auditor that the audit committee group expects to be advised if there are any areas that require its special attention.

Guidelines for Selection of the External Auditor

Treadway emphasizes that one of the primary responsibilities of the audit committee is the selection of an independent external auditor for the company. Normally, the external auditor is proposed by management, with the audit committee confirming management's selection and the shareholders' ratifying the selection. *Treadway* discusses several issues that may need to be considered by the audit committee in the selection of the external auditor. These include:

- Management's and the internal auditor's opinion of the external auditor's performance,
- The audit engagement letter, including the proposed fee,
- The expected level of participation by a partner and other management personnel in the engagement, skills and experience of staff, and staff rotation policy, and
- If a new public accounting firm is to be engaged or is being considered, the steps planned to ensure a smooth and effective transition of external auditors to guard against unexpected complications.

In reviewing various external audit firms, the audit committee should consider the public accounting firm's latest peer review conducted under a professional quality-control program, the litigation problems or disciplinary actions involving the firm, and the firm's overall credentials, capabilities, and reputation, together with a list of clients from the same industry and geographical area.

Guidelines for Post-Audit Review

Treadway also provides a significant number of guidelines regarding post-audit review. The audit committee should:

- Obtain explanations from management for all significant variations in the company's financial statements between years (consider performing this review at a meeting of the entire board).
- Consider whether the significant variations are consistent with Management's Discussion and Analysis (MD&A) in the annual report.[3]

---

[3] As discussed in Chapter 12, "Relationship with the External Auditor," the external auditor may be engaged to examine or review MD&A.

- Obtain from financial management and the external auditor an explanation about changes in accounting standards or rules having an effect on the financial statement.
- Inquire about the existence and substance of significant accounting accruals, reserves, or estimates made by management that had a material impact on the financial statements.
- Inquire of management and the external auditor about any significant financial reporting issues discussed during the accounting period and how they were resolved.
- Hold a private meeting with the external auditor to request the external auditor's opinion on various matters, including the quality of financial accounting personnel and the internal audit staff.
- Ask the external auditor about his or her greatest concerns about the company and if the external auditor believes anything else should be discussed with the committee.
- Review the management representation letter given to the external auditor and inquire as to whether the external auditor encountered any difficulties in obtaining the letter or any portion thereof.
- Discuss with management and the external auditor the substance of significant issues relating to litigation, contingencies, claims, or assessments, and understand how such matters are reflected in the financial statements.
- Determine the open federal income tax years, be aware if there are any significant items that have been or might be disputed by the Internal Revenue Service (or other tax authorities), and inquire as to the status of the related tax reserves.
- Review with management the MD&A section of the annual report and ask the extent to which the external auditor reviewed MD&A.
- Inquire of the external auditor if the other sections of the annual report to shareholders are consistent with the information reflected in the financial statements.
- Consider whether the external auditor should meet with the full board to discuss any matters relating to the financial statements and to answer any questions the other directors might have.

Management's Responsibility for the Financial Statements and Underlying Controls

In another section of the 1987 report, *Treadway* recommends that management be required to state annually its responsibilities for preparing financial statements and for maintaining an adequate system of internal control, including a description as to how such responsibilities are fulfilled. In addition, *Treadway* recommends that management provide an assessment of the effectiveness of the company's internal controls. The assessment encompasses the entire internal control system, not just the internal accounting control required to comply with the Foreign Corrupt Practices Act.

A Post-Mortem

While no formal action on the 11 recommendations was taken for a number of years, a number of the recommendations were implemented voluntarily by many public companies. More recently, the recommendations were reemphasized by the 1999 *Report and Recommendations of the Blue Ribbon Committee on Improving the Effectiveness of Corporate Audit Committees* and implemented thereafter as discussed in Chapter 5.

Here is a summary of the recommendations of the National Commission on Fraudulent Financial Reporting pertaining to audit committees:

1. The boards of directors of all public companies, regardless of size, should be required by SEC rules to establish audit committees composed solely of independent directors.
2. Audit committees should be informed, vigilant, and effective overseers of the financial reporting process and the company's internal controls.
3. All public companies should develop a written charter of the audit committee's duties and responsibilities. The board should approve the charter, review it periodically, and modify it as necessary.
4. Audit committees should have adequate resources and authority to discharge their responsibilities.
5. The audit committee should review management's evaluation of factors related to the independence of the company's external auditor. Both the audit committee and management should assist the external auditor in preserving their independence.
6. Before the beginning of each year, the audit committee should review management's plans for engaging the company's independent auditor to perform consulting services during the coming year, considering both the types of services that may be rendered and the projected fees.

7. A company's audit committee should annually review the management program to monitor compliance with the code of corporate conduct.

8. Management and the audit committee should ensure that the internal auditor's involvement in the audit of the entire financial reporting process is appropriate and properly coordinated with the external auditor.

9. All public companies should be required by SEC rules to include in their annual reports to shareholders a letter signed by the chairman of the audit committee describing the committee's responsibilities and activities during the year.

10. Management should advise the audit committee when it seeks a second opinion on a significant accounting issue.

11. Audit committees should oversee the quarterly reporting process.

CHAPTER 4
ADDITIONAL DEVELOPMENTS
FROM *TREADWAY* TO 2001

As discussed in Chapter 3, *Treadway* focused attention on the function of audit committees in corporate accountability. Because of the continuing incidence of unexpected business failure, management fraud, and financial surprises, legislators, regulators, and business and professional organizations have mandated or encouraged companies to follow accountability practices aimed at ensuring that certain standards of compliance are achieved. Since the issuance of *Treadway,* actions by the above groups have further defined and expanded the roles and responsibilities of audit committees. However, from 1987 until 1998, the Securities and Exchange Commission (SEC) was surprisingly quiet about audit committees, particularly given the logic for stronger audit committees articulated in *Treadway.* As discussed later in this chapter, the SEC, especially in 1999, has clearly made up for lost time in considering requirements for audit committees of public companies. This chapter presents the significant audit committee developments from the issuance of *Treadway* in 1987 to the year 2001.

Institute of Internal Auditors Issues Position Statement and Research Report on Best Practices

In 1987, the Institute of Internal Auditors (IIA) issued a position statement, *Internal Auditing and the Audit Committee: Working Together toward Common Goals.*[1] The IIA recommended that every public company have an audit committee, organized as a standing committee of the board, consisting solely of outside directors independent of management. The IIA also encouraged the establishment of audit committees in other organizations, including not-for-profit and public sector entities.

According to the IIA position statement, the audit committee should expect the internal auditor to examine and evaluate the adequacy and effectiveness of the company's internal control system and the quality of performance in carrying out assigned responsibilities. Further, the IIA recognizes that the internal auditor could be used as a source of information about major frauds or irregularities and compliance with laws and regulations. These

---

[1] *Internal Auditing and the Audit Committee: Working Together toward Common Goals* (The Institute of Internal Auditors, 1987).

recommendations and others are discussed in Chapter 11, "Relationship with the Internal Auditor."

In response to concern about corporate responsibility and accountability, in 1993, the IIA Research Foundation published a research report prepared by Price Waterhouse (currently PricewaterhouseCoopers) entitled *Improving Audit Committee Performance: What Works Best.*[2] The research targeted progressive organizations to identify the practices of their audit committees. Perhaps the report's most important finding was that audit committee members must be provided with more background information and training to enable them to be more effective. The report found that additional background and training would enable audit committees to address the full range of issues related to internal control, organizational governance, and management reporting.

Other findings from the research report were that audit committees:

- Should assess their effectiveness periodically.
- May want to be more involved in the interim reporting process, including reviewing interim financial reports before they are filed with regulators.
- Should follow the *Treadway* and the Public Oversight Board of the SEC Practice Section (discussed later in this chapter) recommendations and include a letter in the annual report describing their activities and responsibilities. (According to the IIA research findings, less than one percent of the publicly held companies in the United States covered in their survey included reports or letters from their audit committees in annual reports.)

Additional findings from *Improving Audit Committee Performance: What Works Best* are presented in other chapters, especially Chapter 11, "Relationship with the Internal Auditor."

National Association of Securities Dealers Adopts Requirement

The National Association of Securities Dealers (NASD) first adopted a requirement, effective in August 1987, for issuers of securities traded on the NASD Automated Quotation system that were deemed to be National Mar-

---

[2] *Improving Audit Committee Performance: What Works Best* (The Institute of Internal Auditors Research Foundation, 1993).

ket System companies to establish and maintain an audit committee, having a majority of independent directors.[3] Smaller companies having securities traded on NASD's Automated Quotation system were not required to have audit committees.

AICPA Issues SAS 61 to Require Communications to Audit Committees

In 1988, the AICPA's Auditing Standards Board, primarily in response to the concerns expressed in *Treadway,* issued Statement on Auditing Standards 61 (SAS 61), *Communication with Audit Committees.*[4] SAS 61 applies to communications between an external auditor and (1) entities that either have an audit committee or that have otherwise formally designated oversight of the financial reporting process to a group equivalent to an audit committee; and (2) all SEC reporting companies.

SAS 61 established a requirement for the external auditor to determine that certain matters related to the conduct of an audit are communicated to the audit committee. The external auditor must communicate some of the matters; management or the internal auditor may communicate others. The communication may be oral or written. The external auditor has a responsibility to determine that the audit committee knows about significant audit adjustments, disagreements with management, difficulties encountered in performing the audit, and other audit-related matters.

The objective of SAS 61 is to increase the flow of useful information to the audit committee. The clear implication of SAS 61 is that the audit committee has a responsibility to follow up on any matters of concern included in a SAS 61 communication from the external auditor. SAS 61 is discussed in detail in Chapter 12, "Relationship with the External Auditor."

Canadian Institute of Chartered Accountants Issues MacDonald Report

As discussed in Chapter 2, Canada exerted leadership in mandating the establishment of audit committees for publicly held companies. In 1988, the Commission to Study the Public's Expectation of Audits (known as the

---

[3] NASD Bylaws, Part II, Schedule D, Section 5(d) and (h) (1987).

[4] "Communication with Audit Committees," *Statement on Auditing Standards No. 61* (AICPA 1988, amended in 1999).

MacDonald Commission) issued its final report, which included several recommendations relating to corporate accountability and strengthening the audit environment and audit committees.[5]

The MacDonald Commission recommended that the Canadian Institute of Chartered Accountants (CICA) enlist the support of interested bodies to seek legislation requiring that all public companies have audit committees composed entirely of outside directors. In addition, the MacDonald Commission urged the CICA to provide written guidance about (1) matters that should be communicated by an external auditor to the audit committee and (2) actions an external auditor should take when not satisfied with the results of such communications. The MacDonald Commission also recommended that the CICA urge changes in the law to require publication by the board of directors of a formal statement of responsibilities of the audit committee and to require audit committees to report annually to shareholders as to how their mandate was fulfilled. In addition, the MacDonald Commission urged that legislation be sought to require that audit committees review both interim financial statements and annual financial statements before publication.

American Stock Exchange Amends Listing Requirements

In 1989, the American Stock Exchange (AMEX) proposed an amendment to its rules to require that listed companies establish and maintain an audit committee; the SEC approved the rule in 1991.[6] Under the amendment, a majority of audit committee members were required to be outside directors. With the change in the rule, the AMEX moved closer to the requirements of the New York Stock Exchange (NYSE) and the NASD.

United States Federal Sentencing Guidelines Are Issued

In November 1991, the U.S. Federal Sentencing Commission issued the Federal Sentencing Guidelines for Organizations (Sentencing Guidelines) for judges to use in sentencing organizations convicted of crimes.[7] The Sentencing Guidelines, which apply to virtually every type of organization (such

---

[5] Commission to Study the Public's Expectation of Audits, *Report of the Commission to Study the Public's Expectations of Audits* (Toronto, Canada: CICA, 1988).

[6] Exchange Act Release No. 39796 (October 8, 1991).

[7] *United States Sentencing Guidelines,* Guidelines Manual, Ch. 8. (The Federal Sentencing Guidelines went into effect in 1987 and were amended in 1991 to apply to companies and other business entities.)

as corporations and partnerships) and every type of business crime (such as antitrust, securities violations, wire and mail fraud, commercial bribery, money laundering, and kickbacks), provide specific rules for sentences of organizational defendants. Penalties under the guidelines range from heavy fines that can reach hundreds of millions of dollars to a possible "death penalty" for an entity. In addition to paying fines, companies can be ordered to make restitution to victims and may be subject to supervised probation.

The Sentencing Guidelines provide for substantial mitigation of penalties if an entity has an effective internal compliance program that is designed to prevent and discover criminal violations of laws. An audit committee overseeing the company's compliance program may be an important mitigating factor under the Sentencing Guidelines.

To have an effective program to prevent and detect violations of the law, the Sentencing Guidelines list the steps that entities should follow to demonstrate exercise of due diligence. Those steps are presented in Exhibit 4-1.

Exhibit 4-1
Compliance Program Requirements under
the Federal Sentencing Guidelines

1. Establish standards and procedures reasonably capable of reducing the prospect of criminal conduct.
2. Appoint designated individual(s) within the organization's high-level personnel to oversee compliance.
3. Avoid giving substantial discretionary authority to individuals whom the organization knows (or should know) have a propensity to engage in illegal activity.
4. Communicate the standards and procedures (in 1 above) to all employees and agents through required training programs and publications.
5. Strive to achieve compliance with the standards through monitoring and auditing systems.
6. Have a reporting system for employees and agents to report criminal conduct of others within the organization without fear of reprisal.
7. Have appropriate disciplinary mechanisms in place so that individuals responsible for failures to detect offenses can be disciplined when appropriate.
8. Take all appropriate steps after detecting an offense to respond and prevent further offenses (modification of the program may be appropriate to prevent similar offenses).

The Sentencing Guidelines' compliance program requirements are generally being accepted and adopted as good corporate practice. **Careful attention should be given to the Sentencing Guidelines by all (for-profit, not-for-profit, and public sector) audit committees.**

Federal Deposit Insurance Corporation Mandates Audit Committees

In December 1991, the Federal Deposit Insurance Corporation Improvement Act (FDICIA) was enacted.[8] The FDICIA is significant because it is the first U.S. federal legislation to mandate audit committees. Among other things, the FDICIA requires that federally insured banks and other depositories with total assets of $500 million or more must have an audit committee composed of outside independent directors. Audit committees of depositories with total assets of $3 billion or more must have (1) members with relevant banking or financial experience, (2) access to their own outside counsel, and (3) no large customers as members. The FDICIA and related regulations do not define "independence," "relevant banking or financial experience," or "large customer."

The FDICIA regulations also require that management (of institutions having $500 million or more of total assets) make assessments of, and report on, the effectiveness of internal controls over financial reporting and the institution's compliance with laws and regulations relating to loans to insiders and dividend restrictions of the Federal Deposit Insurance Corporation.

A federally insured depository's external auditors are required to examine and publicly report on management's representations relating to internal controls over financial reporting. The FDICIA also specifically requires that the audit committee review with management and the external auditor the basis for the accountant's report on management's representations. The external auditor's report on internal control over financial reporting is discussed in Chapter 12, "Relationship with the External Auditor."

Committee of Sponsoring Organizations of the Treadway Commission Issues Reports on Internal Control, Derivatives, and Fraud[9]

In 1992, the Committee of Sponsoring Organizations of the Treadway Commission issued a report entitled *Internal Control — Integrated Framework*

---

[8] Title 1, Public Law No. 102-242 (December 19, 1991).

[9] The COSO publications are available at www.coso.org.

(*COSO Report*).[10] The *COSO Report* resulted from the recommendation of *Treadway* that the sponsoring organizations (American Accounting Association, American Institute of CPAs, Financial Executive Institute, Institute of Internal Auditors, and Institute of Management Accountants) work together to integrate the various internal control concepts and definitions used by those organizations and develop a common control framework. The *COSO Report* also contains guidance to help companies judge the effectiveness of their internal controls over: (1) financial reporting, (2) compliance with laws and regulations, and (3) operations.

In the *COSO Report,* an audit committee is part of the control environment component of a company's internal control system. The audit committee can significantly influence the control environment and the "tone at the top," depending upon the audit committee's independence from management, the experience and the stature of its members, the extent of its oversight activities, and its interactions with the internal and the external auditor.

As discussed in Chapter 9, "The Audit Committee's Oversight of Internal Control," the *COSO Report* focused on the ever-changing and expanding definition of internal control. No longer will companies and their boards of directors merely be able to oversee internal control as it relates to financial reporting and meet the requirements of the various audiences to which they are responsible. Accordingly, the *COSO Report* is a significant document that must be carefully considered by each audit committee in discharging its delegated functions. The *COSO Report* takes on even more significance in light of the *Caremark* decision (see Chapter 10, "The Potential Impact of the *Caremark* Decision on Audit Committees").

In 1996, the Committee of Sponsoring Organizations of the Treadway Commission issued *Internal Control Issues in Derivatives Usage: An Information Tool for Considering the COSO Internal Control — Integrated Framework in Derivatives Applications.*[11] The derivatives framework is a non-authoritative reference document that illustrates how the *COSO Report* can be applied by end users to evaluate the effectiveness of internal controls surrounding the use of derivative products. The board of directors is responsible for overseeing the company's policies for managing risk and using derivatives. Therefore, according to the derivatives document, the audit

---

[10] Committee of Sponsoring Organizations of the Treadway Commission, *Internal Control — Integrated Framework* (1992).

[11] Committee of Sponsoring Organizations of the Treadway Commission, *Internal Control Issues in Derivatives Usage: An Information Tool for Considering the COSO Internal Control — Intergrated Framework in Derivatives Applications* (1996).

committee should understand the scope of internal and external audit testing of compliance with approved risk management policies, procedures, and limits relating to derivatives. Furthermore, the audit committee should become comfortable that controls appear to be working and should be alert to the risk that such controls could be circumvented.[12]

Finally, in 1999, the Committee of Sponsoring Organizations of the Treadway Commission issued a research report, *Fraudulent Financial Reporting 1987–1997: An Analysis of U.S. Public Companies.*[13] According to the research report, the majority of the financial fraud cases brought by the SEC during the period studied involved small companies with total assets of less than $100 million. Twenty-five percent of the 200 companies in which fraudulent financial reporting was alleged did not have an audit committee, and in those companies having an audit committee, the members of such committee met only once a year. In 65 percent of the cases, the audit committee members did not appear to be certified in accounting or have current or prior work experience in accounting or finance positions. Boards of directors in the 200 companies investigated tended to be dominated by insiders with significant equity ownership and little experience serving on boards. The companies also tended to have a number of family relationships among directors and officers, and individuals often had multiple positions with incompatible functions (for example, CEO and CFO). Top senior executives were frequently involved in the financial statement fraud. Significantly, all sizes of CPA firms were associated as auditors with the companies committing fraud.

United Kingdom Issues Cadbury Report

In December 1992, the United Kingdom's Committee on the Financial Aspects of Corporate Governance (Cadbury Committee) sponsored by the Financial Reporting Council, the London Stock Exchange, and the accounting profession, issued a report regarding the financial aspects of corporate gov-

---

[12] *Ibid.*, 5.

[13] Mark S. Beasley, Joseph V. Carcello, and Dana R. Hermanson, *Fraudulent Financial Reporting: 1987-1997 An Analysis of U.S. Public Companies,* A Research Report Commissioned by the Committee of Sponsoring Organizations of the Treadway Commission (1999). The study is summarized at *www.aicpa.org/news/p032699b.htm.* The research analysis is extended by Beasley, *et al.,* in *Fraud-Related SEC Enforcement Actions Against Auditors, 1987-1997* (AICPA, 2000).

ernance.[14] The Cadbury Committee established a Code of Best Practice that has been adopted by the London Stock Exchange. The Code describes the conduct of boards of directors and requires UK-listed companies to state in their reports whether they complied with the Code and to identify and give reasons for any areas of non-compliance. The external auditor is required to review the company's statement of compliance before publication.

The Code of Best Practice requires companies to establish an audit committee of at least three non-executive directors (a majority should be independent of the company) with written terms of reference (that is, a charter) which deal clearly with its authority and duties. The audit committee should normally meet at least twice a year. The membership of the committee should be disclosed in the annual report and the chairperson of the committee should be available at the annual meeting to answer questions.

Public Oversight Board Issues Special Report and Publishes a Report on the Professionalism of the External Auditor

On March 5, 1993, the Public Oversight Board (POB) of the AICPA's SEC Practice Section issued a special report entitled *In the Public Interest: Issues Confronting the Accounting Profession.*[15] The POB special report recognized that, in a number of instances where the responsibility for scrutiny of financial statements had been delegated by boards to an audit committee, the audit committee did not perform its duties adequately, and, in many cases, did not understand its responsibilities. To overcome this problem, the POB recommended that audit committees should have the following responsibilities relating to a SEC registrant's preparation of annual financial statements:

1. Review the annual financial statements.
2. Confer with management and the external auditor about the financial statements.
3. Receive from the external auditor all information that the auditor is required to communicate under auditing standards.
4. Assess whether the financial statements are complete and consistent with information known to the audit committee.

---

[14] *Report of the Committee on the Financial Aspects of Corporate Governance* (United Kingdom, 1992).

[15] *A Special Report by the Public Oversight Board of the SEC Practice Section, AICPA* (March 5, 1993).

5. Assess whether the financial statements reflect appropriate accounting principles.

In addition, the POB recommended that the SEC require registrants to include, in a document containing the annual financial statements, a statement or report by the audit committee (or by the board if there is no audit committee) that describes its responsibilities and discloses how those responsibilities were discharged. Such disclosure should state whether the audit committee carried out the five duties listed above. The special report stated that to reduce the liability of audit committee members, the audit committee report should not be considered "solicited material" or "filed" under the Securities Exchange Act of 1934.

Finally, concerning audit fees, the POB special report recommended that: "The audit committee or the board of directors should be satisfied that the audit fee negotiated by it or management for the entity's audit is sufficient to assure that the entity will receive a comprehensive and complete audit."

In September 1994, the Advisory Panel on Auditor Independence (Kirk Panel) published *Strengthening the Professionalism of the Independent Auditor.*[16] According to the Kirk Panel, stronger, more accountable corporate boards of directors will (1) strengthen the professionalism of the external auditor, (2) enhance the value of the audit, and (3) serve the investing public. To increase the value of the audit, boards and their audit committees must hear from the external auditors their views about the:

- Appropriateness of the accounting principles used or proposed to be adopted by the company,
- Clarity of the company's financial disclosures, and
- Degree of aggressiveness or conservatism of the company's accounting principles and underlying estimates.

The Kirk Panel also indicated that external auditors must assume the obligation to communicate qualitative judgments about accounting principles, disclosures, and estimates to boards and their audit committees. And fundamentally, external auditors should look to the representatives of the shareholders — the board of directors — as their client, not company management.

---

[16] Report to the Public Oversight Board of the SEC Practice Section from the Advisory Panel on Auditor Independence, *Strengthening the Professionalism of the Independent Auditor* (1994).

American Law Institute Drafts Tentative Principles

For many years, the American Law Institute has been studying corporate governance. In early 1993, it issued a preliminary version of "Principles of Corporate Governance: Analysis and Recommendations" (ALI Principles).[17] The duties and responsibilities of audit committees are included in the many aspects of corporate governance covered in the ALI Principles.

The ALI Principles recommended that large (2,000 or more shareholders and $100 million or more of assets) and small (500 or more shareholders and $5 million or more of assets) public companies create an audit committee to implement and support the oversight function of the board by reviewing, on a periodic basis, the company's processes for producing financial data, its internal controls, and the independence of the company's external auditor. The ALI Principles further recommended that the audit committee be made up of at least three members who are neither employed by the company nor have been employed by the company within the two preceding years. In addition, a majority of the members of the committee should have no significant relationship with the company's senior executives.

According to the ALI Principles, an audit committee supports the oversight function of the board of directors by:

1. Providing focused oversight over financial reporting, controls over financial reporting, and the external audit.
2. Reinforcing the independence of the external auditor and assuring that the auditor will have free rein in the audit process.
3. Providing a forum for regular, informed, and private discussions with the external auditor, thereby encouraging the external auditor to raise potentially troublesome issues at an early stage.
4. Reinforcing the objectivity of the internal auditor.

SEC Chairman Delivers Major Speech on Earnings Management

On September 28, 1998, Arthur Levitt, Jr., Chairman of the SEC, made a major speech to address earnings management.[18] The presentation has had,

---

[17] ALI, "Principles of Corporate Governance: Analysis and Recommendations" *(Prepublication Edition)* (1993). To date, the final version of the principles has not been issued.

[18] Arthur Levitt, "The Numbers Game" at New York University for Law and Business, September 28, 1998. The speech is available at www.sec.gov/news/speeches/spch220.txt.

and is having, a major effect on those having responsibilities for financial reporting, including audit committees. Chairman Levitt expressed significant concerns about the quality of earnings of public companies. He indicated that a qualified, committed, independent, and tough-minded audit committee represents the most reliable guardian of the public interest. He stated:

> Sadly, stories abound of audit committees whose members lack expertise in the basic principles of financial reporting as well as the mandate to ask probing questions. In fact, I've heard of one audit committee that convenes only twice a year before the regular board meeting for 15 minutes and whose duties are limited to a perfunctory presentation.
>
> Compare that situation with the audit committee which meets twelve times a year before each board meeting; where every member has a financial background; where there are no personal ties to the chairman or the company; where they have their own advisers; where they ask tough questions of management and outside auditors; and where, ultimately, the investor interest is being served.

Chairman Levitt identified "five of the more common accounting gimmicks" that companies use to manage earnings. These five accounting gimmicks are summarized in Exhibit 4-2. He also announced in his speech a nine-point action plan, summarized in Exhibit 4-3, to enhance the credibility and transparency of financial reporting. The action plan was a public-private sector initiative that involved regulators, standards setters, boards of directors and their audit committees, company management, and the entire financial community. In fact, the action plan called for a fundamental cultural change for company management and the financial community. In concluding his remarks, Chairman Levitt stated that we must rededicate ourselves to a fundamental principle: **Markets exist through the grace of investors.**

Exhibit 4-2
Accounting Gimmicks Used to Manage Earnings:
An SEC Perspective

1. "Big Bath" restructuring charges that companies used to "clean up" their balance sheets are often overstated. If the restructuring charges are overstated in terms of amounts or items accrued, the extra cush-

ion can be used to create income in the future when estimates change or future earnings fall short.

2. Creative acquisition accounting or "merger magic" is used to (a) convert an ever-growing portion of the acquisition price to in-process research and development, which can be written off as a one-time charge, thereby removing any charge to future earnings, and (b) record inappropriate liabilities in a purchase business combination to protect future earnings.

3. Miscellaneous "cookie jar reserves" result from establishing or adjusting estimated liabilities or valuation accounts for such items as sales returns, loan losses, or warranty costs in a period in which creation of such liabilities or valuation accounts is not justified.

4. Misusing "materiality" by not adjusting financial statements because of errors that are less than a defined percentage or materiality level. Some companies misuse materiality by intentionally recording errors below materiality and then arguing that the effect on the bottom line is too small to matter.

5. "Revenue recognition" abuse is used by some companies to record revenue before (a) a sale is complete, (b) the product is delivered to a customer, or (c) the time when the customer still has options to terminate, void, or delay the sale.

Exhibit 4-3
The SEC's Nine-Point Action Plan

Improving the Accounting Framework

1. The SEC will require well-detailed disclosures about the impact of changes in accounting assumptions and accruals for losses.

2. The AICPA will provide auditing guidance related to purchased in-process research and development, restructuring liabilities, large acquisition write-offs, and revenue recognition.

3. The SEC will publish guidance on materiality that will consider qualitative, not just quantitative, factors. Materiality is not a bright line cutoff of three or five percent.

4. The SEC will publish guidance on revenue recognition and also determine whether the revenue recognition standards for the software industry apply to other service companies.

5. The accounting standards setters will take action where current standards are inadequate. The FASB should clarify the definition of a liability.

6. The SEC Division of Corporate Finance and the Division of Enforcement will formally target reviews of companies that announce restructuring liability reserves, major write-offs, or other practices that appear to manage earnings.

Improved Outside Auditing in the Financial Reporting Process

7. The Public Oversight Board of the SEC Practice Section will sponsor the Panel on Audit Effectiveness (to include all major participants in the financial reporting process) to review the way audits are performed and assess the impact of recent trends in auditing on the public interest.

Strengthening the Audit Committee Process

8. The NYSE and the NASD will sponsor the Blue Ribbon Committee on Improving the Effectiveness of Corporate Audit Committees. The Blue Ribbon Committee will examine how we can get the right people to do the right thing and ask the right questions. (See Chapter 5 for a discussion of the final report.)

Need for a Cultural Change

9. Company management and Wall Street should re-examine the current environment with a view toward creating a cultural change in corporate management. Management should focus on the integrity of the numbers and the transparency of financial statements. Wall Street should focus more on long-term prospects and less on the latest quarter.

Independence Standards Board Requires Communications with Audit Committee

The Independence Standards Board (ISB), which sets independence rules for public companies, issued its first standard in January 1999.[19] ISB Stan-

---

[19] The Independence Standards Board (ISB) was formed in 1997 through an agreement of the SEC and the accounting profession. The SEC, in Financial Reporting Release No. 50,

dard 1, *Independence Discussions with Audit Committees,* requires the external auditor at least annually to discuss with the audit committee any relationships with the company that, in the auditor's judgment, may reasonably be thought to bear on independence.[20] The auditor is also required to include a description of such relationships and confirm the firm's independence in a letter to the audit committee. The external auditor, in turn, is required to discuss independence with the audit committee. These requirements are discussed in more detail in Chapter 12, "Relationship with the External Auditor."

Blue Ribbon Committee on Improving the Effectiveness of Corporate Audit Committees Issues Report

On February 8, 1999, the Blue Ribbon Committee on Improving the Effectiveness of Corporate Audit Committees issued the *Report and Recommendations of the Blue Ribbon Committee on Improving the Effectiveness of Corporate Audit Committees (Blue Ribbon Report).*[21] The New York Stock Exchange and the National Association of Securities Dealers sponsored the committee at the request of Arthur Levitt, SEC Chairman. The formation of the Blue Ribbon Committee was announced in the September 28, 1998 speech discussed previously. Because of the significance of the Blue Ribbon Committee and its report, all of Chapter 5 is devoted to a discussion and analysis of its recommendations. The recommendations were directed to regulators and standard-setting bodies — the NYSE, NASD, AMEX, SEC, and the AICPA — that have the authority to mandate the suggested practices.

In December 1999, in response to the *Blue Ribbon Report,* the NYSE, NASD, AMEX, SEC, and the AICPA's Auditing Standards Board all issued new requirements. In summary, those changes (with certain exceptions for small companies) were as follows (the requirements are discussed in various chapters of this book):

---

dated February 18, 1998, recognized the establishment of the ISB. Its purpose is to establish, in the public interest, independence standards applicable to auditors of public companies. The ISB, an independent body funded by the AICPA SEC Practice Section, is currently comprised of eight members — four from the public and four from the accounting profession. (The Panel on Audit Effectiveness has recommended that the composition of the ISB be changed so that a majority of the members of the ISB would be from outside the profession.) William Allen, who was chancellor of the Court of Chancery in Delaware and author of the *Caremark* decision (discussed in Chapter 10), is the first chairperson of the ISB.

[20] *Independence Standards Board Standard 1 — "Independence Discussions with Audit Committee."* The standard can be found at www.cpaindependence.org.

[21] *Report and Recommendations of the Blue Ribbon Committee on Improving the Effectiveness of Corporate Audit Committees,* published by the New York Stock Exchange and the

- The NYSE, NASD, and AMEX strengthened the independence requirements for audit committee members, established a three member minimum size for the committee, and required listed companies to adopt a written audit committee charter that is reviewed annually.
- The SEC required companies to disclose whether they had a charter and to present the charter in proxy statements at least every three years, required an annual report from audit committees to be included in proxy statements, and mandated that all public companies have their quarterly financial statements reviewed on a timely basis by external auditors.
- The AICPA amended its Statements on Auditing Standards to expand the external auditor's required communications to include information about the quality of accounting principles, to include unrecorded audit adjustments, and to require communication of SAS 61 matters in quarterly review engagements.

POB Issues Report from the Panel on Audit Effectiveness

In October 1998, the POB appointed the Panel on Audit Effectiveness at the request of Arthur Levitt, Jr., Chairman of the SEC. Chairman Levitt identified the need for the Panel in his September 28 speech (discussed previously) as part of the SEC's nine point action plan (Exhibit 4-3). The Panel, in its final report (issued in August 2000), made a number of recommendations involving audit committees.[22] Some of the recommendations reiterated those made by others that are discussed previously. However, some of the recommendations are significant in that the emphasis is different or the point is unique. As a result of the survey, focus groups, quasi peer reviews (in-depth reviews of the quality of 126 audits of SEC registrants in 28 offices of the largest CPA firms), and interviews conducted, the Panel stated that:

- There is clear evidence that the frequency of contact and substantive interaction between the external auditor and the audit committee can and should be improved.
- Other opportunities for improvement include more frequent audit committee meetings, a higher level of committee activity, and the need for explicit committee expectations of the external auditor.
- Required external auditor communications should be more respon-

---

National Association of Securities Dealers (February 1999). The complete report may be found online at http://www.nyse.com/content/publications/NT0001873E.html or www.nasd.com/docs/textapp.pdf.

[22] *The Panel on Audit Effectiveness Report and Recommendations,* August 31, 2000.

sive and substantive, especially communications about information systems and financial statement risks, internal control, earnings management, and compliance with laws and regulations.

- Audit committees should consider certain factors in evaluating the engagement of the external auditor to perform non-audit services and should pre-approve significant non-audit services.

The above recommendations and other suggestions made by the Panel are discussed in various chapters in this book, especially in Chapter 12.

SEC Requires Disclosure of Non-Audit Fees

In November 2000, in response to concerns about the kinds of and volume of non-audit services performed by a company's principal external auditor, the SEC approved disclosure requirements for fees related to audit, review, and non-audit services (that is, any service other than audit and review of financial statements).[23] The rules require companies to disclose current-year fees in their proxy statements. A company must disclose fees from its principal auditor for (1) the annual audit and quarterly reviews of its financial statements, (2) non-audit services related to financial information systems work, and (3) all other fees. Furthermore, registrants must disclose whether their audit committee considered all non-audit services and their effect on the principal auditor's independence. Additional details about the SEC's new rule on auditor independence are discussed in Chapter 12.

Here is a summary of the important milestones from 1987 to 2001 in the evolution of audit committees:

1987

- Treadway Commission publishes a specific set of good practice guidelines for audit committees.
- NASD adopts a requirement to establish and maintain an audit committee having a majority of independent directors for all issuers of securities traded on the NASD Automated Quotation system that are National Market System companies.
- IIA issues a position statement, *Internal Auditing and the Audit Committee: Working Together toward Common Goals,* to elaborate on its 1985

---

[23] SEC Release Nos. 33-7919 and 34-43602.

position statement that recommended that every public company have an audit committee.

1988

- AICPA's Auditing Standards Board issues SAS 61, *Communication with Audit Committees,* to require the external auditor to determine that certain matters (e.g., audit adjustments, disagreements with management, and difficulties encountered in performing the audit) are known to the audit committee.
- Canadian Institute of Chartered Accountants' Commission to Study the Public's Expectation of Audits (MacDonald Commission) issues final report, which includes recommendations relating to strengthening the audit environment and audit committees.

1991

- AMEX obtains approval of a requirement that listed companies establish and maintain an audit committee having a majority of outside directors.
- Federal sentencing guidelines for organizations become effective. (Audit committees may qualify as an effective measure to mitigate penalties for entities subject to federal criminal prosecution.)
- Federal Deposit Insurance Corporation Improvement Act becomes law, representing the first U.S. federal legislation to mandate audit committees. The Act's implementing regulations require certain banks and other depositories to have audit committees consisting solely of outside directors. For large depositories, the audit committee is required to include members with banking or financial management expertise.

1992

- United Kingdom's Committee on the Financial Aspects of Corporate Governance (Cadbury Committee) issues recommendation that all listed companies should comply with Code of Best Practices, which includes a requirement to establish an audit committee. The London Stock Exchange requires all listed companies to describe their compliance with the Code.
- COSO issues *Internal Control—Integrated Framework* to provide a common ground for understanding and a common criteria for assessing internal controls over financial reporting, compliance with laws and regulations, and operations.

1993

- Institute of Internal Auditors Research Foundation publishes a research report, *Improving Audit Committee Performance: What Works Best.*

Among other things, the research found that audit committees need more background information and training to be more effective.

- AICPA's Public Oversight Board of the SEC Practice Section issues a special report, *In the Public Interest: Issues Confronting the Accounting Profession.* The special report recognizes that in a number of instances audit committees do not perform their duties adequately and do not understand their responsibilities. The POB recommends certain tasks for audit committees, including providing a report from the committee in the company's annual report.
- American Law Institute issues a preliminary version of *Principles of Corporate Governance: Analysis and Recommendations.* The report recommends that large and small public companies create audit committees, having at least three outside independent members, to implement and support the oversight function of the board by reviewing the company's processes for producing financial data, its internal controls, and the independence of the company's external auditor.

1994

- Public Oversight Board of the SEC Practice Section issues *Conclusions from Strengthening the Professionalism of the Independent Auditor* (Kirk Panel). The report indicates that external auditors must view the board of directors, not company management, as their client, and that audit committees must hear from external auditors their views about the quality and not just the acceptability of a company's accounting principles.

1996

- COSO issues *Internal Control Issues in Derivatives Usage: An Information Tool for Considering the COSO Internal Control — Integrated Framework in Derivatives Applications.* The non-authoritative reference document illustrates how the 1992 COSO Framework can be used to evaluate the effectiveness of control surrounding the use of derivative products by end users.

1998

- SEC Chairman delivers a speech entitled "The Numbers Game" to call attention to problems relating to the quality of earnings and the quality of financial reporting of public companies. The Chairman emphasizes that a qualified, committed, independent, and tough-minded audit committee represents the most reliable guardian of the public interest.

1999

- Independence Standards Board issues Standard 1, *Independence Discussions with Audit Committee,* to require the external auditor to: (1) disclose to the audit committee in writing all relationships between the auditor and the company that bear on independence, (2) confirm in the letter that the auditor is independent, and (3) discuss independence with the audit committee.
- Blue Ribbon Committee on Improving the Effectiveness of Corporate Audit Committees issues *Report and Recommendations of the Blue Ribbon Committee on Improving the Effectiveness of Corporate Audit Committees.* The report is intended to effect pragmatic, progressive changes in the functions and expectations placed on corporate boards, audit committees, senior and financial management, the internal auditor, and the external auditor regarding financial reporting and the oversight process.
- NYSE, NASD, AMEX, SEC, and AICPA finalize major rule changes to implement recommendations of the Blue Ribbon Committee. Changes include strengthened independence requirements for audit committee members, minimum size requirements for audit committees, required charters and disclosure thereof, required timely reviews of quarterly financial statements, and expanded external auditor required communications in audit and review engagements.
- Committee of Sponsoring Organizations of the Treadway Commission issues *Fraudulent Financial Reporting 1987–1997: An Analysis of U.S. Public Companies.* The research report shows that the majority of the financial fraud cases brought by the SEC during the 11-year period analyzed involved small companies with total assets of less than $100 million.

2000

- The Panel on Audit Effectiveness issues its report stating, among other things, that the audit committee should pre-approve significant non-audit services to be performed by the external auditor.
- The SEC issued new rules on external auditor independence that require disclosure of (1) external audit, review, and non-audit fees performed by the principal external auditor and (2) whether the audit committee considered the non-audit services and whether the performance of those services was compatible with maintaining the auditor's independence.

CHAPTER 5
THE 1999 BLUE RIBBON COMMITTEE ON IMPROVING THE EFFECTIVENESS OF CORPORATE AUDIT COMMITTEES— ANOTHER MAJOR MILESTONE

In September 1998, the New York Stock Exchange (NYSE) and the National Association of Securities Dealers (NASD) asked John C. Whitehead, former Deputy Secretary of State and retired Co-Chairman and Senior Partner of Goldman, Sachs & Co., and Ira Millstein, Senior Partner of Weil, Gotshal & Manges LLP, to chair the 1999 Blue Ribbon Committee on Improving the Effectiveness of Corporate Audit Committees (Committee). On February 8, 1999, the 1999 Committee's report entitled *Report and Recommendations of the Blue Ribbon Committee on Improving the Effectiveness of Corporate Audit Committees* (*Blue Ribbon Report*) was issued.[1]

The Committee's focus was on the significant gray area where management discretion and subjective judgments bear on the quality of financial reporting. The Committee emphasized the need for financial management to make sound financial judgments and recognized the need for a formal process by which external auditors and audit committees evaluate such judgments. The report was intended to effect pragmatic, progressive changes in the functions and expectations placed on corporate boards, audit committees, senior and financial management, the internal auditor, and the external auditor regarding financial reporting and the oversight process.

The chapter presents the recommendations made by the *Blue Ribbon Report* and the guiding principles for best practices. The committee identified the guiding principles as common sense fundamentals that apply to audit committees regardless of a company's individual situation.

Overview and Recommendations

The *Blue Ribbon Report* states that the starting point for the development of audit committee guidelines is recognition of the audit committee's position in the larger governance process as it relates to the oversight of financial re-

---

[1] The Blue Ribbon Committee that issued the report discussed in the chapter should not be confused with the Report of the NACD Blue Ribbon Commission on *Audit Committees: A Practical Guide* that was issued in 2000. Recommendations from the latter report are discussed at appropriate points throughout this book.

porting. The *Blue Ribbon Report* recognizes that it is not the job of the audit committee to prepare financial statements, or be involved in the numerous decisions required in the preparation of those statements. The audit committee's task is clearly one of oversight and monitoring, not auditing the auditors. In carrying out its task, the audit committee must rely on senior financial management, the internal auditor, and the external auditor.

The *Blue Ribbon Report* describes the three main groups responsible for financial reporting (the board of directors, including the audit committee; financial management, including internal auditors; and the external auditor) as a "three-legged stool" that supports responsible financial disclosure and active and participatory oversight. The audit committee is "first among equals" in the process since the audit committee is an extension of the board and, hence, the ultimate monitor of the process.

The recommendations of the *Blue Ribbon Report* are built on two essential factors. First, the audit committee must have actual practices and overall performance that reflect the professionalism embodied by the full board of which it is a part. Secondly, a legal, regulatory, and self-regulatory framework must exist that emphasizes disclosure, transparency, and accountability. The *Blue Ribbon Report* emphasizes that while the recommendations are made separately, the ten recommendations are an integrated set of objectives that must be adopted in their entirety to accomplish the intended results.

The ten recommendations are discussed below. The implementation status of each recommendation is presented after the discussion of the particular recommendation.[2]

---

[2] The recommendations concerning the stock exchanges are addressed to the NYSE and NASD. The American Stock Exchange (AMEX) was not *explicitly* addressed. However, AMEX is covered, because at the time of issuing the *Blue Ribbon Report,* NASD and AMEX had agreed to merge. Subsequent thereto, the merger was terminated.

Recommendation 1 — Meaning of Independence

The NYSE and NASD should adopt the following definition of independence for purposes of service on audit committees for listed companies with a market capitalization above $200 million or a more appropriate measure for identifying smaller-size companies as determined jointly by the NYSE and the NASD (hereinafter referred to as "a more appropriate small-company measure").

Members of the audit committee will be considered independent if they have no relationship with the company that may interfere with the exercise of their independence from management and the company. Examples of unacceptable relationships include a director:

- Being employed by the company or any of its affiliates for the current year or any of the past five years;
- Accepting any compensation from the company or any of its affiliates other than compensation for board service or benefits under a tax-qualified retirement plan;
- Being a member of the immediate family of an individual who is, or has been in any of the past five years, employed by the company or any of its affiliates as an executive officer;
- Being a partner in, a controlling shareholder in, or an executive officer of, any for-profit business organization to which the company may make, or from which the company receives, payments that are or have been "significant" to the company in any of the past five years;
- Being employed as an executive of another company (Co. B) where any of the company's executives serve on Co. B's compensation committee.

According to the *Blue Ribbon Report,* a director who has one or more of the above relationships may be appointed to the audit committee, if the board, under exceptional and limited circumstances, determines that membership on the committee by the individual is required for the best interests of the company and its shareholders. If the board decides to appoint such a director to the audit committee, the board should disclose in the next annual proxy statement the nature of the relationship and the reasons for the decision.

Status: NYSE, NASD, and the American Stock Exchange (AMEX) amended their rules on independence along the lines suggested above. The variations in the definitions of independence among the exchanges is presented in Chapter 7, "Appointing and Educating the Audit Commit-

tee." The exchanges made a significant exception from the recommendations relating to the years for disqualification for a former employee or
immediate family member — those individuals should be independent
after three years, not five years. NYSE revised its listing standards to apply to all U. S. companies listing common stock and rejected the $200
million market capitalization exception. NASD and AMEX revised standards apply the independence rules to all SEC entities.

Recommendation 2—All Independent Directors

The NYSE and the NASD should require listed companies with a market
capitalization above $200 million (or a more appropriate small-company
measure) to have an audit committee comprised solely of independent directors. The NYSE and the NASD should maintain their respective current
audit committee independence requirements and their respective definitions
of independence for listed companies with a market capitalization of $200
million or below (or a more appropriate small-company measure).

Status: The NYSE rejected the exemption for companies under $200 mil-
lion market capitalization. Their revised rules require audit committee
members to be independent with one exception permitted. That exception may be applied in exceptional and limited circumstances to one director who is not independent because of the former employee and immediate family member rules. The NASD and AMEX revised standards
permit one director who is not independent because of any rule to be on
the audit committee in exceptional and limited circumstances. The SEC
revised rules require all companies with securities listed on NYSE, AMEX,
or quoted on Nasdaq to disclose whether audit committee members are
independent and to disclose additional information if a company has exercised an independence wavier for a director.

Recommendation 3 — Minimum Size and Expertise

The NYSE and the NASD should require listed companies with a market
capitalization above $200 million (or a more appropriate small-company
measure) to have an audit committee comprised of a minimum of three di-

rectors, each of whom is financially literate (as described in the next paragraph) or becomes financially literate within a reasonable period of time after appointment to the audit committee. In addition, at least one member of the audit committee should have accounting or related financial management expertise. The NYSE and the NASD should maintain their current audit committee requirements for smaller companies.

Because of the audit committee's responsibility for overseeing accounting and financial controls and reporting, the committee should have at least one member with accounting or related financial expertise — meaning past employment experience in finance or accounting, professional certification in accounting, or any other comparable experience or background that results in an individual's financial sophistication, including being or having been a chief executive officer or other senior officer with financial oversight responsibilities. While all of the members of the audit committee need to be able to ask probing questions about the company's financial risks and accounting, a director's ability to ask and intelligently evaluate the answers to such questions may not require "expertise," but rather hinges upon intelligence, diligence, a probing mind, and a certain basic "financial literacy." Such "literacy" signifies the ability to read and understand fundamental financial statements, including a company's balance sheet, income statement, and cash flow statement. Directors who have limited familiarity with finance can achieve such "literacy" through training programs.

While the *Blue Ribbon Report* does not address the issue, the "financial literacy" requirement may be very significant in selecting all members of the board of directors if audit committee memberships are rotated at frequent intervals. If all, or substantially all, directors are not "financially literate," rotation may be made more difficult and the advantages and disadvantages of extended or even lifetime audit committee appointments should be seriously considered by the entire board. As a result of the "financial literacy" recommendation, the nominating committees of boards of directors will need to be diligent in examining the financial qualifications, as well as other qualifications, of prospective board members to give the board maximum flexibility in assigning and rotating committee memberships.

Status: NYSE, NASD, and AMEX adopted the recommendations about (1) the minimum size of the audit committee and (2) one member having accounting or related financial management expertise (with NASD and AMEX exceptions for both (1) and (2) for small business filers).* The exchanges adopted the recommendation about financial literacy with some variation in their definitions, which are discussed in Chapter 7.

---

*A small business filer is an issuer that (1) has revenue of less than $25 million and public float of less than $25 million, (2) is a U.S. or Canadian issuer, and (3) if the entity is a majority-owned subsidiary, the parent company is a small business issuer.

Recommendation 4—Formal Written Charter

The NYSE and the NASD should require the audit committee of each listed company (1) to adopt a formal written charter that is approved by the full board of directors and that specifies the scope of the committee's responsibilities, and how it carries out those responsibilities, including structure, processes, and membership requirements, and (2) to review and assess the adequacy of the audit committee charter on an annual basis.

A well-functioning audit committee will be concerned about, and spend a significant amount of time defining, the scope of its oversight responsibilities and how it discharges its duties. Accordingly, the *Blue Ribbon Report* recommended that a good audit committee memorialize its understanding of its role, responsibilities, and processes in a charter.

Status: NYSE, NASD, and AMEX require every company to adopt a written charter that is approved by the board of directors and reviewed and reassessed annually.

Recommendation 5 — Disclosure of Information about Charter

The SEC should promulgate rules that require the audit committee of each reporting company to disclose in the company's proxy statement for its annual meeting of shareholders whether the audit committee has adopted a formal written charter, and, if so, whether the audit committee satisfied its responsibilities during the prior year in compliance with its charter. Furthermore, the company should disclose its charter at least triennially in the annual report to shareholders or proxy statement and in the next annual report to shareholders or proxy statement after any significant amendment to that charter.

The *Blue Ribbon Report* indicates that disclosure will guide the committee to responsible practices. Although it was not the intention or belief of the Committee that such additional disclosure requirements impose greater liability on the audit committee or the full board under state law, the current standards for liability under the business judgment rule — in essence, gross negligence — would continue to apply. While the Committee believed that a "safe harbor"[3] presumably exists in the context of a state-law fiduciary duty claim, the *Blue Ribbon Report* recommends that the SEC adopt a "safe harbor" under the federal securities laws similar to the one now applicable to the executive compensation committee's report that appears in the proxy statement.

Status: The SEC amended its rules to require companies to disclose in their proxy statements whether the audit committee has a written charter and to file a copy of the charter with the proxy statement every three years. The SEC does not require a statement about compliance with the charter. However, NYSE, NASD, and AMEX require listed companies to confirm that certain charter provisions (for example, independence discussions with the external auditor) have been followed.

Recommendation 6—Accountability of External Auditor

The listing rules for both the NYSE and the NASD should require that the audit committee charter of every listed company specify that the external auditor is ultimately accountable to the board of directors and the audit committee, as representatives of the shareholders, and that these shareholder representatives have the ultimate authority and responsibility to select, evaluate, and, when appropriate, replace the external auditor (or to nominate the external auditor to be proposed for shareholder approval in the proxy statement).

The audit committee, as the delegate of the board, is responsible for oversight of the accounting and financial reporting process. Given the interrelated functions regarding accounting and financial reporting, the *Blue Ribbon Report* states that the relationship of the external auditor with both management and the audit committee should be clarified.

Since the external auditor is ultimately responsible to the board and the

---

[3] A "safe harbor" is merely a standard of conduct that, if met, will protect a person or committee from allegations of violations of a particular law.

audit committee, the audit committee has an obligation to review regularly the relationship between management and the external and internal auditors. Furthermore, the audit committee charter should make it clear in all cases that the board of directors and the audit committee have the ultimate authority and responsibility to select, evaluate, and, when appropriate, replace the external auditor.

Status: NYSE, NASD, and AMEX amended their listing requirements to require that these items be included in the audit committee charter.

Recommendation 7 — Statement from External Auditor Disclosing all Relationships to Company

The listing rules for both the NYSE and the NASD should require the audit committee charter for every listed company to specify that the audit committee is responsible for ensuring that it receives from the external auditors a formal written statement delineating all relationships between the auditor and the company, consistent with Independence Standards Board (ISB) Standard 1 (as discussed in the next paragraph), and that the audit committee also be responsible for actively engaging in a dialogue with the external auditor about any disclosed relationships or services that may impact the objectivity and independence of the auditor and for taking, or recommending that the full board take, appropriate action to ensure the independence of the external auditor.

Because the external auditor is responsible for attesting to the fair presentation of the company's financial statements in accordance with generally accepted accounting principles (GAAP), the external auditor's objectivity must not be compromised. The ISB issued its first standard in January 1999, *Independence Discussions with Audit Committees,* mandating that the external auditor of a public company: (1) disclose in writing to the company's audit committee all relationships with the company that could affect the auditor's independence; (2) confirm its view that it is independent of the company; and (3) discuss such matters with the audit committee. This disclosure and discussion should be a two-way exchange of views. That is, to ensure a useful examination of the independence and objectivity of the external auditor, the audit committee must be an active participant in this process.

Status: NYSE, NASD, and AMEX amended their listing requirements to require coverage of ISB Standard 1 and related independence discussions in the audit committee charter. In addition, the SEC amended its proxy requirements to mandate that the ISB standard be addressed in the audit committee's report to shareholders.

Recommendation 8 — External Auditor's Judgments about Quality of Accounting Principles

Generally accepted auditing standards (GAAS) should require a company's external auditor to discuss with the audit committee the external auditor's judgments about the quality, not just the acceptability, of the company's accounting principles as applied in its financial statements. The discussion should include such issues as the clarity of the company's financial disclosures, the degree of aggressiveness or conservatism of the company's accounting principles and underlying estimates, and other decisions made by management in preparing the financial disclosure and reviewed by the external auditor. This requirement should be written in a way to encourage open, frank discussion and to avoid boilerplate. While some observers believe that this information should be provided to the audit committee in writing, it appears that such written reports could become "boilerplate" and that the openness sought could be seriously compromised.

Status: The Auditing Standards Board issued a Statement on Auditing Standards (SAS 90, *Audit Committee Communications,* which amended SAS 61, *Communication with Audit Committees*) to require the external auditor to discuss the quality of the company's accounting principles, but not their aggressiveness or conservatism, with the audit committee.

Recommendation 9—Report from Audit Committee

The SEC should require all reporting companies to include a letter from the audit committee in the company's annual report to shareholders and the Form 10-K (or Form 10-KSB) annual report disclosing whether for the prior fiscal year: (1) management has reviewed the audited financial statements with the audit committee, including discussion of the quality of the accounting principles applied and significant judgments affecting the company's financial statements; (2) the external auditor has discussed with the audit committee the external auditor's judgments of the quality of those principles as applied in (1) above; (3) the members of the audit committee have discussed among themselves, without management or the external auditor present, the information disclosed to the audit committee described in (1) and (2); and (4) the audit committee, in reliance on the review and discussions conducted with management and the external auditor pursuant to (1) and (2) above, believes that company's financial statements are fairly presented in conformity with generally accepted accounting principles (GAAP) in all material respects. The *Blue Ribbon Report* also recommends that the SEC adopt a "safe harbor" provision applicable to any disclosure required by this recommendation.

The Committee supported a "middle ground" approach between a full-fledged report and a meaningless disclosure requirement. General disclosure about the audit committee's review of the entire audit process highlights that the audit committee is in place to assure shareholders that procedures that promote accountability are integrated into the roles and practices of all the other relevant participants. A formal disclosure by the audit committee as to its view of the company's financial statements that is consistent with the board's existing duty to sign the Form 10-K will serve to raise public awareness of the importance of the audit committee's role as well as underscore its importance for audit committee members. The Committee recognized the impracticality of having the audit committee do more than rely upon information it receives, questions, and assesses in making this disclosure. Again, the audit committee has an oversight responsibility, not an audit responsibility.

Status: The SEC established a requirement for companies to include a report from their audit committees in their proxy statements relating to annual meetings at which directors are elected. The report must indicate if the audit committee recommended to the board of directors that the audited financial statements be included in Form 10-K . The report is not required to explicitly address GAAP. The names of each audit committee member must be presented below the required disclosures in that report. The SEC also adopted a safe harbor for the report;

the report will not be considered to be "filed" with the SEC unless the company specifically requests that the report be filed or makes a reference to the report in a filed document.

Recommendation 10—Required Timely Interim Reviews

The SEC should require a reporting company's external auditor to conduct a Statement on Auditing Standard (SAS) 71, *Interim Financial Information,* review prior to the company's filing its Form 10-Q or Form 10-QSB (the company's quarterly report to the SEC). The *Blue Ribbon Report* further recommends that SAS 71 be amended to require that a reporting company's external auditor discuss with the audit committee, or at least its chairman, and a representative of financial management, in person or by telephone conference call, the matters described in SAS 61, *Communications with Audit Committees,* prior to filing the Form 10-Q (and preferably prior to any public announcement of financial results), including significant adjustments, management judgments and accounting estimates, significant new accounting policies, and disagreements with management. The Committee believed that increased involvement by the external auditor and the audit committee in the interim financial reporting process should result in more credible interim reporting.

An increased level of monitoring of the interim reporting process can be achieved by requiring regular interim communications by the external auditor with financial management and the audit committee. The *Blue Ribbon Report* fully expects that financial management and the audit committee will engender the appropriate diligence, initiative, and commitment to participate in such communications. The audit committee's discussion with the external auditor regarding the quarterly review should always be held prior to public disclosure to the extent practical.

Status: The SEC amended its rules to require the external auditor to review interim financial statements before they are filed. Also, the Auditing Standards Board amended SAS 71 to require that the matters in SAS 61, *Communication with Audit Committees,* be communicated to audit committees prior to the filing of the 10-Q or as soon thereafter as practical.

Guiding Principles for Audit Committee Best Practices

The Committee determined that, in lieu of setting forth a list of best practices to which every audit committee should adhere, "Guiding Principles" for best practices were developed. The Committee emphasized that ". . . the specifics of how any audit committee conducts its business should be self-determined." But the Committee, in outlining the five guiding principles, indicated that the principles are common sense fundamentals that apply to all companies. The five guiding principles are summarized below.

Principle 1: The Audit Committee's Key Role in Monitoring the Other Component Parts of the Audit Process

The audit committee should affirm the existence of necessary interaction between the participants in the financial reporting process — management, internal auditor, and external auditor. The audit committee should learn the roles and responsibilities of each of the three participants in the process. The roles and responsibilities of each party should be commonly understood and agreed to by each of the participants — preferably in writing. With a basic understanding of the various roles and responsibilities, the audit committee should be in a position to devise appropriate questions (not merely a "checklist") as to how each participant carries out its functions, with strong emphasis on the requirements for the particular company involved.

Principle 2: Independent Communication and Information Flow between the Audit Committee and the Internal Auditor

Responsible financial reporting is derived in large part from a system of internal controls, and according to the *Blue Ribbon Report,* the internal auditor is in the best position to evaluate and report on the adequacy and effectiveness of those controls. The Committee recommended that there be formal mechanisms in place to facilitate confidential exchanges between the internal auditor and the audit committee, such as regular meetings or regular confidential memoranda or reports circulated only to the audit committee. Confidential meetings and correspondence should be the norm, not an exception to standard operating procedure.

The audit committee must establish and support a culture that promotes open disclosure on the part of the internal auditor and recognition that if the internal auditor identifies a problem and cannot obtain the support of management, he or she has a duty to the audit committee, the board, and the shareholders to disclose the relevant information to the audit committee. Management should more than acquiesce in this duty to disclose; in fact, management should encourage and support such disclosure by word and deed.

Principle 3: Independent Communication and Information Flow between the Audit Committee and the External Auditor

Every audit committee should adopt, consistent with Recommendation 7 (statement from external auditor disclosing all relationships to company), additional voluntary measures to ensure the objectivity of the external auditor. Regular meetings should be held, and regular reports should be received by the audit committee from the external auditor. Such reports and meetings should be independent of management. The audit committee should promote a culture that values objective and critical analysis of management and the internal auditor in its communications with the external auditor. The audit committee should ask important and penetrating questions regarding the information provided to the audit committee by the external auditor and not merely accept reports without question. As discussed in Chapter 12, "Relationships with the External Auditor," communications required by GAAS may be written or oral and some may be made by management, if the auditor ensures that they were made.

Principle 4: Candid Discussions with Management, the Internal Auditor, and the External Auditor Regarding Issues Implicating Judgment and Impacting Quality

The audit committee will normally work closely with, and rely on, senior management, particularly those representing financial management, in developing the dialogue suggested in Principles 2 and 3 above. Management should apprise the committee of the company's overall business environment and risks and its system of internal controls, and provide an explanation of the company's financial statements. Specifically, management should provide the audit committee with:

1. Timely, periodic reviews of the financial statements and related disclosure documents prior to filing with the SEC.
2. Presentations concerning:
   a. Any changes in accounting principles or financial reporting policies from a prior year;
   b. The accounting treatment accorded significant transactions; and
   c. Any significant variations between budgeted and actual numbers in a particular account.

3. Information regarding any "second" opinions sought by management from another external auditor about the accounting treatment of a particular event or transaction.
4. Management's response to the assessments provided by the internal and external auditors.

After the audit committee has received the foregoing information from management, it should review the material with the internal auditor and external auditor to verify management's compliance with process and procedures and seek additional input on any significant judgments made. Adequate dialogue should be developed to ensure that the committee has received all necessary and pertinent information.

The audit committee may use a checklist to review various aspects of the company's financial reporting and internal control systems with management, the internal auditor, and the external auditor. However, the *Blue Ribbon Report* cautions against using a checklist as a substitute for conducting the audit committee's own investigation and analysis.

Illustrative questions may cover:

- The accounting implications of new, significant transactions.
- Changes in, or the continued propriety of, elective accounting principles.
- The methods of application of such principles and their aggressiveness or conservatism.
- The use of reserves and accruals.
- Significant estimates and judgments used in the preparation of the financial statements.
- Internal and external auditors' methods for risk assessment and the results of those assessments.
- Changes in the scope of the audit as a result of such risk assessments.
- The emergence or elimination of high-risk areas.
- The effect of any external environmental factors (economic, industrial, or otherwise) on financial reporting and the audit process.
- Any other questions addressing topics that the audit committee believes may influence the quality of the financial statements, including any other issues the external auditor must address under GAAS.

Principle 5: Diligent and Knowledgeable Audit Committee Membership

As suggested by Recommendations 2 (all independent directors) and 3 (size of the audit committee and financial literacy of its members), the Committee expects that audit committees will carefully consider independence and financial qualifications for members of the committee. The company may distribute to nominees to the audit committee a written description of qualifications, diligence, and time commitment the board expects of members, as well as a clear statement of the expectation that audit committee members will recognize the seriousness of the committee's purpose and will fulfill their duties accordingly. The *Blue Ribbon Report* suggests that audit committee members might warrant higher compensation than that accorded other board members. While this suggestion does not seem appropriate as to basic board remuneration, adequate compensation should be provided for the extra duties and time required for audit committee members. Perhaps audit committee meeting fees could be used to accomplish the need to compensate audit committee members for their increased responsibility and time commitments.

The audit committee should also consider training and education programs to ensure that its membership has the proper background and knowledge about relevant material. Professionals within the company may conduct training, but the company may also choose to engage outside advisors for educational programs.

The *Blue Ribbon Committee* indicates that the audit committee may wish to consider limiting the term of audit committee service by automatic rotation or by other means.

Here is a summary of the 10 governance recommendations from the *Blue Ribbon Report* (including the status of their implementation):

Strengthening Independence

1. Independence means that an audit committee member has no relationship to the company that may interfere with exercising independence from management and the company.
2. The audit committee should be comprised solely of independent directors with an exception for one member in exceptional and limited circumstances.

Improving Effectiveness

3. The audit committee should have a minimum of three directors each of who is or becomes financially literate. Further, one member should have accounting or related financial management expertise.

4. The audit committee should have a formal written charter that is approved by the full board and that specifies its responsibilities, structure, process, and membership requirements. The charter must be reviewed and reassessed annually.

5. The company's proxy statement for its annual meeting must indicate if the audit committee has adopted a charter and whether the committee complied with the charter. The charter should be disclosed at least triennially in the annual report or proxy statement and in the next annual report or proxy statement after significant amendment.

Accountability among Audit Committee, External Auditor, and Management

6. The charter should state that the external auditor is ultimately accountable to the board and the audit committee, which has the ultimate authority to select, evaluate, and replace the external auditor.

7. The audit committee is responsible for ensuring that it receives from the external auditor a formal written statement delineating all relationships between the auditor and the company and for actively engaging in a dialogue with the auditor about any disclosed relationship or service that may affect the auditor's objectivity and independence.

8. The external auditor must discuss with the audit committee the quality, not just the acceptability, of the company's accounting principles.

9. The audit committee should present a letter in the company's annual report and the Form 10-K disclosing whether: (a) management has reviewed the audited financial statements with the audit committee, including a discussion of the quality of accounting principles and significant judgments made, (b) the external auditor has discussed the quality of accounting principles and significant judgments with the committee, (c) the audit committee has discussed the matters in (a) and (b) above in private among themselves, and (d) the committee believes that the company's financial statements are fairly presented in conformity with GAAP.

10. The external auditor must conduct a SAS 71 interim financial review before the company files its Form 10-Q.

The NYSE, NASD, AMEX, SEC, and AICPA (Auditing Standards Board) have generally implemented the above broad recommendations except for:

• Recommendation 5: The SEC does not require the audit committee report to indicate whether the committee complied with its charter.

- Recommendation 9: The audit committee has to indicate in its report whether the committee recommended publication of the financial statements in Form 10-K, not whether those financial statements are fairly presented in accordance with GAAP.

CHAPTER 6
CREATING AN AUDIT COMMITTEE

This chapter discusses the various ways that a company and its board of directors may establish an audit committee. When the committee is created, the board has to make decisions about the size of the committee and term of office of its members. In addition, the company has to develop a charter setting forth the responsibilities of the committee.

Resolution to Establish the Audit Committee

An audit committee is a standing committee of the board of directors created to provide, on behalf of the board, oversight of:

- The integrity of the company's financial statements and the risks and controls underlying financial reporting.
- The independence and objectivity of the external auditor and the internal auditor.
- The external and internal audit processes.

The board of directors may create an audit committee by board resolution, by bylaw amendment, or less frequently, by amendment to the articles of incorporation. The easiest approach is via board resolution. In fact, the audit committee is usually created by board resolution unless otherwise required by state law.

The board resolution (along with the appended audit committee charter) should specify the purpose and responsibilities of the committee, its size, its chairperson, and the terms of service of the members of the committee. Appendix 2 presents an example of a board resolution to create an audit committee.

Size of the Committee

The audit committee typically includes between three and six members. The size, beyond the minimum requirements of the stock exchanges, depends on the company and its culture, the responsibilities delegated to the committee by the board of directors, the size of the board, and the qualifications of its members.

An audit committee of three to six members should serve the purposes of most companies. However, some larger companies now have larger audit committees. While a larger audit committee allows an increased diversity of experience and skills to be included on the committee, large committees can be difficult to control effectively and may create a situation where some of the members do not actively participate.

The authors believe that it is preferable to form a small (three to six members) audit committee with members having the requisite independence, financial literacy, and experience needed by the committee and the company and required by the stock exchanges. The committee should be small enough to allow the individual members to participate actively in meetings and activities of the committee so that members will have a thorough understanding of the responsibilities included in the scope of the committee's work. If a larger committee is established, smaller subcommittees should be used to oversee various aspects of the responsibilities of the committee to actively involve all members. The size of the committee should be carefully studied before the committee is created, taking into account the capabilities and experience available from potential members.

The NYSE, NASD, and AMEX require audit committees to have at least three members (see Exhibit 6-1). However, NASD and AMEX provide an exception for small business filers (generally a U.S. or Canadian issuer having revenues of less than $25 million and public float of less than $25 million). Small business filers must have an audit committee of at least two members.

Exhibit 6-1
Requirements of Stock Exchanges for Size of Audit Committee

NYSE

Each audit committee shall consist of at least three directors, all of whom have no relationship to the company that may interfere with the exercise of their independence from management of the company.

NASD and AMEX

Each issuer must have, and certify that it has and will continue to have, an audit committee of at least three members, comprised solely of independent directors.

Term of Office

There is significant merit to having no term limits so that audit committee members benefit from experience gained over time. However, the board of directors must have a means of replacing audit committee members who are not interested and willing to commit the necessary time or who become stale or out of touch with committee activities. While normal turnover at the board may solve some of these concerns, the board should have a means of rotating audit committee members regardless of the defined term of service.

If a board of directors has enough qualified and interested candidates to fill its audit committee, the board may appoint the individual members for one-year terms. However, the "financial literacy" requirements of the stock exchanges may seriously limit a company's ability to rotate audit committee members on a short-term basis. The impact of the financial literacy requirements should be positive since audit committee members should become more effective with longer terms, provided again that the board has a means of rotating stale or noncontributing members.

As discussed in Chapter 15, "Evaluating the Audit Committee," the charter of the audit committee or the board resolution creating the audit committee should provide for an annual assessment of each committee member's performance so that the board of directors can identify and make needed replacements.

The Audit Committee Charter

At the same time that the board of directors creates an audit committee by resolution or by bylaw amendment, the board/committee should develop a charter for the committee. The charter serves as a guide to the committee in carrying out the responsibilities delegated to it by the board and the responsibilities required by the stock exchanges.

The designated chairperson of the audit committee and the committee members, the internal auditor, the external auditor, the company's legal counsel, and financial management should participate in drafting the charter so that it will be specifically tailored to the company. The use of a "boilerplate" charter will probably lead to serious interpretation problems at a later date. A tailor-made charter, which provides flexibility, will allow easier committee administration over a longer period of time. Even a tailor-made charter will need to be changed as circumstances of the company change. The charter should be reviewed, revised, and updated annually by the audit committee and submitted to the full board of directors for approval after such revisions.

The NYSE, NASD, and AMEX require every listed company to have an audit committee charter. The audit committee also must review and reassess the adequacy of the charter every year. The charter content requirements of the stock exchanges are substantially the same. The audit committee charter should specify:

1. The scope of the committee's responsibilities and how it carries out those responsibilities.
2. That the external auditor is ultimately accountable to the board of directors and its audit committee.
3. That the committee and the board have the ultimate authority and responsibility to select, evaluate, and, when appropriate, replace the external auditor.
4. That the committee is responsible for ensuring that the external auditor submits to the committee a written statement delineating all relationships between the auditor and the company.
5. That the committee is responsible for actively engaging in a dialogue with the external auditor about the disclosures in 4. above that may affect the independence of the auditor and for recommending that the board take appropriate action to ensure the external auditor's independence.

Under the NYSE requirements, the charter must be approved by the board of directors, and as recommended previously, this is a best practice for all companies. The NYSE also requires the company to annually confirm whether the charter was reviewed and reassessed for its adequacy. In contrast, NASD and AMEX require only a one-time charter review confirmation. The SEC requires all registrants to disclose in their annual proxy statement whether they have an audit committee charter. Each company has to append a copy of its charter to its proxy statement at least every three years.

Appendix 3 presents a basic (bare bones) audit committee charter that was developed by Weil, Gotshal & Manges to satisfy the stock exchange requirements, the SEC disclosure requirements, and the requirements set out in the AICPA's Statements on Auditing Standards. Appendix 4 presents a more detailed illustrative charter that encompasses the various recommendations made in this book, particularly those in Chapter 8, "The Responsibilities of an Audit Committee." Appendices 3 and 4 are designed to assist a company in developing its own charter that recognizes the unique culture of the company. Every company should tailor-make its own audit committee charter and should not simply copy a sample charter or one from another company.[1]

Finally, whether an audit committee should have a charter or not is not debatable — every audit committee should be governed by a charter that is approved by the board of directors. The only downside of having a charter is that charters can and will be used against boards and audit committees in legal actions. Therefore, it is essential to determine that the charter is complete and that the audit committee complies with the responsibilities as articulated in the charter.

Here is a summary of the important points of this chapter:

Resolution to Establish the Audit Committee

1. The board of directors usually creates the audit committee by board resolution (unless otherwise required by state law).

Size of the Audit Committee

2. The audit committee typically includes between three and six members.
3. The NYSE, NASD, and AMEX require audit committees to have at least three members with an exception for small business filers, which are required to have at least two members.

Term of Office

4. There is significant merit to having no term limits for audit committee members. However, the board should have a means of rotating members regardless of the defined term of service.

The Audit Committee Charter

5. Every company that has an audit committee should develop a charter for the committee. The charter should be approved by the board.
6. The charter serves as a guide to the audit committee in carrying out the responsibilities delegated to it by the board and the responsibilities required by the stock exchanges.

---

[1] When creating or updating an audit committee charter, companies may want to refer to charters of other companies. An excellent source that presents charters of various companies is Financial Executive Online (at www.fei.org/finrep/audit.cfm).

7. The audit committee charter should be tailored to the company.
8. The NYSE, NASD, and AMEX require every listed company to have an audit committee charter.
9. The NYSE, NASD, and AMEX require the charter to contain:
   a. The responsibilities and how they are carried out.
   b. A statement that the external auditor is ultimately accountable to the board and the audit committee.
   c. A statement that the audit committee and the board have the ultimate authority and responsibility to select, evaluate, and replace the external auditor.
   d. A statement that the audit committee is responsible for ensuring that the external auditor submits an independence letter.
   e. A statement that the audit committee is responsible for actively discussing the independence letter and recommending that the board take any needed action to ensure the external auditor's independence.
10. The SEC requires all listed companies to disclose in their annual proxy statement whether they have an audit committee and to append the charter of such committee to the proxy statement at least every three years.

CHAPTER 7
APPOINTING AND EDUCATING
THE AUDIT COMMITTEE

This chapter discusses characteristics of effective audit committee members, including their need for independence from management and the company, and their need for financial literacy. After presenting the essential attributes for committee members, the chapter focuses on the process of appointing committee members and the committee chairperson. The chapter concludes with a brief discussion of the initial and continuing educational needs of audit committee members.

Characteristics of Effective Audit Committee Members

To be an effective audit committee member, an individual should have certain characteristics. First, the individual should have a general understanding of the company's major economic, operating, and financial risks. In addition, the individual should have a broad awareness of the interrelationship of the company's operations and its financial reporting, including risks and controls related to financial reporting. Obviously, an inquiring attitude, independence, and sound judgment are essential for a person serving in this important capacity. Further, as highlighted in Exhibit 7-1, an audit committee member should understand the difference between the oversight function of the audit committee and the decision-making function of management.

Exhibit 7-1
Vigilant, Informed, and Effective Audit Committees*

The audit committee must be vigilant, informed, diligent, and probing in fulfilling its oversight responsibilities. The audit committee must, of course, avoid unnecessary or inappropriate interventions with the prerogatives of corporate management; but the oversight must be effective.

---

*From the National Commission on Fraudulent Financial Reporting, *Report of the National Commission on Fraudulent Financial Reporting* (October, 1987), p. 41.

As indicated in the 1999 *Blue Ribbon Report* (see Chapter 5), audit committee members must have the ability to, and must, ask probing questions about the company's financial risks and accounting. According to the *Blue Ribbon Report,* a director's ability to ask and intelligently evaluate the answers to the necessary questions hinges on intelligence, diligence, a probing mind, and certain financial literacy. In fact, according to the international recruiting firm, Korn/Ferry, the number one attribute of a "good director" (not just a member of the audit committee) is a willingness to challenge management when necessary.[1] Stated another way, that means "independence." Independence is the backbone of what a directorship is all about, especially an outside director who serves on the audit committee.

Independence Requirements

Over the past twenty years, the question of audit committee member independence has generated a significant amount of discussion. Obviously, since the audit committee is responsible, on behalf of the board of directors, for oversight of the financial integrity of the company and must from time to time question the actions and judgments of management, a committee that is not independent will probably not properly discharge its responsibilities. Again, it bears repeating that independence is the backbone of the audit committee.

The essence of independence is an audit committee member's mental objectivity. Thus, a committee member should have no relationship to the company that could interfere with the exercise of his or her independence from management and the company. In addition to mental objectivity or independence in fact, independence also involves the appearance of objectivity. Before appointing a director to the audit committee, the board of directors should consider whether a shareholder, having knowledge of all the relationships that the director has to the company, would consider the individual independent. It is widely recognized and commonly accepted that each audit committee member should be independent in fact and in appearance unless otherwise discussed by the board and disclosed in proxy statements when required. The need for independence is also supported by research that shows a higher degree of active oversight and a lower incidence of fraudulent financial reporting emanating from companies having independent audit committees.

In response to concerns about independent directors, the *Blue Ribbon Re-*

---

[1] Korn/Ferry International, *26ᵗʰ Annual Board of Directors Study,* p. 31.

port recommended that the New York Stock Exchange (NYSE) and the National Association of Securities Dealers (NASD) tighten their independence rules. In response to that recommendation, the NYSE, the NASD, and the American Stock Exchange (AMEX) passed new requirements in December 1999. According to the NYSE, NASD, and AMEX requirements (see Appendix 5, "Stock Exchanges' Independence Requirements for Audit Committee Members of U.S. Companies"), directors who should not be appointed to an audit committee, **because they are not considered independent,** include the following:

1. A current employee of the company or its affiliates (includes a subsidiary, sibling company, predecessor, parent company, or former parent company).
2. A former employee of the company/affiliate anytime during the last 3 years.
3. An immediate family member (includes a person's spouse, parents, children, siblings, fathers- and mothers-in-law, sons- and daughters-in-law, brothers- and sisters-in-law, and anyone other than an employee who shares such person's home) of an executive of the company.
4. A director/executive of another company when any of the company's executives serve on the other company's compensation committee. (These relationships are referred to as "cross compensation committee links.")
5. A partner, controlling shareholder, or executive officer of a company (Co. B) that has a business relationship with the company (Co. A):
    a. (NYSE) Unless the board determines in its business judgment that the relationship does not interfere with the individual's independence.
    b. (NASD and AMEX) If a company (Co. B) makes or receives payments that exceed 5 percent of its consolidated gross revenues or $200,000 (of Co. A or Co. B), whichever is more, in any of the past 3 years.
6. A director who has a direct business relationship with the company (for example, a consultant):
    a. (NYSE) Unless the board of determines in its business judgment that the relationship does not interfere with the individual's independence.
    b. (NASD and AMEX) If the director receives from the company/affiliate in excess of $60,000 during the year, excluding compen-

sation for board service, benefits under a tax-qualified retirement plan or non-discretionary compensation.

The NYSE, NASD, and AMEX allow one non-independent director to serve on the audit committee. For the NYSE, the exception relates to items 2 and 3 above for a past employee or an immediate family member of a past executive who is not independent because of the three-year restriction. To invoke the exception, the board must determine in its business judgment that the director's membership on the audit committee is in the best interest of the company and its shareholders. In addition, the company must disclose in its next annual proxy statement the nature of the non-independent relationship and the reasons for the board's decision.

NASD and AMEX permit an exception for items 2 through 6 above for a non-independent director under exceptional and limited circumstances when it is in the best interests of the company and its shareholders. NASD and AMEX require the same proxy disclosure as the NYSE for the exception or waiver.

A director may be independent according to the rules above but have a conflict of interest relating to a matter under consideration by the audit committee. In those situations, the director's objectivity may be impaired from either a factual or from an appearance perspective. Therefore, the director should disclose the conflict to the committee and generally not participate in the discussion of the matter.

As recognized in the Federal Deposit Insurance Corporation Improvement Act of 1991, an independence issue can arise from the inclusion of a large shareholder on the audit committee. While it is appropriate for all members of the board of directors to have a financial interest in the company through share ownership, there are a number of circumstances where a large ownership position could create a conflict of interest, or at least a perception of a conflict of interest, for an audit committee member. The board of directors should make the final judgment about whether a large shareholder can truly be independent in his or her service as a member of the audit committee.

Financial Literacy and Accounting/Financial Expertise

Good audit committee members ask probing questions about financial information and related risks and controls underlying such information. This means that committee members, in order to ask such questions, must have a basic level of knowledge about financial statements — "financial literacy."

As shown in Appendix 6, "Financial Literacy Requirements for Audit Committee Members," the NYSE, NASD, and AMEX require all members of the audit committee to be or to become financially literate. In addition, at least one member of the committee must possess accounting or financial expertise.[2] The only exception to this requirement by the stock exchanges is an exclusion for small business filers (generally a U.S. or Canadian issuer having revenues of less than $25 million and public float of less than $25 million).

The meaning of financial literacy and accounting/financial expertise varies between the NYSE, NASD, and AMEX. The NYSE leaves the decision about whether an individual has financial literacy and accounting/financial expertise up to the board of directors and its judgment. In contrast, NASD and AMEX define financial literacy to mean a member who is able to read and understand basic financial statements, including a balance sheet, income statement, and cash flow statement. NASD and AMEX define accounting/ financial expertise as past experience in finance or accounting or other comparable experience or background that results in financial sophistication. The latter, according to NASD and AMEX, would include being or having been a CEO, CFO, or other senior officer with financial oversight responsibilities.

The meaning of financial literacy, even as defined by NASD and AMEX, is vague. At a minimum, the authors believe that each audit committee member should have a general knowledge of generally accepted accounting principles (GAAP). This knowledge is essential if committee members are to ask probing questions about financial information and are able to analyze responses to those questions. Depending upon the level of financial accounting background and experience of committee members, members should take whatever steps are necessary to remain knowledgeable, including attending seminars and conferences that address current accounting topics and issues. The board of directors should recognize this need and provide whatever educational resources are appropriate for committee members.

Process for Appointing Committee Members and the Chairperson

The board of directors or its nominating (governance) committee should appoint audit committee members. Because of the need for audit committee

---

[2] The Federal Deposit Insurance Corporation Improvement Act of 1991 requires large financial institutions ($3 billion or more of assets) to also have audit committee members with banking or related management experience (see Section 36(g)(2) of the FDIC Act).

members to be independent, the authors believe that it is inappropriate for the chief executive officer, or any of the company officers or inside directors serving on the board, to appoint members to the audit committee. Since one of the committee's principal obligations is to perform management oversight, it is inappropriate for the persons subject to the oversight (that is, members of management) to appoint the persons to perform the oversight. Unfortunately, the CEO/chairperson, according to Korn/Ferry, still plays a dominant role in appointing committee members and the committee chairpersons. That practice does, however, appear to be declining.[3] In appointing committee members, the board or its nominating committee may, of course, seek recommendations from the CEO/chairperson, the CFO, and inside directors.

The board of directors or its nominating committee should likewise appoint the chairperson of the audit committee. The selection of the right chairperson for the committee is critical since this person is the most important member of the committee. In fact, the National Association of Corporate Directors' *Audit Committees: A Practical Guide,* states emphatically that: "A key determinant of the effectiveness of an audit committee is the independence, competence, dedication, and leadership skills of the audit committee chair."[4] Given the importance of the position, the authors believe that the chairperson should normally have an accounting/financial management background so that he or she can properly direct the discussions during the committee meetings and guide the activities of the committee.

Educating the Audit Committee

The 1999 *Blue Ribbon Report* clearly emphasizes the importance of initial training and continuing education for audit committee members. The company and its board of directors should ensure that committee members have the proper background and current knowledge about developments in accounting, risks, controls, and auditing. Management, the internal auditor, and the external auditor should express their views on the committee members' knowledge needs related to the committee's oversight responsibilities and the committee's need to have and maintain financial literacy. Professionals within the company may conduct training, but the committee should be able (1) to engage outside experts for educational programs and (2) to attend external programs and seminars at the company's expense.

Obviously, whenever an audit committee is created, or new members are

---

[3] Korn/Ferry International, p. 31.
[4] Report of the NACD Blue Ribbon Commission, *Audit Committees: A Practical Guide* (Washington, D.C., The National Association of Corporate Directors, 2000) p. 11.

selected or appointed to an existing audit committee, certain basic information about the company and the audit committee should be made available to them, including the following:

1. The board resolution creating the audit committee.
2. The audit committee charter.
3. Annual reports of the company for the past three years and filings with the Securities and Exchange Commission for the past three years.
4. Interim financial reports of the company for the last four quarters.
5. Minutes of the audit committee for the past three years.
6. Copies of communications between the audit committee and external auditors during the past three years and communications between the internal auditor and the audit committee for the same period.
7. Information from legal counsel about pending litigation and contingent liabilities.
8. Biographical sketches of senior financial management and members of the internal audit staff.
9. The internal audit charter.
10. General information about the size and scope of activities of the internal audit function.
11. A copy of the current year internal audit plan.
12. The current audit engagement letter from the external auditor.
13. A list of types of reports and the timing thereof to be issued by the external auditor.
14. A summary of work performed by the external auditor other than the annual audit and quarterly reviews.
15. Any written material about committee activities and meeting schedules for the next year.

It is good practice for a company to conduct an introductory session for new audit committee members to familiarize them with the above information. The length of the introductory session will obviously depend on the volume of material and complexity of the operations of the company. The new member orientation may include presentations by the chairperson of the committee, representatives of the company's financial management function, and the internal auditor. In addition, the company's general counsel should explain and discuss the standards of liability applicable to audit committee members.[5]

---

[5] Financial Executive Online contains an illustrative orientation packet for new audit committee members (see *www.fei.org/finrep/files/acorientation.doc*).

Periodic briefings should be held for all audit committee members on specific aspects of the business operations and the financial operations of the company so that committee members can become familiar with and can have a more in-depth understanding of various aspects of the company's operations. Although financial management will report periodically to the full board of directors regarding the financial operations of the company, the audit committee should undertake special briefings to focus on details such as contingencies, accounting changes, reserves, and similar matters. A board of directors does not ordinarily focus on such details, but to carry out its oversight of financial reporting, the audit committee must discuss these issues on a regular and frequent basis.

The external auditor and financial management should periodically update the audit committee on new accounting and auditing standards having a potential affect on the company's financial statements. In addition, the audit committee should be made aware of any changes that may be mandated because of the changes in regulatory requirements related to financial reporting.

Even before the issuance of the *Blue Ribbon Report*, education of the board of directors and its committees was receiving significant attention as illustrated in a *New York Times* article that discussed various director training programs being conducted by universities.[6] In addition, the National Association of Corporate Directors, a trade association formed in 1977 which is based in Washington, D.C., provides seminars and educational materials not only for boards of directors in general, but specifically for audit committees.[7] A board of directors should consider sending at least one member of its audit committee to selected seminars each year so that the audit committee will be aware of the best practices being used by audit committees generally.

Here is a summary of the important points of this chapter:

Characteristics of Effective Audit Committee Members

1. An effective audit committee member should have:
   a. Independence.
   b. Financial literacy.

---

[6] "For Corporate Directors, Board Room Survival 101," *The New York Times* (March 29, 1998), p.1 (business section).

[7] NACD's seminars and publications are available at www.nacdonline.org.

   c. A general understanding of the company's major economic, operating, and financial risks.

   d. A broad awareness of the interrelationship of the company's operations and its financial reporting.

   e. An inquiring attitude.

   f. Sound judgment.

   g. An understanding of the difference between the oversight function of the audit committee and the decision-making function of management.

   h. A willingness to challenge management when necessary.

Independence Requirements

2. An audit committee member should have no relationship to the company that could interfere with the exercise of independence from management and the company.

3. In December 1999, the NYSE, NASD, and AMEX passed new independence rules. The rules are complex and generally indicate that the following directors are not or may not be independent:

   a. Current employees.

   b. Former employees during the last three years.

   c. Immediate family members of an executive of the company.

   d. Directors of other companies when there are cross compensation committee links.

   e. Partners, controlling shareholders, or executives of companies that have business relationships with the company.

   f. Directors who have direct business relationships with the company.

4. A director may be independent but have a conflict of interest related to a given matter that may impair objectivity.

Financial Literacy and Accounting/Financial Expertise

5. All audit committee members should be or become financially literate within a reasonable period of time after appointment to the committee.

6. Generally, financial literacy means the ability to read and understand basic financial statements, including a balance sheet, income statement, and cash flow statement.

7. At least one member of the audit committee should have accounting/financial expertise such as past experience in finance or accounting or other experience that results in financial sophistication.

Process for Appointing Committee Members and the Chairperson

8. The board of directors or its nominating (governance) committee should appoint audit committee members and the committee chairperson.

Educating the Audit Committee

9. The company and its board of directors should ensure that the audit committee members have the proper background and current knowledge about developments in accounting, risks, controls, and auditing.

10. Professionals within the company may conduct training, but the audit committee should be able to engage outside experts for educational programs and to attend external programs at company expense.

11. The company should conduct an orientation session for new audit committee members and should hold periodic briefings for all committee members on specific aspects of business and financial operations of the company.

12. The external auditor and financial management should periodically update the audit committee on new accounting and auditing standards and regulatory requirements that will affect the company's financial statements.

CHAPTER 8
THE RESPONSIBILITIES OF AN AUDIT COMMITTEE

As the audit committee concept has become more broadly accepted, the role of the committee has expanded considerably. There is no comprehensive set of audit committee responsibilities or duties mandated by legislation or regulation; thus, the responsibilities vary from company to company. Obviously, the responsibilities of a particular audit committee should be focused on the needs and unique culture of the company that the committee serves. According to the *Blue Ribbon Report* (Chapter 5), "one size can't fit all."

Responsibilities assigned via the audit committee charter are dependent on factors such as the size and structure of the company, the industry in which the company operates, activities delegated by the board of directors to other board committees, capability and time commitment of committee members, and the age of the committee.

When boards of directors delegate responsibilities to audit committees, they should follow two cardinal principles:

1. Each company should tailor the responsibilities of its audit committee to meet the company's unique needs and its culture.
2. The audit committee should not be overloaded with activities or the committee may lose sight of its major objectives or perform its duties superficially.

The second principle is especially important if the board of directors has recently created the committee.

This chapter discusses the most commonly delegated responsibilities of an audit committee and additional responsibilities that boards of directors frequently assign to the committee. The board of directors commonly delegates the following responsibilities to the committee:

1. Selecting, evaluating, and replacing the external auditor.
2. Reviewing the external audit plan.
3. Evaluating the annual audited financial statements.
4. Overseeing the external audit process and audit results.
5. Monitoring the external auditor's independence.
6. Monitoring internal control over financial reporting.
7. Overseeing the internal audit function.
8. Evaluating interim financial statements and the external auditor's review of those statements.

The board of directors also frequently assigns additional responsibilities to the audit committee involving the oversight of the company's:

- Code of ethical conduct.
- Special investigations involving possible fraud and related problems.
- Compliance with laws, rules, and regulations.
- Litigation matters.
- Officer and director expense accounts and perquisites.
- Business risks.
- Self-assessment of performance.

Finally, the board of directors in every company should explicitly assign the audit committee the responsibility to (1) evaluate the committee's charter, and (2) if required by law, regulation, or the company's audit committee charter, report annually to shareholders. Chapter 6, "Creating an Audit Committee," discusses the audit committee charter, and the responsibility to prepare an annual report is discussed later in this chapter.

Selecting, Evaluating, and Replacing the External Auditor

In every company, it is imperative that the external auditor recognizes that the external audit firm is accountable to the audit committee and the board of directors. In fact, the stock exchanges require listed companies to specify in their charters that the external auditor is ultimately accountable to the board and that the board and its audit committee have the authority to select, evaluate, and replace the external auditor. In some companies, the audit committee is authorized by the board of directors to select the external auditor. More commonly, the committee recommends an external audit firm to the full board for formal approval. Also, a number of companies seek ratification of the selection of the external auditor by the shareholders via the proxy statement.

As the audit committee evaluates the performance of the external auditor, the committee should consider the quality of the audit and other services rendered and the efficiency of services provided. The audit committee should specifically review the expertise of the external auditor in relationship to the company's business and the industry in which it operates, and the benefits obtained from the external auditor's recommendations for improvements to controls and operations. Obviously, the committee must be assured that the external audit firm is independent and that the external audit firm has appropriate means of monitoring its independence. Each year, the committee should assess the overall external auditor relationship (see Appendix 17, "External Auditor Assessment by Audit Committee"), including fees charged (which the committee should approve in advance) versus level of service received, to determine if a change in external auditors should be considered. As discussed in Chapter 14, "Termination of the External Auditor," if the committee believes it is appropriate to consider a change in external auditors, the process should not be taken lightly. Chapter 14 should aid an audit committee in determining if and how the consideration of a change in external auditors should be undertaken.

Reviewing the External Audit Plan

Before reviewing the external audit plan, the audit committee should discuss and understand the level of responsibility assumed by the external auditor under generally accepted auditing standards (GAAS) for internal control and the financial statements. The audit committee should also understand that the concept of "reasonable assurance" in the standard audit report (see Exhibit 12-2) means that the auditor provides a high level of assurance, not an absolute guarantee, that the financial statements are fairly presented in accordance with generally accepted accounting principles (GAAP).

Although the scope of the annual audit is based upon the external auditor's professional judgment and the auditor's obligation to adhere to GAAS, the audit committee should generally understand the basis for the auditor's plan and the scope of planned audit work. Although the committee normally reviews the audit scope, its members do not, and normally will not, have a detailed understanding of the many and complex decisions that the external auditor makes about how the audit will be performed. Simply stated, the committee's review of the audit plan for the annual financial statements with the external auditor is intended to satisfy the committee that the audit will meet the needs of the company's board of directors and its shareholders. In considering the scope of the external auditor's work, the committee should discuss and understand the external auditor's responsibility for information that will surround the audited financial statements (that is, other information such as management's discussion and analysis of financial condition and results of operations).

Most audit committees hold a pre-audit meeting to discuss the audit plan with the external auditor. After reviewing the audit plan, the committee may request the external auditor to perform additional work, such as expanded tests of internal controls at foreign locations or at other high-risk locations. Further discussions with the external auditor prior to the commencement of the audit, or early in the audit, serves to enhance the communications between the external auditor and the committee. Also, it allows the committee to identify areas that should be audited or analyzed by the internal auditor so that the internal auditor can make a report on such areas at a later audit committee meeting.

If the company recently retained the external auditor, the audit committee should inquire about any major issues (for example, issues about the application of GAAP or GAAS) that were discussed with management in connection with engaging the auditor. This inquiry and discussion should also take place every year at the pre-audit meeting to cover recurring engagement of the external auditor.

Evaluating the Annual Audited Financial Statements

The audit committee should discuss the annual financial statements with the chief financial officer (CFO), the internal auditor, and the external auditor before they are filed or distributed. In fact, the audit committee or its chairperson should be alerted to any significant accounting or disclosure issues that were identified by the external auditor during interim audit work. Early identification of significant issues enables the audit committee to resolve complex matters on a timely basis. The committee should consider the following items for discussion during its review of the annual financial statements.

Accounting Policies. If there are new accounting policies (for example, a method for depreciating plant and equipment) or new methods of applying existing accounting policies (for example, changes in asset depreciation lives), the audit committee should be aware of those matters and understand the nature and effect of the new or changed accounting policies and their application.[1] The committee should also be aware of the effect and implications of existing accounting policies in controversial or emerging areas, such as revenue recognition for new and complex transactions. In fact, the audit committee should understand all of the company's significant accounting policies and procedures.

Significant Fluctuations and Unusual Transactions. As part of the evaluation of the annual financial statements, the audit committee should discuss and understand the reasons for major fluctuations, as compared to the prior year(s), in asset, liability, equity, revenue, and expense accounts. In addition,

---

[1] Accounting policies are the specific accounting principles and the methods of applying those principles that a company uses to prepare its financial statements. A company is required by GAAP to disclose its significant accounting policies in its financial statements.

the committee should review unusual transactions reflected in the financial statements, such as discontinued operations.

Differences in Financial Statement Presentation Format. If there are significant differences in the presentation of information in the financial statements as compared to reports to governmental agencies or others, as well as significant differences in format or disclosures from the prior year(s) or from financial statements of other companies in the industry, the CFO and the external auditor should explain those differences to the audit committee, and the committee should be satisfied about the reasons for the differences.

Accounting Estimates (and Reserves). For significant accounting estimates (for example, net realizable value of inventory and accounts receivable, pension and warranty expenses, losses expected from litigation) in the financial statements, the CFO should inform the audit committee about the processes the company uses to formulate those estimates.[2] Afterwards, the external auditor should inform the audit committee about the audit approaches used to determine that the accounting estimates and changes therein were reasonable and fairly presented in the financial statements in accordance with GAAP.

Disagreements with Management about Accounting Matters. The external auditor should advise the audit committee about the nature and resolution of any accounting or disclosure disagreements between the external auditor and management, including any such matters that were the subject of consultation (for example, second opinions) between the company and other external accountants. The committee should determine that such difficulties did not unduly influence the financial statements.

Audit Adjustments. The audit committee should be informed about any significant adjustments and disclosures that the external auditor proposed — both those made by the company and those not made. The committee should also review and discuss the external auditor's summary of uncorrected adjustments (for example, passed or waived adjustments) that management concluded were immaterial and therefore were not recorded by the company.

Quality of Accounting Principles. The external auditor is required by GAAS for each SEC client to discuss the quality of accounting principles with the audit committee. In addition, an audit committee of an SEC report-

---

[2] An accounting estimate is an approximation of a financial statement element, item, or account. Accounting estimates are presented in financial statements because (a) the measurement of some amounts is uncertain, pending the outcome of future events, and (b) data needed for events that have already occurred cannot be obtained on a timely, cost-effective basis.

ing company is required to indicate in the annual report whether they discussed the company's financial statements with management. Therefore, it is certain that the committee will have discussions about GAAP and their quality with the external auditor and management. The quality-of-accounting-principles discussion should be tailored to the company's specific circumstances and should cover, among other things, the:

- Consistency of the company's accounting policies and their application.
- Clarity and completeness of the company's financial statements, including related disclosures.
- Items that have a significant affect on representational faithfulness,[3] verifiability,[4] and neutrality[5] of accounting information, such as:
  — Selection of new, or changes in, accounting policies.
  — Accounting policies relating to significant financial statement items.
  — Estimates, judgments, and uncertainties.
  — Unusual transactions.

Other Information. Finally, the audit committee should understand what procedures the external auditor performed to determine if the other information surrounding the financial statements was factually presented and consistent with the financial statements. Chapter 12, "Relationship with the External Auditor," discusses the external auditor's responsibility for other information that surrounds the audited financial statements.

Overseeing the External Audit Process and Audit Results

In separate private meetings with the CFO and the external auditor, the audit committee should oversee the external audit process and the results of that process, including the written reports that are generated by the external auditor. Concerning the audit process, the committee should focus on significant departures from the audit plan and the corresponding effect on expanded audit scope. The committee should ask both the CFO and the external auditor about the degree of cooperation experienced during the audit and

---

[3] Representational faithfulness means that the amounts and disclosures in the company's financial statements represent what really happened.

[4] Verifiability means that accountants using the same measurement method would obtain similar results.

[5] Neutrality means that information in financial statements cannot be selected to favor one set of financial statement users over another.

any differences of opinion between them about GAAP or the application of GAAS during the engagement. The committee should pay special attention to any situation in which the company obtained a second opinion about GAAP or GAAS from another external accountant.

During the separate meeting with management, the audit committee should not only inquire about management's assessment regarding the overall service provided by the external auditor and the quality of the audit, but about management's assessment of the external auditor's knowledge of the company, its industry or industries, and its business risks. If management is uncomfortable with any aspect of the external auditor's knowledge, such concern may be a signal that changing the external auditor should be considered.

In meeting with the external auditor, the audit committee should make sure that they understand the reasons for any changes or modifications to the standard audit report (that is, the three-paragraph unqualified opinion). In addition, the committee should discuss any significant deficiencies in internal control that the external auditor identified during the audit. The committee should also read and discuss other communications received from the external auditor relating to fraud, illegal acts, and other matters that are required to be communicated by GAAS. Finally, the committee should discuss with the external auditor the capabilities and depth of the company's financial management, including accounting, internal audit, and other personnel.

Monitoring the External Auditor's Independence

Under Independence Standards Board Standard (ISB) 1, *Independence Discussions with Audit Committees,* the external auditor of an SEC reporting company is required, at least annually, to: (1) disclose, in writing, independence issues to the audit committee, (2) confirm to the committee, in writing, that the external audit firm is independent, and (3) discuss with the committee the external auditor's independence. The objective of the requirement from the perspective of the committee and corporate governance is to deepen the committee's understanding of audit independence and to assist the committee in satisfying themselves that the company has engaged an independent external auditor. As discussed later in this chapter, the committee is required by the SEC in its annual report to shareholders to indicate whether they received the external auditor's disclosures about independence and discussed independence with the external auditor.

Finally, as mandated by the SEC, the audit committee must consider the performance of non-audit services by the company's principal auditor and whether that work was compatible with maintaining the external auditor's independence. The company is required to disclose in its proxy statement whether the audit committee considered the non-audit services.

Overseeing Internal Control over Financial Reporting

Internal control is a process, effected by the company's board of directors and its audit committee, management, internal auditors, and other company personnel, and designed to provide reasonable assurance about the company's:

1. Financial reporting reliability.
2. Compliance with applicable laws and regulations.
3. Effectiveness and efficiency of operations.

One of the responsibilities that a board of directors commonly delegates to an audit committee is to oversee the company's internal control over financial reporting (historically referred to as "internal accounting control"), which is identified in item 1 above. As discussed later, under "Additional Responsibilities — Business Risks," audit committees are increasingly involved in overseeing controls in areas 2 and 3 above.

In overseeing internal control over financial reporting, the audit committee, if it wishes to be proactive, generally obtains an understanding of significant risks related to financial reporting reliability and controls that management establishes to address those risks. The committee obtains its understanding of risks and controls over financial reporting by discussing risks and controls with management, the internal auditor, and the external auditor. In obtaining this understanding, the committee is concerned that the assets of the company are safeguarded and that transactions are appropriately authorized and properly recorded in the company's books and records to facilitate the preparation of reliable financial reports for internal and external use.

During the review of the external audit plan at the pre-audit planning meeting, one of the items that is typically discussed is the external auditor's planned reliance on (or assessment of) internal control over financial reporting. One of the primary reasons for discussing the external auditor's planned reliance is to identify significant controls that the external auditor does not plan to test. Armed with this information and with knowledge of significant controls over financial reporting that the internal auditor has tested or plans to test, the audit committee is in position to request the external auditor to expand his or her test of controls to significant areas or to request the internal auditor to expand his or her planned work on controls.

At the post-audit meeting, the audit committee should discuss the external auditor's management or reportable conditions letter. That letter (or oral communications, if not in writing) identifies, among other things, all significant deficiencies or reportable conditions in the company's design or operation of its internal control over financial reporting that have come to the external auditor's attention during the audit. The letter may also suggest corrective actions for the company to consider. The audit committee should understand, via discussion with the external auditor, how the external auditor adjusted his or her audit scope to determine that the control deficiencies did not permit a material misstatement to affect the audited financial statements. The audit committee should also discuss the control deficiencies with management to determine their plans for corrective actions. In addition, if any of the deficiencies are deemed to be material weaknesses, the audit committee should discuss such deficiencies with in-house legal counsel to assess potential violations of the Foreign Corrupt Practices Act (see Exhibit 2-1).[6]

In some companies, the audit committee may take a more passive approach to overseeing internal control over financial reporting by simply reviewing control deficiencies identified in internal and external audit work and monitoring management's actions to correct such deficiencies. The major weakness of this approach is that the committee does not have an overall understanding of control risks related to financial reporting reliability. Furthermore, the external auditor does not, and is not obligated to, search for significant deficiencies and may not test and rely on a number of significant controls over financial reporting in an audit of the financial statement. Therefore, the committee would not necessarily know that certain controls should be more effective.

Because of the significance of internal control is its broadest dimensions to boards of directors and audit committees, Chapter 9, "The Audit Committee's Oversight of Internal Control" presents an overview of what an audit committee member should know about internal control. As indicated in Chapter 9, the concept of internal control encompasses more than control over financial reporting. The audit committee should be sensitive to the expanding concept of internal control and be sure that it is discharging its responsibilities appropriately. The board of directors should carefully consider the scope of internal control responsibility delegated to the committee. If responsibility for "overall" internal control (that is, internal control over finan-

---

[6] A material weakness in internal control is a reportable condition that creates a significant risk of material misstatement in the company's financial statements.

cial reporting, compliance, and operations) is not delegated to the committee (and it probably should not be), the board of directors must be sure that areas of internal control related to significant business risks outside the financial area are being adequately monitored by the board or other board committees.

Overseeing the Internal Audit Function

The internal audit function is an important tool to aid the audit committee in discharging its responsibilities. The internal auditor can assist the audit committee in gaining the needed understanding of the company's risks and controls and the reliability of the company's financial information. The committee can also use the work and reports of the internal auditor to supplement the work performed by the external auditor. Thus, the committee should review, at least annually, the scope and effectiveness of the internal auditor and the capacity of the internal audit function to fulfill its objectives.

To have an effective internal audit function, the internal auditor must have direct and unrestricted access to the audit committee. Accordingly, the 1999 *Blue Ribbon Report* (discussed in Chapter 5) indicated in its "Guiding Principles for Audit Committee Best Practices," that the internal auditor should have regularly scheduled and confidential exchanges with the committee. The committee should also specifically instruct the internal auditor that they should be advised immediately of any areas requiring the committee's attention.

Ideally, at each meeting, the audit committee should have a private session with the internal auditor to provide a mechanism for raising issues that may not be appropriate for discussion in the general meeting of the committee. The committee should schedule a private session at each meeting, even if not needed, to establish a routine procedure and mechanism for confidential exchanges. As discussed in Chapter 11, "Relationship with the Internal Auditor," the Institute of Internal Auditors (IIA) recommends a private meeting at least once a year.

As discussed later in this chapter, the internal auditor can also be useful to the audit committee in conducting special investigations of matters of concern or of interest to the committee. For example, the internal auditor can investigate suspected fraud and report to the audit committee on a confidential basis.

At a minimum, the internal auditor should attend each audit committee meeting. At the meeting, the audit committee should review the planned internal audit work, all reports of completed work, and the implementation status of recommendations made to management in those reports. To monitor other activities of the internal auditor, the audit committee should:

- Periodically review the company's internal audit charter, including the independence and objectivity of the internal audit function.
- Oversee the appointment, performance, and termination of internal audit personnel, especially the senior internal audit executive (for example, the director of internal auditing).
- Review the budget and staffing for the internal audit function.
- Review the plans for internal audit activities and subsequent changes in those plans.
- Monitor the coordination of audit work between the internal auditor and the external auditor.
- Review internal audit reports and management's response to those reports.
- Consider whether the internal auditor complies with the standards issued by the IIA.

Chapter 11, "Relationship with the Internal Auditor," discusses these matters in more detail.

Reviewing Interim Financial Statements

As discussed in Chapter 5, on December 15, 1999, the SEC, in response to Recommendation 10 (Required Timely Interim Reviews) of the 1999 *Blue Ribbon Report,* adopted a rule that requires public companies to engage their external auditors to review their interim or quarterly financial statements before those statements are filed. This is frequently referred to as a SAS 71 review (after Statement of Auditing Standards 71, *Interim Financial Information*). The purpose of the requirement is to facilitate early identification and resolution of significant accounting issues and to decrease the frequency of fourth quarter adjustments.

As discussed in Chapter 12, "Relationship with the External Auditor," a review of interim financial statements differs significantly from an audit of annual financial statements. In a review engagement, the external auditor does not have a basis for expressing an audit opinion because of the limited work that is performed. The external auditor may identify material misstatements from GAAP based on the review procedures applied. However, a review does not provide the level of assurance that all of the material misstatements that would be discovered in an audit would be identified.

Delegating Additional Responsibilities

Over the years, as the importance of the audit committee continues to expand, boards of directors have used the committee for overseeing matters in addition to the previously discussed responsibilities. Some of these commonly delegated additional responsibilities are presented in this section. A board of directors, in delegating additional responsibilities to its audit committee, should consider whether the committee has the capability, time, and resources to handle expanded duties. Otherwise, if the board of directors inappropriately delegates a responsibility to the committee, the result from a liability perspective may be worse than if no assignment had been made in the first place.

A. Code of Ethical Conduct

Perhaps the most commonly delegated additional duty of audit committees today is to oversee the company's code of ethical conduct. In fact, *Treadway*, in its 1987 report, indicated that (1) all public companies should develop and enforce effective, written codes of conduct, and (2) the audit committee should annually oversee the program that the company establishes to monitor compliance with the code.

In overseeing the code of ethical conduct, the audit committee may:

1. Review, approve, and periodically assess the code of ethical conduct.
2. Review the company's process for implementing the code, including how the code is disseminated in the company and how employees are trained.
3. Oversee the company's process for (a) monitoring compliance with the code and (b) carrying out disciplinary actions.

While handling oversight responsibility for the company's code of ethical conduct, which typically covers conflicts of interest (for example, outside employment and employee personal investments), including related-party transactions, and sensitive payments (for example, wire transfers and fees paid to consultants and agents), the audit committee may expand its oversight (if charged by the board to do so) to:

1. Review the company's policies for conflicts of interest, related-party transactions, and sensitive payments.
2. Inquire about the risks and controls that apply to these items.
3. Oversee the company's processes for monitoring compliance with the policies in 1 above.
4. Direct the internal auditor to evaluate internal controls over conflicts of interest, related parties, and sensitive payments.
5. Receive and evaluate internal audit reports and consider external audit findings that address the above areas.

Oversight of the code of ethical conduct by the board of directors, its audit committee, or another board committee is very important because of the Federal Sentencing Guidelines (discussed in Chapter 4) and the *Caremark* decision (discussed in Chapter 10). The development of a monitoring system whereby the audit committee or another board committee can use the internal auditor or the external auditor for assistance is important in demonstrating the high level of oversight required by the Federal Sentencing Guidelines.

The board of directors may choose to not delegate the code of ethical conduct oversight responsibility to the audit committee. In that case, the committee should at least periodically review those items in the company's code of ethical conduct that apply to financial statements and related risks and controls. In addition, the committee should review those items in the code of ethical conduct that relate to other responsibilities delegated to it. Appendix 7 presents a list of items that are typically included in a company's code of ethical conduct.

B. Special Investigations

Also of increased importance for audit committees is the performance or supervision of special investigations regarding possible fraud and illegal acts, violations of the code of ethical conduct, and material unintentional accounting errors. Sometimes the committee uses the internal auditor and the company's general counsel, with assistance from an independent law firm and the external auditor, to perform the special investigation. However, if there is an allegation of management fraud or misconduct, the committee should use external parties, including another external audit firm, and should limit dissemination of information during the investigation. The committee should oversee and monitor the progress of the special investigation and should receive a complete report from the parties conducting the investigation upon its completion.

C. Laws, Rules, and Regulations

Audit committees in some companies are involved in overseeing compliance matters pertaining to significant laws, rules, and regulations. For example, many committees may oversee, on an annual basis, the environmental compliance of the company and its federal and state income tax status. Also, a number of committees oversee employee benefit plans and compliance with applicable federal and state laws.

D. Litigation Matters

In some companies, the audit committee may be charged with overseeing legal claims and settlements of lawsuits against the company and decisions by the company to file lawsuits. This responsibility may be delegated to the committee because its members are independent outside directors.

E. Expense Accounts and Perquisites

Audit committees also frequently monitor officers' and directors' expense accounts and perquisites,[7] because these items are susceptible to abuse. Typically, the internal auditor performs these reviews and reports the results to the committee. Then the committee can focus on matters that are unusual or questionable or that appear to be abusive. The review of perquisites is particularly important for the top five officers of public companies for whom the information must be disclosed in proxy material.

F. Business Risks

As discussed earlier in this chapter, the audit committee has oversight responsibility for risks related to financial reporting, including fraud risks. However, in some companies, the board of directors has delegated responsibility to the audit committee to monitor the company's overall business risk. In these situations, the committee has to become well-informed of the overall business risks and exposures facing the company and the controls that management has implemented to mitigate those risks.

To identify the business risks, management should periodically update the audit committee about the company's risks and exposures, including the company's strategic plans. The committee should also make inquires of the internal and external auditors about their understanding and identification of business risks. Having identified the company's business risks, the committee is then in a position to monitor the company's processes for controlling those risks. Those controls not related to financial reporting fall within categories 2 and 3 of internal control — controls relating to compliance with laws and regulations and controls over effectiveness and efficiency of operations.

---

[7] Perquisites are expenditures made by the company for the personal benefit of an executive that are unrelated to the company's business.

G. Self-Assessment of Performance

Finally, as discussed in Chapter 15, "Evaluating the Audit Committee," the board of directors may charge — as a good practice — the audit committee with periodically performing a self-assessment of the committee's performance.

Reporting to Shareholders

Audit committees of SEC reporting companies are required to report in proxy statements (relating to the annual meeting of shareholders) whether the committee has:

1. Reviewed and discussed the audited financial statements with management.
2. Discussed the matters required to be communicated by Statement on Auditing Standards (SAS) 61, *Communication with Audit Committees,* (refer to Appendix 16, which contains the SAS 61 communications plus other communications required by GAAS).
3. Received from the external auditor the independence disclosures and discussed independence with the external auditor as required by ISB 1.
4. Considered the non-audit services provided by the external auditor and the impact of those services on the external auditor's independence.
5. Recommended to the board of directors, based on the reviews and discussions above, that the audited financial statements be included in the company's annual report on Form 10-K to be filled with the SEC.

The SEC mandates audit committee reporting in the belief that the report will better communicate to shareholders the committee's responsibility for overseeing the financial reporting process. The report has to appear over the printed names of the committee members. That requirement, according to the SEC, emphasizes the role of the audit committee to shareholders.

The SEC believes that the required report to shareholders will not increase the liability of committee members. The report is based on a process involving discussions with management and the external auditor that enables the committee to make a business judgment, consistent with state corporate law, about filing the company's financial statements. The requirement is consistent with the *Blue Ribbon Report* (discussed in Chapter 5), which indicates that the audit committee can do no more than rely upon the information that it receives, questions, and assesses. Finally, the SEC adopted a "safe harbor" whereby the report is not considered soliciting material that is filed with the Commission (unless the company requests that it be treated as such). Exhibit 8-1 presents a report from an audit committee to shareholders that meets the minimum SEC requirements.

Exhibit 8-1
Example Audit Committee Report to Shareholders

The audit committee reviewed and discussed the audited financial statements, dated December 31, 20X1, and discussed those financial statements with management of XYZ Company. In addition, the committee discussed with the Burke & Guy, CPAs, the independent auditors, the matters required to be communicated by Statement on Auditing Standards No. 61, "Communication with Audit Committees." The committee also received and discussed with Burke & Guy the matters required by Independent Standards Board No. 1, "Independence Discussions with Audit Committee." The independence discussions also included whether the non-audit services provided by the external auditor were compatible with maintaining independence. Based on the review and discussions above, the committee recommended to the Board of Directors that the audited financial statements be included in the Annual Report on Form 10-K (or Form 10-KSB) filed with the Securities and Exchange Commission.

Here is a summary of the responsibilities that the board of directors may delegate to the audit committee:

General Observations

1. The responsibilities of an audit committee vary from company to company.
2. When boards of directors delegate responsibilities to an audit committee, they should:
   a. Tailor the responsibilities of the audit committee to meet the company's unique needs.
   b. Not overload the audit committee with activities.

Primary Responsibilities

3. The primary responsibilities that are delegated to the audit committee are:
   a. Selecting, evaluating, and replacing the external auditor.
   b. Reviewing the external audit plan.
   c. Evaluating the annual audited financial statements.
   d. Overseeing the external audit process and audit results.
   e. Monitoring the external auditor's independence.
   f. Monitoring internal control over financial reporting.
   g. Overseeing the internal audit function.
   h. Evaluating interim financial statements and the external auditor's review of those statements.
   i. Evaluating the committee charter.
   j. Performing a self-assessment.

Additional Responsibilities

4. The board of directors frequently delegates additional responsibilities to the audit committee, such as responsibility for overseeing:
   a. Code of ethical conduct.
   b. Special investigations involving possible fraud and related problems.
   c. Compliance with laws, rules, and regulations.
   d. Litigation matters.
   e. Officers and directors expense accounts and perquisites.
   f. Business risks.

Reporting to Shareholders

5. Audit committees of SEC reporting companies are required to report in their proxy statements whether the committee has:
   a. Reviewed and discussed the audited financial statements with management.
   b. Discussed the matters required to be communicated by SAS 61, *Communication with Audit Committees.*
   c. Received from the external auditor the independence disclosures and discussed independence with the external auditor as required by ISB 1.
   d. Recommended to the board of directors that the audited financial statements be included in the company's annual report on Form 10-K to be filed with the SEC.

CHAPTER 9
THE AUDIT COMMITTEE'S OVERSIGHT
OF INTERNAL CONTROL

As discussed in Chapter 2, "Early History of the Audit Committee Concept — 1939 to 1987," the Foreign Corrupt Practices Act (FCPA) was enacted in 1977. While the FCPA received most of its notoriety because of its anti-bribery provisions, it also contained stringent internal control provisions. Under the FCPA, management is required to maintain accurate books and records and to have a system of internal accounting control sufficient to provide reasonable assurances about proper execution and recording of transactions and protection of assets. By including internal control provisions, the FCPA brought internal control out of the accounting departments and into the boardrooms of U.S. companies.

This chapter discusses the audit committee's oversight responsibilities for internal control. First, internal control is defined. Second, the board of directors' and the audit committee's oversight responsibilities for internal control are discussed. In carrying out its responsibilities, the audit committee relies on management, the internal auditor, and the external auditor. Accordingly, the responsibilities of each of these groups for internal control are discussed.

Definition of Internal Control

Treadway (see Chapter 3, "The 1987 Treadway Commission Report — A Defining Event") recognized that varying interpretations of the meaning of internal control existed. In fact, management, internal auditors, and external auditors did not have a common framework to use when discussing internal control or control weaknesses. Thus, *Treadway* urged its sponsoring organizations to work together to integrate the various internal control concepts and definitions, and develop a common reference point. The 1992 COSO Report *Internal Control — Integrated Framework* (*COSO Report*) was a result of that recommendation.[1]

The *COSO Report* defines internal control and provides criteria for evaluating the effectiveness of internal control. Today, the *COSO Report* is gen-

---

[1] COSO refers to the Committee of Sponsoring Organizations of the Treadway Commission. As discussed in Chapter 3, "The 1987 Treadway Commission Report — A Defining Event," the sponsoring organizations are the American Institute of CPAs, the American Ac-

erally recognized as providing acceptable criteria. In 1996, the Committee of Sponsoring Organizations (COSO) published *Internal Control Issues in Derivatives Usage* to provide specific guidance on risks and controls over derivative activities. In order to properly carry out their fiduciary duties, all boards of directors and audit committees should have a general understanding of the COSO definition of internal control and a general awareness of the various COSO publications. Exhibit 9-1 lists COSO's publications to date and provides COSO's website address.

Exhibit 9-1
COSO Publications and Website

Publications: (available free of charge)
- *Internal Control — Integrated Framework* (1992)
- *Internal Control Issues in Derivatives Usage* (1996)
- *Fraudulent Financial Reporting: 1987–1997 — An Analysis of U.S. Public Companies* (1999)

Website: www.coso.org

The *COSO Report* defines internal control as a process, effected by a company's board of directors, management, internal auditors, and other personnel, designed to provide reasonable assurance about the achievement of objectives in the following categories:

1. Reliability of financial reporting.
2. Compliance with laws and regulations, and
3. Effectiveness and efficiency of operations.

Although a company's internal control addresses objectives in each of the these categories, the controls relating to compliance and operations objectives generally are not directly relevant to a company's internal and external financial reports. Exhibit 9-2 presents a summary of the limitations of internal control.

---

counting Association, the Financial Executives Institute, the Institute of Internal Auditors, and the Institute of Management Accountants.

Exhibit 9-2
What Internal Control Can and Cannot Accomplish

Internal Control Can:

- Promote reliable internal and external financial reporting.
- Help safeguard a company's assets.
- Promote compliance with laws and regulations.
- Help a company achieve its performance and profitability targets.
- ***Bottom Line*** — Internal control can help a company get to where it wants to go and avoid pitfalls and surprises along the way.

Internal Control Cannot:

- Guarantee the reliability of financial reporting and compliance with laws and regulations. (But it can provide reasonable assurance on these matters.)
- Guarantee a company's success or survival. (But it can help a company better achieve its objectives and provide quality information about the company's progress.)
- ***Bottom Line*** — Internal control is not a panacea.

Components of Internal Control

The *COSO Report* identifies *five interrelated components* of internal control that are necessary for the objectives to be achieved. They are: the control environment, risk assessment, control activities, information and communication, and monitoring. The *COSO Report* applies the five components to each of the three categories of control previously discussed to judge whether internal controls in that category are effective.

The *control environment* is the foundation for all the other components. It sets the tone of the company and influences the control consciousness of its employees. Control environment factors include the attention and direction provided by the company's board of directors and its audit committee, the integrity and ethical values of management, management's commitment to competence, management's philosophy and operating style, the company's organizational structure, the way management assigns authority and responsibility, and human resource policies and practices.

As discussed in Chapter 1, "The Need for an Audit Committee," in order for a company to achieve its objective of reliable financial reporting, a proper tone at the top is a must. A proper tone at the top insists upon accuracy in financial reporting. A board of directors and its audit committee must play an important part in establishing a proper tone at the top by making sure that senior management demands truthfulness in financial reporting.

Risk assessment is management's process of identifying, analyzing, and managing risks (including fraud risks as presented in Appendix 14, "Illustrative Fraud Risk Factors") that are relevant to the achievement of objectives. Once risks are identified, management considers their significance, the likelihood of their occurrence, and how they should be managed. Management may initiate plans, programs, or actions to address specific risks or it may decide to accept a risk because of cost or other considerations.

A company's risk assessment for financial reporting purposes is its identification, analysis, and management of risks relevant to the preparation of financial statements that are fairly presented in conformity with generally accepted accounting principles. For example, risk assessment may address how the company considers the possibility of unrecorded transactions or identifies and prepares significant estimates recorded in the financial statements. Risks relevant to financial reporting include external and internal events such as the following:

- *Changes in operating environment.* Changes in the regulatory or operating environment can result in changes in competitive pressures and significantly different risks.
- *New personnel.* New personnel may have a different focus on, or understanding of, controls over financial reporting.
- *New or revamped information systems.* Significant and rapid changes in information systems can change the risk relating to controls over financial reporting.
- *Rapid growth.* Significant and rapid expansion of operations can strain controls and increase the risk of a breakdown in financial controls.
- *New technology.* Incorporation of new technologies into production processes or information systems may change the risk associated with controls over financial reporting.
- *New lines, products, or activities.* Entering into business areas or transactions with which a company has little experience may introduce new risks associated with controls over financial reporting.
- *Corporate restructurings.* Restructurings may be accompanied by staff reductions and changes in supervision and segregation of duties that may change the risk associated with controls over financial reporting.

- *Foreign operations.* The expansion or acquisition of foreign operations carries new and often unique risks that may impact controls over financial reporting, for example, additional or changed risks associated with foreign currency transactions.
- *Accounting pronouncements.* Adoption of new accounting principles or changing accounting principles may affect risks in preparing financial statements.

Control activities are the policies and procedures that help ensure that the necessary actions are taken to address risks related to achieving the company's objectives. Control activities have various objectives and occur throughout the company at all levels and in all functions. Control activities that are relevant to the achievement of the objective of reliable financial reporting include: performance reviews, general controls over data center operations and system software, applications controls over transactions, security of assets, and segregation of duties.

Information and communication involves timely identification, capture, and communication of internal and external information that enable the company's personnel to carry out their responsibilities. Information systems should produce reports containing financial, compliance, and operational information that make it possible to run and control the company. All personnel should receive a clear message from top management that control responsibilities must be taken seriously at all levels. Each employee should understand his or her role in the internal control system, as well as how individual activities relate to the work of others. A mechanism must be provided for communicating significant information upstream, as well as to external parties such as suppliers, customers, regulators, and shareholders.

Monitoring is a process that assesses the quality of internal control over time. This process is accomplished through ongoing monitoring activities and separate evaluations. Ongoing monitoring activities occur in the course of operations and include regular management and supervisory activities. For example, managers of sales, purchasing, and production at divisional and corporate levels are in touch with operations and may question reports that differ significantly from their knowledge of operations. In addition, internal auditors often perform separate evaluations. The scope and frequency of evaluations of the control system depend primarily on an assessment of risk and the effectiveness of the ongoing monitoring procedures. Obviously, a mechanism must be provided for reporting internal control deficiencies upstream, with serious matters being reported to top management and the board of directors or its audit committee.

The urgency with which companies should approach assessing their monitoring of their internal control systems has been accelerated by a 1996 decision in Delaware in the *Caremark* case. The implications of the *Caremark* case and the impact on the future activities of audit committees are presented in the next chapter.

The Audit Committee's Responsibilities For Internal Control

A company faces numerous risks (including fraud risks) related to its business such as risks pertaining to competitive, environmental, financial, legal, administrative and operational, regulatory, strategic, and technological factors. The board of directors bears ultimate responsibility for overseeing all of the company's significant business risks and controls related to those risks. As discussed above, internal control is a broad concept that encompasses a wide range of risks and controls related to objectives in three categories: financial reporting, compliance with laws and regulations, and operations. Thus the question arises, is the audit committee responsible for overseeing all internal control?

Clearly the audit committee has responsibility for overseeing risks and controls over financial reporting. In some cases, the audit committee has some responsibility for risks and controls over compliance with certain laws and regulations. For example, there appears to be a trend among audit committees to oversee tax, environmental, legal, and certain other regulatory and compliance matters relevant to the company's business simply because these items can have a material affect on financial reporting. However, the audit committee does not have responsibility for overseeing risks and controls over compliance with laws and regulations and operations unless the board of directors specifically delegates such responsibility to the audit committee. The board should recognize its responsibility for overall business risks and related controls and should be very specific in delegating risks and controls responsibility to the audit committee.

In fulfilling its oversight responsibilities for risks and controls over financial reporting (and other risks and controls delegated to it), the audit committee relies on representations made by management to the committee about risks and controls. However, the audit committee should recognize that management might not fully disclose all deficiencies in financial reporting control either because management is not aware of the deficiencies or because management is reluctant to divulge that uncontrolled risks exist within the company. Thus, the audit committee should make inquiries of the internal and external auditors not only to corroborate management's representations about risks and controls over financial reporting, but also to gain additional information about those risks and controls.

To make effective inquiries and to evaluate the responses to those inquiries, the audit committee must understand the responsibilities of management, the internal auditor, and the external auditor for business risks and internal controls related to those risks. These responsibilities are discussed next.

Report of Management to Shareholders

While the board of directors has oversight responsibility for all significant business risks and controls, it is generally recognized that management has the responsibility for identifying business risks and for designing, implementing, and monitoring controls. Since the passage of the FCPA in 1977, various groups have recommended that management report to shareholders information about the effectiveness of internal control over financial reporting. These recommendations have come from a variety of groups in both the private and public sector, including: (1) the Cohen Commission in 1978; (2) the SEC in 1979 and again in 1988; (3) the Treadway Commission in 1987; and (4) the Public Oversight Board of the AICPA SEC Practices Section in 1993. In some cases, these recommendations have called for auditor reporting on the effectiveness of internal control over financial reporting. To date, the SEC does not require management or auditor reporting on the effectiveness of control over financial reporting.

Although publicly held companies, other than certain financial institutions, are not required by law or regulation to include in their annual reports to shareholders specific disclosures about internal control, the management of many companies will provide such information in a report of management that is included in the company's annual report, typically presented next to the auditor's report. Since there are no laws or regulations except for financial institutions that require reports of management in annual reports, the specific disclosures included in these reports vary.[2] However, reports of management typically discuss one or more of the following items:

- Management's responsibility for financial reporting.
- Management's responsibility for internal control over financial reporting.
- The audit committee role in the oversight of financial reporting.

---

[2] The Federal Deposit Insurance Corporation Improvement Act of 1991 requires management of certain financial institutions to report on the effectiveness of the institution's internal control over financial reporting. The Act requires the auditor to examine management's report about the effectiveness of internal control over financial reporting. The auditor's report is generally provided only to the company and its regulators.

- The internal auditor's role in monitoring the effectiveness of internal control.
- The name of the external auditor and an explanation that the financial statements were audited in accordance with generally accepted auditing standards.
- Management's representation as to the effectiveness of internal control over financial reporting.

Management's representation about the effectiveness of internal control over financial reporting may be unaudited or audited. (The external auditor's responsibilities regarding management reports are discussed later under the auditor's responsibilities.)

The Panel on Audit Effectiveness (*Panel*) recently observed that confusion exists among shareholders and other users of the annual report about the nature of the work performed and the responsibilities assumed by the external auditor for internal controls over financial reporting.[3] To reduce this confusion, the *Panel* recommended that if management is required to report to shareholders on the effectiveness of controls over financial reporting, the SEC should require either the external auditor to report on those controls or management to explicitly state that the external auditor does not express an opinion on internal control.

Appendix 8, "Example of Report of Management," presents a report by management on financial statements and internal control over financial reporting. In this sample report, management has engaged the auditor to examine and report on management's representations about internal control.

Management Representation to the Audit Committee

Although the audit committee should obtain a copy of the report of management to shareholders if one exists, the audit committee needs additional information from management. The *Panel* recommended that audit committees should obtain written representations from management on the ef-

---

[3] As discussed in Chapter 4, "Additional Developments from *Treadway* to 2001," in September 1998, at the request of the chairman of the SEC, the Public Oversight Board of the AICPA SEC Practice Section appointed the Panel on Audit Effectiveness. The Panel conducted a review and evaluation of auditing practice to explore the efficacy of the audit process for public companies. The Panel's final report was issued in September 2000 and is available at www.pobauditpanel.org.

fectiveness of control over financial reporting. According to the *Panel,* the written report is necessary for the effective discharge of the audit committee's responsibilities and will serve as a catalyst for its more substantive involvement in the area of internal control and a more meaningful dialogue with the internal and external auditors about controls.

The National Association of Corporate Directors' *Audit Committees: A Practical Guide* (*NACD Guide*) also recommended that management provide written representations to the audit committee. The representation letter suggested by the *NACD Guide* covers financial statements, controls, and the quality of earnings. The letter should be signed by the chief executive officer, the chief financial officer, and the chief accounting officer. According to the *NACD Guide,* management should affirmatively acknowledge to the audit committee its responsibility for the integrity of the control and financial reporting systems and processes, and its beliefs about the quality of controls and financial reports. The purposes of these written representations are to: (1) confirm the representations given explicitly or implicitly to the audit committee, (2) reduce the possibility of misunderstanding concerning the matters that are the subject of the representations, and (3) explicitly recognize management's responsibility to the committee in the two areas. These written representations from management should be provided annually before the annual report is issued. Appendix 9, "Excerpt From Management Representation Letter to the Audit Committee," presents the section of the *NACD Guide* representation letter that addresses controls. The excerpt may be used to supplement the management letter that the external auditor is required to obtain. As discussed in Chapter 12, "Relationship with the External Auditor," the required audit management representation letter addresses financial statements, not controls.

The Internal Auditor's Responsibility for Internal Control

The internal auditor plays a significant role in monitoring the risks and controls over financial reporting, compliance, and operations. According to *Treadway,* "internal auditing gives management and the audit committee a way to monitor the reliability and the integrity of financial and operating information." The internal auditor's specific authority and responsibility for internal control should be set forth in the internal audit charter that is approved by management and the audit committee. Chapter 11, "Relationship with the Internal Auditor," discusses the internal auditor's responsibilities under the internal audit charter and professional standards issued by the Institute of Internal Auditors.

The External Auditor's Responsibility for Internal Control in a Financial Statement Audit

The auditor's report on financial statements does not address internal control (including any of the three *COSO Report* categories of control) or provide any assurance about internal control. However, to say that the auditor has no responsibilities for internal control is incorrect. As explained below, the auditor must perform some internal control work on every audit engagement.

When performing an audit of financial statements, the external auditor has to obtain an understanding of a company's risks and controls over financial reporting. The auditor obtains this understanding by making inquiries of the company's personnel, observing activities within the company, and inspecting documents. For example, to obtain an understanding about monitoring controls over the financial reporting process, the auditor might inspect the budget and inquire about how management followed up on significant variances. Or, to obtain an understanding of control activities over sales transactions, the auditor might inspect the procedures manual that describes the processing of sales transactions, and then clarify that understanding by making inquiries of the company's personnel and observing their activities.

The auditor uses his or her understanding about risks and controls over financial reporting to design an audit approach for each significant account in the company's financial statements. The auditor may choose a "substantive" approach whereby the auditor does not test the effectiveness of the controls for certain financial statement accounts. Instead, the auditor will directly test the accounts in the financial statements. The auditor will choose this approach if the auditor believes that the company's controls over financial reporting for a given account are not effective or if the auditor concludes it would be more efficient to directly test the financial statement account.

On the other hand, if the auditor believes that the controls over financial reporting for a given account are properly designed and are being used by the company, the auditor may choose to "rely on internal control." Under this approach, the auditor performs "tests of controls" on the account balance to determine whether the controls are effective. If the controls are in fact effective, the auditor will have evidence about the reliability of that financial statement account. Thus, the auditor's direct tests of that account in the financial statements will be reduced.

Recently, some CPA firms have adopted a business risk approach to auditing financial statements. In a business risk approach, the auditor strives to obtain an understanding of the company's overall business strategy and objectives, attempts to identify risks that would prevent the company from achieving its objectives, and obtains an understanding of how management controls these risks. The business risk approach is similar to the approach described above based on reliance on controls. It differs from the reliance on controls in that the auditor attempts to obtain an understanding of all significant business risks, not just risks associated with financial reporting. When performing tests of controls, the auditor tests only those controls that relate to financial reporting. However, the tests typically focus on high level controls. High level controls are those associated with the control environment (for example, the role of the audit committee) and monitoring (for example, reviews of actual performance versus budgets) as opposed to specific control activities (for example, inspection of sales transaction documents such as customer orders, shipping documents, and sales invoices for evidence that control procedures related to the sales transaction were performed). After performing tests of controls, if the auditor believes there are uncontrolled risks that could affect the financial statements, the auditor performs additional "risk-reducing procedures" by testing the account balances in the financial statements directly.

Understanding the approach that was taken by the external auditor can assist the audit committee in framing and evaluating questions about internal control such as: What risks, especially those related to financial reporting, did the external auditor identify when performing the audit? Are there controls in place to mitigate those risks? Did the auditor test those controls?

SAS 60 Letters (Management Letters)

Although the external auditor performs procedures to understand risks and controls over financial reporting and frequently performs tests of controls on various accounts in the financial statements, the auditor does not have a responsibility to perform procedures to identify control deficiencies. However, when performing the audit, the auditor may become aware of significant deficiencies in controls over financial reporting. SAS 60, *Communication of Internal Control Related Matters Noted in an Audit,* refers to significant deficiencies in internal control as reportable conditions. Some reportable conditions may be of such magnitude that they are called material weaknesses.

A reportable condition may involve any of the five components of internal control over financial reporting. The following are examples of reportable conditions:

- Inadequate procedures for appropriately assessing and applying accounting principles.

- Evidence of failure to safeguard assets from loss, damage, or misappropriation.
- Evidence of intentional override of internal control by those in authority.
- Absence of a sufficient level of control consciousness within the company.

Because the board of directors is a factor that makes up the control environment, the authors believe that an audit committee that is not properly executing its oversight duties constitutes a reportable condition.

The auditor is required to communicate reportable conditions to the audit committee either orally or in writing. The authors believe that the communication should be in writing. A written communication identifying reportable conditions may be called (1) an SAS 60 letter, (2) a reportable conditions letter, (3) an internal control letter, or (4) a management letter. Such letters, especially the management letter, may be more inclusive than an SAS 60 letter because it contains items other than reportable conditions related to financial reporting. For example, a management letter may identify problems noted in operational and administrative areas such as the need to develop better strategic plans. Appendix 10, "Example of SAS 60 Letter," contains a sample reportable conditions letter.

Although the auditor is not required to separately identify which reportable conditions are material weaknesses, the auditor may choose to do so or the audit committee may request the auditor to do so. In fact, if the letter does not address material weaknesses, the authors believe that the audit committee should explicitly ask the external auditor if he or she believes that any of the reportable conditions are material weaknesses. If material weaknesses exist, the audit committee should determine that the material weaknesses have been referred to the company's legal counsel for evaluation. The material weaknesses may have legal ramifications under the FCPA.

Based on the reviews of actual audit engagements, the *Panel* observed that auditors communicated reportable conditions and material weaknesses in only a few instances. In fact, it is very common for auditors to report that the audit did not identify any material weaknesses. The *Panel* provides several explanations for the minimal communications regarding internal controls, including: (1) a lack of such conditions on the audits reviewed, (2) the limited amount of internal control work performed by the external auditors, and (3) the subjectivity of the criteria for identifying reportable conditions and material weaknesses. Exhibit 9-3 presents definitions of "reportable condition" and "material weakness."

Exhibit 9-3
Reportable Conditions vs. Material Weaknesses

- A **reportable condition** is a significant deficiency in the design or operation of internal control that comes to the external auditor's attention that could cause the financial statements to be misstated.
- A **material weakness** is a reportable condition that produces a risk of misstatement in the financial statements that is not low.

The *Panel* concluded that audit committees seldom ask management and the external auditors in-depth questions about internal control. Consequently, the *Panel* recommends that audit committees should establish specific expectations with management and the internal and external auditors about the information needs of the committee related to internal control. The audit committee should understand management's and the auditor's views on (1) the control environment and (2) the controls (or lack thereof) over financial reporting, with particular attention to the controls in higher risk areas of the company's information systems. Discussions that the audit committee has should include the effects of technology on current and future information systems.

External Auditor's Attest Report on Internal Control over Financial Reporting

An auditor may be engaged to express an opinion about the effectiveness of a company's internal control over financial reporting under Statements on Standards for Attestation Engagements (SSAE) 2, *Reporting on an Entity's Internal Control over Financial Reporting.* In order for the CPA to evaluate the effectiveness of a company's internal control, criteria must be established for assessing the effectiveness. As previously stated, the *COSO Report* is the most commonly used criteria for reporting on the effectiveness of internal control over financial reporting.

The examination of controls over financial reporting to express an opinion may be made separately from, or in conjunction with, an audit of a company's financial statements. This type of report can be dated differently from the CPA's audit report on the financial statements. A report expressing an unqualified opinion on a company's internal control over financial reporting is presented in Appendix 11, "Example of External Auditor's Attest Report on Internal Control Over Financial Reporting."

Agreed-Upon Procedures Reports on Internal Control over Compliance

A CPA may also be engaged to perform agreed-upon procedures to assist a company or its audit committee in evaluating the effectiveness of the company's internal controls over compliance with some aspects of a rule, law, or regulation. These engagements are performed under Statements on Standards for Attestation Engagements 3, *Compliance Attestation.*

Here is a summary of the important points in this chapter:

Internal Control — The Company's Responsibility

1. A company faces numerous risks (including fraud risks) related to its business, such as risks pertaining to competitive, environmental, financial, legal, administrative and operational, regulatory, strategic, and technological factors.
2. The board of directors is responsible for overseeing all of the company's significant business risks and controls related to those risks.
3. The *COSO Report* subdivides internal control into three categories: (A) control over financial reporting, (B) control over compliance with laws and regulations, and (C) control over operations. (Business risks may also be classified into the same categories.)
4. Management has the responsibility to monitor and control (when cost beneficial) all significant business risks; thus, management designs, implements, and monitors controls relevant to those risks.
5. Management may acknowledge its responsibility for internal control over financial reporting and comment on the effectiveness of internal control in a management report that is included in the company's annual report. The management report may be based on (a) management's best knowledge and belief or (b) an evaluation made by the company using control criteria set forth in the *COSO Report.*

Internal Control — The Audit Committee's Responsibility

1. The board of directors, in delegating oversight responsibility for the integrity of financial reporting to the audit committee, assigns responsibility for risks related to financial reporting (including fraud risk) and controls over financial reporting to the committee.

2. The board of directors may also delegate other oversight responsibilities to the audit committee that relate to risks and controls over compliance with certain laws and regulations (for example, tax and environmental compliance) and risks and controls over operations.
3. The audit committee should not be charged with overseeing all business risks and controls related to those risks.
4. The audit committee, in carrying out its responsibility for oversight of risks and controls over financial reporting (and other risks and controls pertaining to compliance or operations that are explicitly delegated by the board of directors), relies on (a) management, (b) the internal auditor, and (c) the external auditor in identifying risks and inquiring about the existence and effectiveness of controls that pertain to its oversight responsibility.

Internal Control — The External Auditor's Responsibility

1. The external auditor is not required to and does not obtain an understanding of all significant business risks and related controls. (Some CPA firms attempt to obtain an understanding of all significant business risks to plan the audit and add value to the audit.)
2. The external auditor is required by professional standards to obtain an understanding of those risks and controls that relate to financial reporting. The external auditor must obtain this understanding to plan the audit and design an effective audit program.
3. The external auditor may test certain controls over financial reporting and may not test other controls over financial reporting. The external auditor does not test those controls that he or she believes are not effective and does not test controls when it is more efficient to directly test a financial statement account (referred to as "substantive testing").
4. The external auditor is not required to search for or to identify control deficiencies over financial reporting. However, if the external auditor becomes aware of significant deficiencies in controls over financial reporting, he or she is required to report those to the audit committee (significant control deficiencies are called "reportable conditions" and may also be "material weaknesses").
5. The external auditor's report containing significant control deficiencies may be referred to as an SAS 60 letter, reportable conditions letter, internal control letter, or a management letter. Such letters, especially the management letter, may also contain comments about control deficiencies that pertain to controls over compliance or operations.

6. In a financial statement audit, the auditor does not give any assurance on internal control over financial reporting or any other internal control. In fact, the audit report does not even address internal control.
7. An external auditor may be engaged to report on the effectiveness of internal control over financial reporting under Statement on Standards for Attestation Engagements 2, *Reporting on an Entity's Internal Control over Financial Reporting.*
8. An external auditor may also be engaged to perform agreed-upon procedures on the effectiveness of internal control over compliance matters under Statement on Standards for Attestation Engagements 3, *Compliance Attestation.*

Panel on Audit Effectiveness — Recommendations on Internal Control to Audit Committees

Audit committees should:

1. Increase the time and attention that they devote to discussions of internal control with management, the internal auditor, and the external auditor.
2. Obtain written representations from management on the effectiveness of internal control over financial reporting.
3. Establish specific expectations with management and the internal and external auditors about their information needs related to internal control.

CHAPTER 10
THE POTENTIAL IMPACT
OF THE *CAREMARK* DECISION
ON AUDIT COMMITTEES

As discussed in Chapter 4, "Additional Developments from *Treadway* to 2001," the Federal Sentencing Guidelines were amended in 1991 to apply to corporations and other business entities. The Guidelines cover a number of different types of business and white-collar crimes, including antitrust violations, bid-rigging, price fixing, embezzlement, securities violations, mail fraud, and numerous other criminal activities. Even if only one employee is found guilty, companies may face substantial fines under the Federal Sentencing Guidelines. The seriousness of the crime and the culpability of the company affect the amount of the potential fine. The Guidelines do provide for a reduction of fines if a company (1) detects the offense and reports it to the proper authorities or (2) had an effective compliance system in place before the crime was committed.

In 1992, the *COSO Report* (see Chapter 9) established a framework for a broader and uniform concept of internal control. According to the *COSO Report,* internal control is broadly defined as a process, effected by an entity's board of directors, management and other personnel, designed to provide reasonable assurance about achievement of control objectives in the following categories:

- Reliability of financial reporting.
- Compliance with applicable laws and regulations.
- Effectiveness and efficiency of operations.

Applying the broad concept of internal control in the *COSO Report* clearly requires a board of directors to oversee the overall effectiveness of a company's reporting and compliance control systems to help the entity achieve its performance and profitability goals, safeguard assets, ensure reliable financial reporting, and ensure compliance with laws and regulations, thereby avoiding damage to its reputation and other consequences. As discussed later in this chapter, it now appears that at least the Delaware Court of Chancery is adopting the view that a board of directors has an obligation to determine that corporate information and reporting systems exist and are adequate for the needs of the corporation.[1] The purpose of this chapter is to present the

---

[1] Many of the largest companies are incorporated in Delaware, and the Court of Chancery is a respected authority on corporate law that sets precedents for other states.

court decision that articulated the board's responsibility to oversee a company's information and reporting systems.

The *Caremark* Decision

On September 25, 1996, the Delaware Court of Chancery issued a decision, *In Re: Caremark International, Inc. Derivative Litigation,*[2] that gives important guidance to boards of directors about their responsibilities to assure that a company has an adequate corporate compliance information reporting system. Failure by the board to do so may render directors liable for losses caused by non-compliance with applicable legal standards.

In *Caremark,* the company and several of its middle and lower-level employees admitted violating criminal prohibitions relating to kickback payments. No senior officers or directors were accused of participating in the activity. Nevertheless, the directors were sued in derivative actions based on claims that they breached their fiduciary duty in connection with alleged violations of federal and state laws and regulations by Caremark employees.

As a result of the alleged violations, Caremark was subjected to an extensive four-year investigation by the U. S. Department of Health and Human Services (DHHS) and the Department of Justice (DOJ). In 1994, Caremark was charged in an indictment with multiple felonies. Thereafter, Caremark entered into a number of agreements with the DOJ and others, including a plea agreement in which the company pleaded guilty to a single count of mail fraud and agreed to pay civil and criminal fines and to make restitution to various private and public parties. The total payments made by Caremark were approximately $250 million.

The derivative suit was filed in 1994 to seek, on behalf of Caremark, recovery of the approximate $250 million from the individual directors of the company. The *Caremark* decision involved a review of a proposed settlement of the derivative litigation by the Delaware Court of Chancery. The Court's opinion was written by Chancellor William P. Allen, now chairman of the Independence Standards Board.

In considering approval of the proposed settlement, the Court discussed a number of facts. Caremark was created in 1992 as a result of a spin-off from Baxter International, Inc. The business practices that created the legal problems predated the spin-off. During the relevant time period, Caremark

---

[2] Civ. A. No. 13670 (Court of Chancery of Delaware — Newcastle County — September 25, 1996).

was involved in providing patient care and managed care services as part of its patient care business, which accounted for the majority of its revenues. As part of its patient care business, Caremark provided alternative site health-care services, such as infusion therapy and growth hormone therapy. Caremark's managed care services included prescription drug programs and the operation of multi-specialty group practices.

A substantial part of the revenues generated by Caremark's businesses were derived from third-party payments, insurers, and Medicare and Medicaid reimbursement programs. The latter payments are subject to the Anti-Referral Payments Law (ARPL), which prohibits healthcare providers from paying any form of remuneration to induce the referral of Medicare or Medicaid patients. From inception, Caremark (Baxter International prior to 1992 and hereafter referred to simply as Caremark) entered into a variety of agreements with hospitals, physicians, and healthcare providers for advice and services, and with drug manufacturers relative to product distribution. Caremark had a practice of entering into contracts for consulting and research services with physicians, at least some of whom prescribed or recommended services or products that Caremark provided to Medicare recipients and other patients. Such contracts were not prohibited by the ARPL, but they obviously raised the possibility of illegal "kickbacks."

As early as 1989, Caremark issued an internal contract guide to govern its employees in contracting with physicians and hospitals. The guide was reviewed annually and updated by attorneys. Each version of the guide stated as Caremark's policy that no payments would be made in exchange for, or to induce, patient referrals. Nevertheless, the law was unclear and Caremark publicly stated a number of times that there was uncertainty regarding their interpretation of the ARPL.

In 1991, the DHHS issued "safe-harbor" regulations under the ARPL stating conditions under which financial relationships between a healthcare service provider and patient referral sources, such as physicians, would not violate the ARPL. Caremark contended that the narrowly drawn regulations gave limited guidance about the legality of many of their agreements that did not fall within the "safe-harbor." Caremark, however, amended many of its standard forms of agreement with healthcare providers and revised the contract guide in an apparent attempt to comply with the new regulations. After issuance of the regulations in 1991, the DHHS Inspector General initiated an investigation. In subpoenaed materials, it appears that Caremark paid physicians' fees for monitoring patients, including Medicare and Medicaid recipients. Apparently, in some cases, the individuals monitoring patients were referring physicians that raised the ARPL concern.

In 1992, DOJ joined the DHHS Inspector General in the investigation. Investigations were also commenced by several additional federal and state agencies. During the relevant period, Caremark had approximately 7,000 employees and 90 branch operations. By May 1991, however, Caremark claimed that it had begun making attempts to centralize its management structure to increase supervision over its branch operations.

The first action taken by management as a result of the investigation was an announcement that, as of October 1, 1991, Caremark would no longer pay management fees to physicians for services to Medicare and Medicaid patients. Despite this decision, management asserted that it did not believe that such payments were illegal under the existing laws and regulations.

During this period, Caremark's board of directors took several additional steps consistent with an effort to assure compliance with company ARPL policies and the forms in the contract guide. In April 1992, Caremark published a fourth revised version of its contract guide, apparently designed to assure that its agreements either complied with the ARPL regulations or excluded Medicare and Medicaid patients altogether. In addition, in September 1992, Caremark instituted a policy requiring its regional officers to approve each contractual relationship entered into by Caremark with a physician.

While there is evidence that inside and outside counsel advised Caremark's directors that their contracts were acceptable, Caremark recognized that some uncertainty about the interpretation of the law existed. In its 1992 annual report, Caremark disclosed the on-going government investigations, acknowledged that if penalties were imposed on the company, they could have a material adverse affect on the company's business, and stated that no assurance could be given that its interpretation of ARPL would prevail if challenged.

Throughout the period of the investigation, Caremark had an internal audit plan designed to ensure compliance with business and ethics policies. In early 1993, the Ethics Committee of Caremark's board received and reviewed a letter from its external auditor stating that there were no material weaknesses in Caremark's controls. The Committee also adopted a new internal audit charter requiring a comprehensive review of compliance policies and the compilation of an employee ethics handbook covering such policies.

Caremark's board appears to have been informed about this project and other efforts to assure compliance with laws and regulations. Caremark took several steps to determine that contract forms were used properly and payments in exchange for referrals were not made. Caremark continued these policies in subsequent years; employees received revised versions of the ethics handbook and were required to participate in training sessions about compliance matters.

In 1993, Caremark took several additional steps aimed at increasing management supervision, including new policies requiring local branch managers to secure home office approval of all disbursements under arrangements with healthcare providers and to certify compliance with the ethics program. Also, the chief financial officer of Caremark was appointed to serve as compliance officer. In 1994, a fifth revised contract guide was published.

In August 1994, a federal grand jury in Minnesota indicted Caremark, two of its officers and others, for violating ARPL over a lengthy period. Caremark denied any wrongdoing relating to the indictment and indicated that the company believed that the investigation by the DHHS Inspector General would have a favorable outcome. Almost immediately, five stockholder derivative actions were filed in Delaware and consolidated. The derivative actions alleged that Caremark's directors breached their duty of care by failing (1) to supervise adequately the conduct of Caremark employees, or (2) to institute appropriate corrective measures, thereby exposing Caremark to fines and liabilities.

In September 1994, another indictment was issued in Ohio alleging that an Ohio physician had defrauded the Medicare program by requesting and receiving payments for referrals of patients whose medical costs were in part reimbursed by Medicare in violation of ARPL. Caremark was the healthcare provider allegedly making such payments. In October 1994, the stockholder derivative actions were amended to add allegations regarding the Ohio indictment and certain other matters. After each complaint was filed in the derivative actions, the defendants filed a motion to dismiss.

In September 1994, Caremark announced that as of January 1, 1995, it would terminate all remaining financial relationships with physicians for certain activities, including infusion therapy and growth hormone therapy. Caremark also indicated that its restrictive policies were extended to all of its contractual relationships with physicians, including those with Medicare and Medicaid patients. Finally, Caremark terminated its research grant program.

Settlement negotiations commenced with federal and state government entities in May 1995. On June 15, 1995, the Caremark board approved a settlement covering all of the pending federal and state government allegations.

Settlement negotiations in the derivative actions also commenced in May 1995, resulting in a Memorandum of Understanding in June 1995. The Caremark board of directors approved the Memorandum of Understanding that required the board of directors to adopt several resolutions and create a new compliance committee.

After negotiating the settlements, Caremark learned in late 1995 that several insurance companies believed that Caremark was liable for damages to them for allegedly improper business practices. The Caremark board approved a $98.5 million settlement with those insurance companies in March 1996.

After concluding the insurance company settlement, the plaintiffs in the derivative actions decided to continue seeking approval of the proposed settlement agreement. The final settlement agreement contained several significant points, including the following matters relevant to the Caremark board:

1. The board was required to discuss all relevant material changes in government healthcare regulations and their effect on relationships with healthcare providers on a semi-annual basis.
2. The board was required to establish a Compliance and Ethics Committee consisting of four directors, two of whom are non-management directors. The new committee was obligated to meet at least four times a year to effectuate policies and monitor business segment compliance with the ARPL. Finally, the new committee was required to report to the board semi-annually concerning the compliance by each business section.
3. Corporate officers responsible for business segments were required to serve as compliance officers who report semi-annually to the Compliance and Ethics Committee and, with the assistance of outside counsel, review existing contracts and obtain advance approval of any new contract form.

Chancellor Allen analyzed the claims made in light of the foregoing facts to determine if the proposed settlement of the shareholder derivative suit was fair. He began his analysis by noting that director liability can arise either from a board decision that (1) results in a loss because that decision was ill-advised or "negligent," or (2) is a failure by the board to act in circumstances under which due attention would, arguably, have prevented the loss.

Chancellor Allen also noted the confusion surrounding the business judgment rule insofar as it relates to the difference between a board decision and the process employed in making the decision. He stated that the focus should be on the process involved in making a board decision, not the decision itself. This means that when a director exercises a good faith effort to be informed and to exercise appropriate judgment, he or she has satisfied the duty of attention.

In the failure-to-monitor situation at issue in *Caremark,* Chancellor Allen stated that:

> ... a director's obligation includes a duty to attempt in good faith to ensure that a corporate information and reporting system, which the board concludes is adequate, exists, and that failure to do so under some circumstances may, in theory at least, render a director liable for losses caused by noncompliance with applicable legal standards.

The *Caremark* court decided that there was no director liability for a decision that the court believed to be "wrong," "stupid," egregious," or "irrational," so long as the process employed was either rational or employed in a good faith effort to advance corporate interest.

The Court's position in *Caremark* is clear. **Directors, at least in Delaware, have an obligation to ensure that adequate information and reporting systems exist in a corporation.** To be adequate, the systems must be designed to provide timely and accurate information to the board management. *Caremark* concluded that while the directors may not have been totally aware of the activities leading to liability, the board of directors was not guilty of sustained failure to exercise its oversight function. While the Court did not mention the definition of internal control contained in the *COSO Report,* **it clearly implies that the board of directors has responsibility for overall internal control, not just internal control over financial reporting.**

Caremark noted the increasing tendency to use criminal law to ensure corporate compliance with laws and regulations. The Court referred to the Federal Sentencing Guidelines as impacting importantly on the prospective effect criminal sanctions might have on business entities. The Guidelines offer a powerful incentive for companies to have compliance programs to detect violations of law, promptly report violations to the appropriate public officials when discovered, and to take prompt voluntary remedial actions. Chancellor Allen noted in *Caremark* that any rational person attempting in good faith to meet an organizational governance responsibility would be bound to take the Federal Sentencing Guidelines into account.

Caremark and the Audit Committee

While no court or regulatory rulings require audit committees to oversee compliance control systems in a company, based on *Caremark,* boards of directors should seriously consider whether their audit committees should be assigned that oversight function. The audit committee is perhaps best positioned to understand the various control systems in the company and the level of compliance with corporate policy regarding the operations of such systems.[3] Furthermore, the Federal Sentencing Guidelines should be carefully considered in developing the processes and procedures implemented to comply with *Caremark.*[4]

If the audit committee does not extend the scope of its activities to include the oversight of compliance controls suggested by *Caremark,* the board of directors should consider forming a new committee that is charged with oversight responsibility for compliance control systems. In addition, the board should determine that the responsibility for compliance with the code of conduct is assigned either to the audit committee or the new committee.

In any event, whether the responsibility is delegated to the audit committee, a new committee, or carried out by the entire board, *Caremark* makes it clear that boards of directors must receive information they reasonably decide is needed to make informed judgments about compliance with applicable laws and regulations. At a minimum, the board or a designated committee thereof should oversee:

- The overall state of compliance with government and other regulations affecting the company's operations, such as taxation, environmental, employee relations, workplace safety, foreign operations, antitrust, and other industry-specific legal or regulatory requirements.
- The compliance and reporting system to determine that it is in accordance with the Federal Sentencing Guidelines, particularly policies about communication of requirements, training, and internal enforcement.
- Any important whistle-blower reports, as well as management actions taken in response to such reports.
- The overall compliance environment with legal counsel and other specialists to determine that the company's systems are up-to-date.
- Internal and external compliance audits to the extent appropriate.

---

[3] See "Building a Better Audit Committee," *Business Law Today* (January/February 1999), p. 5 for an implication that audit committees should be responsible for compliance with *Caremark.*

[4] "The *Caremark* Decision: Director's Fiduciary Duty in a Sentencing Guidelines World", *The Corporate Counselor* (February 1997), p. 8; see also "Director's Liability for Compliance," *Corporate Board* (July 17, 1997), p. 10, and "An Opportunity for Directors to Help Their Company and Avoid Personal Liability," *Southern California Business* (April 1997), p. 6.

Summary of the *Caremark* Decision:

- In 1994, prosecutors charged Caremark, a healthcare provider, with committing illegal acts by paying doctors and hospitals for referral of Medicare and Medicaid patients. Caremark pleaded guilty to one count of mail fraud and agreed to pay approximately $250 million in fines and restitution.
- The *Caremark* decision was a derivative action brought against the board of directors to recover the above amount.
- The action alleged that the directors breached their fiduciary duties by failing to monitor effectively the conduct of company employees who violated state and federal laws regarding payments to healthcare providers.
- The Delaware Court of Chancery's opinion, dated September 25, 1996, approved the settlement of the consolidated derivative action based upon, according to the Chancellor, a "very low probability" that the directors would have been personally liable for having breached any duty.
- In support of the opinion, the Chancellor cited, among other things, the compliance programs that Caremark had instituted prior to being indicted. Caremark had already implemented, among other things:
  1. A code of employee conduct, including policies for compliance with regulatory requirements.
  2. Procedures for reviewing and amending the code of employee conduct.
  3. Requirements that designated officers review and approve regulated activities.
  4. A compliance officer.
  5. An internal audit plan over compliance with business and ethics policies.
  6. On-going employee training about compliance matters.
- In approving the settlement, Caremark also paid $869,500 in attorneys' fees and was required to improve its compliance systems.

Effect of Caremark *on Boards of Directors and their Audit Committees:*

- Prior to *Caremark,* directors' liability was for breaching the duty of care by failing to properly oversee the actions of corporate officers largely based on applying a general rule to particular facts and circumstances surrounding the alleged breach.
- Because of *Caremark,* directors (at least directors of Delaware corporations) now apparently have a duty to assure that information and reporting systems exist in their companies.

- The information and reporting systems must be reasonably designed to provide timely and accurate information sufficient to allow management and directors to reach informed judgments about their company's compliance with laws and regulations.
- Avoiding *Caremark* liability requires establishing compliance systems for high-risk compliance and regulatory areas. Such systems should be part of a company's control systems and should be administered by high-ranking executives who report regularly to the board or its audit committee.
- Directors or their audit committees (or other specially designated committees) must oversee compliance systems, including receiving reports thereon and reviewing employee training efforts, discipline actions, and the results of compliance audits.
- Properly structured compliance systems will provide a double benefit by (1) protecting a company from material criminal penalties and (2) insulating directors from liability.

CHAPTER 11
RELATIONSHIP WITH THE INTERNAL AUDITOR

The Foreign Corrupt Practices Act (FCPA) of 1977 prompted many companies to establish internal audit functions or to increase the size and quality of their internal audit staff. The FCPA (discussed in Chapter 2, "Early History of the Audit Committee Concept — 1939 to 1987") requires, among other things, publicly held companies to devise and maintain systems of internal accounting controls to provide reasonable assurance that control objectives are being achieved. One method of gaining this assurance is to establish and maintain an effective internal audit function.

Treadway (discussed in Chapter 3, "The 1987 Treadway Commission Report — A Defining Event") recognized the internal auditing function as an important element in preventing and detecting fraudulent financial reporting. According to *Treadway,* "properly organized and effectively operated, internal auditing gives management and the audit committee a way to monitor the reliability and integrity of financial and operating information." [1] *Treadway* made four recommendations regarding internal auditing. [2] Exhibit 11-1 presents those recommendations. They are discussed later in this chapter.

Exhibit 11-1
Treadway on Internal Auditing

1. Public companies should maintain an effective internal audit function staffed with an adequate number of qualified personnel appropriate to the size and the nature of the company.
2. Public companies should ensure that their internal audit functions are objective.
3. Internal auditors should consider the implications of their nonfinancial audit findings for the company's financial statements.
4. Management and the audit committee should ensure that the internal auditors' involvement in the audit of the entire financial reporting process is appropriate and properly coordinated with the independent public accountant.

---

[1] *Report of the National Commission on Fraudulent Financial Reporting* (National Commission on Fraudulent Reporting, October 1987), p. 33.

[2] *Ibid.*, pp. 33-34.

This chapter discusses the relationship between the audit committee and the internal auditor.[3] Topics covered include: the definition of internal auditing; the establishment of an internal auditing function; outsourcing of internal auditing; the Institute of Internal Auditors' (IIA's) role in promoting best practices for internal auditing; the organizational status of the internal auditor; and the audit committee's oversight of the internal auditor. The next chapter discusses the external auditor's relationship with the internal auditor.

Internal Auditing Defined

In June 1999, the IIA's Board of Directors approved a new definition of internal auditing. As shown in Exhibit 11-2, internal auditing is described as an independent, objective activity that provides assurance and consulting services to the company. Assurance engagements include all the traditional internal audit areas such as financial audits, compliance audits, operation audits, and economy and efficiency audits, as well as new areas such as control and risk management audits. Consulting services include control self-assessments, which enlist the support of the employees in diagnosing inefficiencies and implementing improvements, and systems development audits.

Exhibit 11-2
Internal Auditing Defined

Internal auditing is an independent, objective assurance and consulting activity designed to add value and improve an organization's operations. It helps an organization accomplish its objectives by bringing a systematic, disciplined approach to evaluate and improve the effectiveness of risk management, control, and governance processes.

---

[3] The term "internal auditor" is used as an umbrella term to encompass the terms "director of internal auditing" and "internal audit function." The director of internal auditing is the company's chief internal auditor and is sometimes referred to as the "chief audit executive" or the "chief corporate auditor." The internal audit function includes both the director of internal auditing and the internal audit staff. If internal auditing has been outsourced, the internal audit function refers to the director of internal auditing and the outside provider.

Establishing an Internal Auditing Function

There are no specific rules on when to establish an internal auditing function. However, companies in a manufacturing or service business having sales of $50 million or more, 100 or more employees, and assets of $25 million or more should seriously consider creating an internal audit function. Likewise, assets of $30 to $50 million generally indicate a need for an internal auditing function in a bank.[4] Also, if a company goes public, creation of an internal audit function should be given serious consideration regardless of the size of the company. As noted in Exhibit 11-1, *Treadway* recommended that all public companies maintain an effective internal audit function. In the final analysis, the decision to create or not create an internal audit function should be based on a careful review of the facts and circumstances relating to the company. When making a decision about the establishment of an internal auditing function, management and the audit committee should consider questions such as those in Exhibit 11-3.

A formal internal auditing function evolves over time and grows with the company. *Treadway* noted that the optimal size of the internal audit function and the composition of its staff depend on the company's size and nature and the scope of responsibilities assigned to the function. It typically is created by assigning part-time responsibilities for internal auditing to a company employee. Initially, a company may find it helpful to use independent contractors to perform internal audit functions under the supervision of the employee responsible for the activity. As the company grows, management may appoint a director of internal auditing who may be supported by third-party providers or in-house internal auditors. In many companies, employees on a management track are encouraged to spend a tour of duty in internal auditing, because internal auditing is viewed as an outstanding training ground. As growth continues, the company may establish a professionally staffed, in-house internal auditing function. At some point, the company may decide to outsource the internal auditing function based on the company's strategic objectives.

---

[4]Report of the NACD Blue Ribbon Commission on Audit Committees, *Audit Committees: A Practical Guide* (National Association of Corporate Directors, 2000), p. 47.

Exhibit 11-3
Checklist: When to Establish an Internal Auditing Function*

Members of management, the board, and the audit committee would do well to candidly respond to the questions presented below and to quickly implement proactive steps to convert any "No" answers to "Yes" by establishing a fully functioning and appropriately governed internal auditing function.

- Am I able to sleep at night without worrying about risk in the company?
- Am I comfortable that risks have been appropriately addressed?
- Is there a function within the company responsible for assessing and monitoring risk?
- Do I have assurance that controls are operating as planned?
- Is there a thorough and appropriate reporting mechanism within the company that allows for an adequate checks and balances system for fraud prevention and risk management?
- Do I have assurance that financial and other information is reported correctly?
- Are risk management, control, and governance processes being evaluated and reviewed for efficiency and effectiveness on an ongoing basis?
- Do I have a clear understanding of enterprise-wide risk and the company's key areas of vulnerability?
- Does the company have a system for managing risk?
- Are the company's stakeholders provided with reliable assurances that their investment is protected?

---

*Adapted from "When Should Organizations Establish an Internal Auditing Function?" The Institute of Internal Auditors. Available at www3.theiia.org/ecm/guide-ia.cfm?doc_id=1204.

Outsourcing Internal Audit Activities

A company may outsource internal auditing by contracting with a third-party provider to provide some or all of the internal auditing function.[5] The

---

[5] Arguments for and against outsourcing the internal auditing function to a third-party provider are presented in Professional Practices Pamphlet 98-1, *A Perspective on Outsourcing of the Internal Auditing Function*, The Institute of Internal Auditors.

audit committee has a responsibility to provide effective oversight of the internal audit function whether it is housed internally or provided by an outside provider.

A controversial issue associated with the outsourcing decision is whether the company's external auditor should be engaged to perform the internal audit function. This issue has been debated by the IIA, the American Institute of Certified Public Accountants (AICPA), and the Securities and Exchange Commission (SEC). The IIA's position is that the performance of the internal audit services by the external auditor impairs the independence of the external auditor.[6] On the other hand, the AICPA believes that the performance of internal audit services by the external auditor does not impair the external auditor's independence if certain criteria are met.[7] The external auditor must establish an understanding with the company, preferably in writing. The understanding should cover the following items:

- The external auditor may not perform management functions or make management decisions.
- The external auditor may not act, or appear to act, in a capacity equivalent to that of an employee.
- Company management is responsible for establishing and maintaining internal control, including responsibility for ongoing monitoring. (The SEC requires the company to acknowledge this in writing to the external auditor and the audit committee.)
- Company management is responsible for directing the internal audit function.

To fulfill its responsibilities under the outsourcing agreement, management should (as required by the SEC):

- Designate a competent individual (or individuals), preferably within senior management, to be responsible for the internal audit function.
- Determine the scope, risk and frequency of internal audit activities.
- Evaluate the findings and results arising from internal audit activities.
- Evaluate the adequacy of the audit procedures performed and audit findings by obtaining reports from the external auditor and other means.

---

[6] "The Institute Consolidates its Evolving View of Outsourcing Internal Auditing," The Institute of Internal Auditors.

[7] American Institute of Certified Public Accountants, *Code of Professional Conduct,* Interpretation 101-13: Extended Audit Services (ET 101.15).

- Not rely on the external auditor's work as the primary basis for determining the adequacy of internal controls.

On June 27, 2000, the SEC proposed changes to its auditor independence requirements that would preclude the external auditor from performing internal audit services for an audit client unless such services are unrelated to the internal accounting controls, financial systems, or financial statements.[8] However, in its final rule, approved in November 2000, the SEC permits the external auditor to perform internal auditor outsourcing related to financial information. For companies having $200 million or more in total assets, these services cannot be greater than 40 percent of the total hours expended on the company's internal auditor activities for the fiscal year.[9] (The 40 percent rule is effective August 5, 2002.)

The Institute of Internal Auditors and Its Standards

The IIA is the international professional organization of internal auditors. Established in 1941, the IIA now has over 70,000 members in more than 100 countries. The IIA provides valuable guidance to boards of directors, audit committees, senior management, and internal auditors on internal auditing best practices.

Over the years, the IIA has enhanced the professionalism of internal auditors by establishing a program of certification and developing a professional practices framework that includes a definition of internal auditing, a code of ethics for internal auditors, and internal auditing standards.

The Certified Internal Auditor

Since December 1974, the IIA has offered the certified internal auditor (CIA) examination. The examination consists of four parts: internal audit process, internal audit skills, management control and information technology, and the audit environment. To become certified, an internal auditor must not only pass the CIA examination but also generally must have at least two years of experience in auditing. The certification program also requires individuals to meet continuing professional education requirements.

The CIA designation is widely recognized as a mark of excellence in in-

---

[8] Proposed Rule: S7-13-00, *Revision of the Commission's Auditor Independence Requirements,* Securities and Exchange Commission, pp. 36-37.

[9] SEC Releases Nos. 33-7919 and 34-43602.

ternal auditing. Certification is not required to practice internal auditing. However, some companies require the CIA designation for advancement within the internal auditing ranks.

Code of Ethics

In June 2000, the IIA's Board of Directors approved a revised *Code of Ethics (Code)*. The purpose of the *Code* is to promote an ethical culture in the profession of internal auditing. The *Code* is applicable to both entities and individuals that provide internal auditing services. The IIA's ability to enforce compliance with the *Code* extends to members of the IIA and holders of, or candidates for, the CIA certification. Of course, a company may require that its internal auditors comply with the *Code*.

The *Code* consists of two components: (1) principles that are relevant to the profession and practice of internal auditing, and (2) rules of conduct that describe behavior norms expected of internal auditors. The principles and rules encompass four areas: (1) integrity, (2), objectivity, (3) confidentiality, and (4) competency. Exhibit 11-4 presents the *Code* (the complete *Code,* including its introduction, is at www3.theiia.org/ecm/guide-frame .cfm?doc_id=92).

Exhibit 11-4
Code of Ethics

Principles

Internal auditors are expected to apply and uphold the following principles:

Integrity

The integrity of internal auditors establishes trust and thus provides the basis for reliance on their judgment.

Objectivity

Internal auditors exhibit the highest level of professional objectivity in gathering, evaluating, and communicating information about the activity or process being examined. Internal auditors make a balanced assessment of all the relevant circumstances and are not unduly influenced by their own interests or by others in forming judgments.

Confidentiality

Internal auditors respect the value and ownership of information they receive and do not disclose information without appropriate authority unless there is a legal or professional obligation to do so.

Competency

Internal auditors apply the knowledge, skills, and experience needed in the performance of internal auditing services.

Rules of Conduct

1. Integrity

Internal auditors:

1.1 Shall perform their work with honesty, diligence, and responsibility.
1.2 Shall observe the law and make disclosures expected by the law and the profession.
1.3 Shall not knowingly be a party to any illegal activity, or engage in acts that are discreditable to the profession of internal auditing or to the organization.
1.4 Shall respect and contribute to the legitimate and ethical objectives of the organization.

2. Objectivity

Internal auditors:

2.1 Shall not participate in any activity or relationship that may impair, or be presumed to impair, their unbiased assessment. This participation includes those activities or relationships that may be in conflict with the interests of the organization.
2.2 Shall not accept anything that may impair, or be presumed to impair, their professional judgment.
2.3 Shall disclose all material facts known to them that, if not disclosed, may distort the reporting of activities under review.

3. Confidentiality

Internal auditors:

3.1 Shall be prudent in the use and protection of information acquired in the course of their duties.
3.2 Shall not use information for any personal gain or in any manner that would be contrary to the law or detrimental to the legitimate and ethical objectives of the organization.

4. Competency

Internal auditors:

4.1 Shall engage only in those services for which they have the necessary knowledge, skills, and experience.

4.2 Shall perform internal auditing services in accordance with the *Standards for the Professional Practice of Internal Auditing.*

4.3 Shall continually improve their proficiency and the effectiveness and quality of their services.

Standards of Internal Auditing

In 1978, the IIA issued Standards for the Professional Practice of Internal Auditing (Standards). The Standards fall into five broad categories: independence, professional proficiency, scope of work, performance of audit work, and management of the internal auditing department. Exhibit 11-5 presents a summary of the Standards.[10] To provide authoritative interpretations of the Standards, the IIA began issuing Statements on Internal Auditing Standards (SIASs) in 1983. To date, there have been eighteen SIASs issued on a variety of topics, including fraud, risk assessment, quality assurance, and outside service providers.[11]

Exhibit 11-5
Summary of the Standards for the Professional Practice of Internal Auditing

100 Independence— Internal auditors should be independent of the activities they audit.

- 110 Organizational Status — The organizational status of the internal auditing department should be sufficient to permit the accomplishment of its audit responsibilities.

---

[10] In December 2000, the Internal Auditing Standards Board approved new *Standards for the Professional Practice of Internal Auditing.* The new standards are effective for internal audits beginning on or after January 1, 2002. (Earlier adoption is encouraged.) Next year's edition of this book will present the new standards.

[11] A complete listing of the Statements on Internal Auditing Standards (SIASs) is available on the Institute of Internal Auditors' web site at www.theiia.org/standard/sias1.htm.

- 120 Objectivity — Internal auditors should be objective in performing audits.

200 Professional Proficiency — Internal audits should be performed with proficiency and due care.

The Internal Auditing Department

- 210 Staffing — The director of internal auditing should ensure that the technical proficiency and educational background of internal auditors are appropriate for the audits to be performed.
- 220 Knowledge, Skills, and Disciplines — The internal auditing department should possess or should obtain the knowledge, skills, and disciplines needed to carry out its audit responsibilities.
- 230 Supervision — The director of internal auditing should ensure that internal audits are properly supervised.

The Internal Auditor

- 240 Compliance with Standards of Conduct — Internal auditors should comply with professional standards of conduct.
- 250 Knowledge, Skills, and Disciplines — Internal auditors should possess knowledge, skills, and disciplines essential to the performance of internal audits.
- 260 Human Relations and Communications — Internal auditors should be skilled in dealing with people and in communicating effectively.
- 270 Continuing Education — Internal auditors should maintain their technical competence through continuing education.
- 280 Due Professional Care — Internal auditors should exercise due professional care in performing internal audits.

300 Scope of Work — The scope of internal auditing should encompass the examination and evaluation of the adequacy and effectiveness of the organizations' system of internal control and the quality of performance in carrying out assigned responsibilities.

- 310 Reliability and Integrity of Information — Internal auditors should review the reliability and integrity of financial and operating information and the means used to identify, measure, classify, and report such information.
- 320 Compliance with Policies, Plans, Procedures, Laws, Regulations, and Contracts — Internal auditors should review the systems established to ensure compliance with those policies, plans, procedures, laws, regulations, and contracts which could have a significant impact

on operations and reports, and should determine whether the organization is in compliance.

- 330 Safeguarding of Assets — Internal auditors should review the means of safeguarding assets and, as appropriate, verify the existence of such assets.
- 340 Economical and Efficient Use of Resources — Internal auditors should appraise the economy and efficiency with which resources are employed.
- 350 Accomplishment of Established Objectives and Goals for Operations or Programs — Internal auditors should review operations or programs to ascertain whether results are consistent with established objectives and goals and whether the operations or programs are being carried out as planned.

400 Performance of Audit Work — Audit work should include planning the audit, examining and evaluating information, communicating results, and following up.

- 410 Planning the Audit — Internal auditors should plan each audit.
- 420 Examining and Evaluating Information — Internal auditors should collect, analyze, interpret, and document information to support audit results.
- 430 Communicating Results — Internal auditors should report the results of their audit work.
- 440 Following Up — Internal auditors should follow up to ascertain that appropriate action is taken on reported audit findings.

500 Management of the Internal Auditing Department — The director of internal auditing should properly manage the internal auditing department.

- 510 Purpose, Authority, and Responsibility — The director of internal auditing should have a statement of purpose, authority, and responsibility for the internal auditing department.
- 520 Planning — The director of internal auditing should establish plans to carry out the responsibilities of the internal auditing department.
- 530 Policies and Procedures — The director of internal auditing should provide written policies and procedures to guide the audit staff.
- 540 Personnel Management and Development — The director of internal auditing should establish a program for selecting and developing the human resources of the internal auditing department.
- 550 External Auditors — The director of internal auditing should coordinate internal and external audit efforts.

- 560 Quality Assurance — The director of internal auditing should establish and maintain a quality assurance program to evaluate the operations of the internal auditing department.

Source: *Summary of General and Specific Standards for the Professional Practice of Internal Auditing,* The Institute of Internal Auditors. Available at http://www.theiia.org/standard/Summary.htm.

Reporting Relationships

According to Section 110 of the Standards, "the organizational status of the internal auditing department should be sufficient to permit the accomplishment of its audit responsibilities." Sufficient organizational status is a must in order for the internal auditor to achieve a broad range of audit coverage and to ensure adequate consideration of audit results. To have sufficient organizational status, the internal auditor must have a relationship with both senior management and the audit committee.

Senior management has administrative responsibility for the internal auditor. The audit committee has oversight responsibility for the internal auditor. For example, the audit committee should review and concur with the appointment or the dismissal of the director of internal auditing. Oversight responsibilities, which are discussed in the next section of this chapter, allow the audit committee to participate in key administrative decisions involving the internal auditor.

The internal auditor has dual-reporting responsibilities, reporting to senior management on a continuing basis and to the audit committee on a periodic basis (frequently referred to as a dotted-line reporting relationship on organization charts). The importance of communications between the audit committee and the internal auditor is recognized in Section 100 of the Standards, which states that the director of internal auditing should have direct communications with the audit committee. According to the Standards, direct communications require that the director attend and participate in audit committee meetings and meet privately with the board at least once a year. The Standards also identify specific items that the director should report to management and the audit committee. These include:

- A summary of the internal audit work schedule, staffing plan, and financial budget, which should be submitted annually.
- Significant interim changes to the internal audit work schedule, staffing plan, and financial budget.

- Scope limitations along with their potential effects to the audit committee.
- Activity reports, which should be submitted annually or more frequently.

Oversight Relationships

The audit committee exercises an oversight role with respect to the internal auditor. In fulfilling this role, the audit committee performs various activities. These activities are listed in Exhibit 11-6 and discussed in the following paragraphs. Appendix 12 presents a series of questions that the audit committee may use to assess the internal audit function.

Exhibit 11-6
Oversight of the Internal Auditor*

- Review and approve the internal auditing charter
- Review the independence and objectivity of internal auditing
- Review and concur with appointment and termination of the director of internal auditing
- Review the budgets and staffing of internal auditing
- Review the internal auditing plans and subsequent changes in planned activities
- Review internal audit reports and management's response to these reports
- Review internal auditing's compliance with the IIA's Standards

---

*Adapted from *Improving Audit Committee Performance: What Works Best,* The Institute of Internal Auditors Research Foundation, 1993.

The Internal Auditing Charter

The Standards state that the purpose, authority, and responsibility of the internal auditing department should be defined in a formal written charter. [12] The basic internal audit charter should include the:

---

[12] The internal audit charter of Louisiana State University is available on the Institute of Internal Auditors' web site at www3.theiia.org/ecm/guide-ia.cfm?doc_id=115. Louisiana State University is a leading institution in performing research and education in internal au-

- Mission of the internal audit function.
- Scope of work of the internal audit function.
- Accountability of the internal audit function to management and the audit committee.
- Independence of the internal audit function.
- Responsibilities of the internal audit function.
- Authority of the internal audit function.
- Compliance with the IIA's Standards.

According to the Standards, the internal auditor should seek approval of the charter by senior management and the board of directors. The audit committee charter generally is signed by the chairperson of the audit committee, the chief executive officer, and the director of internal audit. The chairman of the board of directors and the chief financial officer may also sign the charter.

The Standards also state that the director of internal auditing should periodically assess whether the purpose, authority, and responsibility, as defined in the charter, continue to be adequate to enable the internal auditing function to accomplish its objectives. The result of this periodic assessment should be communicated to senior management and the audit committee.

Independence and Objectivity of Internal Auditing

The audit committee should oversee the independence and objectivity of the internal function. Internal auditors achieve independence through the organizational status of the internal auditing function and objectivity of the internal auditors. As discussed earlier, the organizational status of the internal audit function should be sufficient to permit the accomplishment of its audit responsibilities. To be sufficient, internal auditors must have the support of both senior management and the audit committee.

Objectivity is an independent mental attitude which internal auditors should maintain in performing audits. To be objective, internal auditors should not subordinate their judgment on audit matters to that of others. According to the Standards, objectivity is enhanced by the following policies:

- Making staff assignments so that potential and actual conflicts of interest and bias are avoided.

---

diting. Also, a sample internal audit charter is included in *Report of the NACD Blue Ribbon Commission on Audit Committees* (The National Association of Corporate Directors, 2000), p. 47.

- Requiring internal auditors to report to the director any situations indicating a possible conflict of interest.
- Rotating staff assignments periodically.
- Prohibiting internal auditors from assuming operating responsibilities unless it is understood that they are not functioning as internal auditors.
- Requiring a reasonable amount of time to elapse before internal auditors are assigned to audit activities they previously performed.
- Prohibiting internal auditors from designing, installing, or operating systems.

Appointment or Termination of the Internal Auditor

The audit committee should review and concur with the appointment, replacement, reassignment, or dismissal of the director of internal auditing. For example, in an appointment decision, the audit committee should determine that the director of internal audit has the knowledge and skills to effectively head up the internal audit function and interact with fellow senior officers.[13] This review ensures the competency of the internal audit function. In a dismissal action, the audit committee should determine that the action does not represent an attempt by management to restrict the scope of internal auditing activities or to suppress the reporting of internal audit findings. This review promotes the independence of the internal auditing function.

Budget and Staffing of Internal Auditing

The audit committee should review the budget and staffing of the internal auditing function. The committee should determine that the budget and staff are adequate to enable the internal audit function to effectively perform its responsibilities. Also, the committee should review the quality of the internal audit staff. *Treadway* recognized that, in order for the function to be effective, the internal auditors must have the appropriate level of education and experience, and conduct themselves in a professional manner. Certifications such as certified internal auditors (CIAs), certified public accountants (CPAs), certified management accountants (CMAs), and certified information systems auditors (CISAs) serve as measures of quality. The company should encourage the development of its internal auditors through continu-

---

[13] A checklist of attributes for evaluating the competency of the director of internal auditing is available at http://www3.theiia.org/ecm/guide-ia.cfm?doc_id=112.

ing professional education programs. The company should strive to retain quality people by offering attractive career paths.

Internal Auditing Plans

The audit committee should review the internal auditing plans and subsequent changes in those plans. The audit committee should inquire whether the internal auditor and management consider the scope of the internal auditing to be appropriate and responsive to the risks within the company. At this point, the audit committee should also inquire about the coordination of the internal auditing and the external audit activities. Depending on its charge, the audit committee may discuss with the internal auditor the audits in such areas as compliance with laws and regulations and compliance with the code of conduct.

Internal Audit Reports

The director of internal auditing should submit activity reports to management and the audit committee. Activity reports should highlight significant audit findings. Significant audit findings include errors, fraud, illegal acts, and control weaknesses. Typically the activity reports are reviewed by management. Management has the responsibility to determine the appropriate action. The audit committee should be informed of significant findings and management's response to those findings.

Activity reports should also report significant deviations from approved audit work schedules, staffing plans, and financial budget, and the reasons for them. Reasons for significant deviations include organization and management changes, economic conditions, legal and regulatory requirements, internal auditing staff changes, management requests, and expansion or reduction of audit scope as determined by the director of internal auditing.

Compliance with the IIA Standards

According to *Treadway,* "Standards of the IIA offer excellent guidance for effective internal auditing and reflect some of the most advanced thinking on fraud prevention and detection." *Treadway* encouraged public companies that have not done so to consider adopting the IIA standards. The audit committee should review the internal auditor's compliance with the IIA's standards. Compliance may be determined by asking the director of internal auditing whether internal auditing activities are in conformity with the standards issued by the IIA.

The audit committee should also determine whether the internal auditing function has undergone an external quality assurance review. The Standards require the director of internal auditor to establish and maintain a quality assurance program to evaluate the operations of the internal auditing function. A quality assurance program includes three elements: supervision, internal review, and external reviews. According to the Standards, external reviews should be conducted at least once every three years. The external reviews may be performed by internal auditors from other companies or by an outside service provider such as a CPA firm. On completion of the external review, a written report should be issued that expresses an opinion about the department's compliance with the Standards and offers recommendations for improvement. *Treadway* endorsed periodic external (peer) reviews of the internal audit function.

Here is a summary of the important points of this chapter:

The Internal Audit Function

1. Internal audit is an independent, objective assurance and consulting activity designed to add value and improve an organization's operations. It helps an organization accomplish its objectives by bringing a systematic, disciplined approach to evaluate and improve the effectiveness of risk management, control, and governance processes.
2. The lifecycle of the internal audit function can be divided into four stages:
   a. The internal audit function is staffed part-time by employees of the company.
   b. The internal audit function is a small function that is staffed full-time. The function has a director. The audit staff may be employed by the company or a third-party provider. (In this stage, the internal auditor may need the services of a third-party provider to obtain necessary knowledge and skills that are not found in a small internal audit function).
   c. The internal audit function is a large function. The director of internal audit may have assistant directors that head up internal auditing in various geographic locations. The staff is in-house and provides the majority of the company's internal auditing needs.
   d. The company decides to outsource part or all of its internal audit function based on the company's strategic goals.
3. The purpose, authority, and responsibility of the internal auditor should be documented in the internal audit charter.

4. To be effective, the internal auditor must be independent. Independence is achieved through the organizational status of the internal audit function and the objectivity of the internal auditor.
5. To be effective, the internal audit function must have a competent director of internal audit and staff.

The Institute of Internal Auditors (IIA)

1. The IIA is the international professional organization of internal auditors.
2. The IIA provides the internal auditor with guidance on internal auditing best practices.
3. The IIA has taken major steps to enhance the professionalism of internal auditing, including:
   a. Establishing a program of certification.
   b. Developing a professional practices framework that includes the definition of internal auditing, the code of ethics, and the standards for the professional practice of internal auditing.

Relationship between the Audit Committee and the Internal Auditor

1. The audit committee must have an effective relationship with the internal auditor to properly discharge its oversight responsibilities for the risks and controls over financial reporting, the integrity of the financial statements, and other responsibilities delegated to it by the board of directors.
2. The audit committee has a reporting relationship with the internal auditor. The internal auditor communicates directly with the audit committee. Direct communications require that the internal auditor attend and participate in audit committee meetings and meet privately with the board at least once a year.
3. The audit committee has an oversight relationship with the internal auditor. To effectively oversee the internal auditor, the audit committee should:
   • Review and approve the internal auditing charter.
   • Review the independence and objectivity of internal auditing.
   • Review and concur with the appointment and termination of the director of internal auditing.
   • Review the budgets and staffing of internal auditing.
   • Review the auditing plans and subsequent changes in planned activities.
   • Review internal audit reports and management's response to these reports.
   • Review internal auditing's compliance with the IIA's Standards.

CHAPTER 12
RELATIONSHIP WITH THE EXTERNAL AUDITOR

One of the primary responsibilities of the audit committee is oversight of the financial accounting and reporting process. The external auditor is in the best position to provide an independent assessment of this process. Thus, the audit committee must maintain clear and open lines of communication with the external auditor.

This chapter discusses the relationship between the audit committee and the external auditor. First, the chapter explains the role of the American Institute of Certified Public Accountants (AICPA) in establishing authoritative requirements for the external auditor. Next, the chapter focuses on the external auditor's professional responsibilities when engaged to audit financial statements and perform other related services. Finally, the chapter discusses the audit committee's responsibilities for overseeing the external audit process.

The AICPA

The AICPA is the national professional organization of CPAs. The AICPA has a current membership of more than 340,000 CPAs in public practice, industry, government, and education. The AICPA also has a Division for CPA Firms, with two sections: the SEC Practice Section (SECPS) and PCPS/ Partnering for CPA Practice Success (formerly known as the Private Companies Practice Section). A CPA firm may belong to both sections, either section, or neither section. However, a member of the AICPA who practices with a CPA firm that audits one or more SEC clients can only practice with a firm that is a member of the SECPS.[1]

In any profession, the members should ensure that the services offered are of an acceptable level of quality. This is certainly true in public accounting. As a consequence, the AICPA has taken steps to ensure the quality of external audits, including: (1) establishing quality control standards, (2) creating a related peer review program, and (3) establishing authoritative standards for external audits and related engagements.

---

[1] Bylaws of the AICPA, Section 230, BL 2.3, "Requirements for Retention of Membership."

Quality Control and Peer Review

Auditing firms are required to establish quality control policies and procedures to provide reasonable assurance of conforming with generally accepted auditing standards (GAAS). The five elements of quality control are: (1) independence, integrity, and objectivity, (2) personnel management, (3) acceptance and continuation of clients and engagements, (4) engagement performance, and (5) monitoring.

Peer review is an examination of one CPA firm's accounting and auditing quality control procedures by another CPA firm or group of CPAs. A CPA firm with an accounting or auditing practice is required to enroll in a peer review program (either the AICPA peer review program or the SECPS peer review program) and undergo a peer review at least once every three years.

The output of the peer review is a report and a letter of comments. The most commonly issued report is a standard report that states, among other matters, the standards used to perform the peer review and the opinion on the CPA firm's quality control system. An opinion may be modified or adverse. Reasons for a modified or adverse opinion include: (1) a limitation on the scope of the peer review, (2) significant deficiencies in the firm's quality control policies and procedures, and (3) lack of compliance with the firm's quality control procedures. Exhibit 12-1 presents an example of an unmodified peer review report.

When the review report is modified or adverse, a letter of comments must be submitted. The letter of comments may also be prepared when the peer reviewer issues an unmodified report but believes there are matters that create a condition in which there is more than a remote possibility that the CPA firm will fail to adhere to professional standards. The letter of comments is similar to the reportable conditions or management letter issued by the external auditor in connection with the financial statement audit. The comments may address (1) the design of the firm's quality control system, (2) noncompliance with the firm's quality control system, or (3) noncompliance with the membership requirements of the section (for example, the SECPS). The letter of comments usually accompanies the peer review report.

If a CPA firm is a member of the AICPA peer review program, the peer review report and letter of comments are not available to the public. However, if a CPA firm is a member of the SECPS peer review program, the peer review report and letters of comment are available in the AICPA public files. In both cases, it is imperative that the audit committee obtain and review the latest peer review report and the related letter of comments (if any).

Exhibit 12-1
Unmodified Peer Review Report

November 1, 20X1

To the Partners of
Burke & Guy, CPAs

We have reviewed the system of quality control for the accounting and auditing practice of Burke & Guy, CPAs (the Firm), in effect for the year ended June, 30, 20X1. Our review was conducted in conformity with standards for peer reviews promulgated by the peer review committee of the SEC Practice Section of the AICPA Division for CPA Firms (the Section). We tested compliance with the Firm's quality control policies and procedures at the Firm's National Office and at selected practice offices in the United States, and with the membership requirements of the Section to the extent we considered appropriate. These tests included the application of the Firm's policies and procedures on selected accounting and auditing engagements. We tested the supervision and control of portions of engagements performed outside the United States.

In performing our review, we have given consideration to the general characteristics of a system of quality control as described in quality control standards issued by the AICPA. Such a system should be appropriately comprehensive and suitably designed in relation to a firm's organizational structure, its policies, and the nature of its practice. Variance in individual performance can affect the degree of compliance with a firm's prescribed quality control policies and procedures. Therefore, adherence to all policies and procedures in every case may not be possible. As is customary in a peer review, we are issuing a letter under this date that sets forth comments related to certain policies and procedures or compliance with them. None of these matters were considered to be of sufficient significance to affect the opinion expressed in this report.

In our opinion, the system of quality control for the accounting and auditing practice of Burke & Guy, CPAs in effect for the year ended June 30, 20X1, met the objectives of quality control standards established by the AICPA, and was being complied with during the year then ended to provide the Firm with reasonable assurance of conforming with professional standards. Also, in our opinion, the Firm was in conformity with the membership requirements of the Section in all material respects.

Signed
Lach and Tatum, CPAs

Statements on Auditing Standards

The external audit of financial statements must be conducted in accordance with GAAS. The AICPA has the primary responsibility for establishing auditing standards, which are published as Statements on Auditing Standards (SASs). The SASs cover a variety of topics, including the external auditor's responsibilities for fraud, illegal acts, and internal control as well as the external auditor's responsibilities for communicating with management, the audit committee, and shareholders. These and other standards are discussed below.

External Auditor Reports

The external auditor's primary responsibility is to express an opinion whether the financial statements are presented fairly, in all material respects, with generally accepted accounting principles (GAAP). The external auditor's opinion is found in the external auditor's report. Because the external auditor's opinion is the most significant element of the external auditor's report, the terms "auditor's report" and "auditor's opinion" are often used interchangeably. Exhibit 12-2 presents the standard report of the external auditor.

The standard report contains three paragraphs: (1) an introductory paragraph that identifies the financial statements audited, (2) a scope paragraph that describes the nature of the external audit, and (3) an opinion paragraph that contains the external auditor's conclusion (that is, opinion) about the financial statements. In the standard report, the external auditor's opinion is always an unqualified opinion. An unqualified opinion is the best opinion that an auditor can express.

In some audit engagements, the external auditor does not issue the standard report because certain conditions exist that should be emphasized. These conditions include going-concern issues, changes in accounting principles, and shared responsibility with another auditor. The external auditor explains these conditions by modifying the wording of the three paragraphs in the standard report (in the case of shared responsibility) or by adding a paragraph after the opinion paragraph. These conditions do not affect the external auditor's conclusion about the financial statements adhering to GAAP. The auditor's opinion is still unqualified.

Exhibit 12-2
External Auditor's Standard Report
on Comparative Financial Statements

Independent Auditor's Report

To the Board of Directors and Shareholders of XYZ Company:

We have audited the accompanying balance sheets of XYZ Company as of December 31, 20X1 and 20X0, and the related statements of income, retained earnings, and cash flows for the years then ended. These financial statements are the responsibility of the Company's management. Our responsibility is to express an opinion on these financial statements based on our audit.

We conducted our audit in accordance with auditing standards generally accepted in the United States of America. Those standards require that we plan and perform the audit to obtain reasonable assurance about whether the financial statements are free of material misstatement. An audit includes examining, on a test basis, evidence supporting the amounts and disclosures in the financial statements. An audit also includes assessing the accounting principles used and significant estimates made by management, as well as evaluating the overall financial statement presentation. We believe that our audits provide a reasonable basis for our opinion.

In our opinion, the financial statements referred to above present fairly, in all material respects, the financial position of XYZ Company as of December 31, 20X1 and 20X0, and the results of its operations and its cash flows for the years then ended in conformity with accounting principles generally accepted in the United States of America.

Burke & Guy, CPAs
February 14, 20X2

Some conditions may cause the external auditor to change the wording of the standard report as well as the external auditor's opinion. The various opinions that the external auditor may issue are the:

- *Unqualified opinion.* An unqualified opinion states that the financial statements conform with GAAP, in all material respects.
- *Qualified opinion.* A qualified opinion states that the financial statements conform with GAAP, in all material respects, except for the effects of the matters to which the qualification relates. Matters that cause the external auditor to issue a qualified opinion include a significant limitation on the scope of the external auditor's work or a material departure in the financial statements from GAAP.
- *Adverse opinion.* An adverse opinion states that the financial statements are not fairly presented in conformity with GAAP. An adverse opinion is issued when there is a very material GAAP departure or when there are multiple GAAP departures and, as a result, the overall financial statements are not reliable.
- *Disclaimer of opinion.* A disclaimer of opinion states that the external auditor does not express an opinion on the financial statements. The external auditor issues a disclaimer when a very significant scope limitation exists. The external auditor is also required to issue a disclaimer if the auditor is not independent.

Independence

To express an opinion on the financial statements, the external auditor must be independent. Independence depends on two factors: the external auditor's basic character (independence in fact) and the public's perception of whether or not the external auditor is independent (independence in appearance).

The AICPA has established specific independence requirements in its *Code of Professional Conduct.* These requirements prohibit certain financial and business relationships with the client as well as management, the board of directors, and shareholders. In addition, the SEC has adopted independence requirements for external auditors who report on financial statements filed with the SEC. Some of the SEC's requirements are more stringent than the AICPA's requirements.[2]

---

[2] The SEC has issued new rules on auditor independence. The full text of the new rules is available at http://www.sec.gov/rules/final/33-7919.htm.

The Independence Standards Board (ISB) was created to establish independence standards for public companies. Under ISB Standard 1, *Independence Discussions with Audit Committees,* the external auditor of an SEC reporting company is required, at least annually, to:

- Disclose to the audit committee, in writing, all relationships between the external auditor and the company that, in the external auditor's judgment, may reasonably bear on independence.
- Confirm in the letter above that the external auditor's firm is independent within the meaning of the Securities Acts administered by the SEC.
- Discuss the external auditor's independence with the audit committee.

The *Blue Ribbon Report* (discussed in Chapter 5) observed that "this disclosure and discussion is a two-way street." As a consequence, the *Blue Ribbon Report* recommended that the listing rules for both the New York Stock Exchange (NYSE) and the National Association of Securities Dealers (NASD) require that the audit committee charter for every listed company specify that the audit committee is responsible for:

- Ensuring receipt from the external auditors of a formal written statement delineating all relationships between the auditor and the company, consistent with ISB 1.
- Actively engaging in a dialogue with the external auditor with respect to any disclosed relationships or services which may impact the objectivity and independence of the auditor.
- Taking, or recommending that the full board take, appropriate action to ensure the independence of the external auditor.

The NYSE, NASD, and American Stock Exchange (AMEX) subsequently adopted the recommendation.[3] The SEC has similar requirements for these independence communications. The SEC requires that the audit committee, in its annual report to shareholders, indicate whether the committee (1) received the external auditor's disclosures about independence and (2) discussed independence with the external auditor.[4]

---

[3] SEC Release No. 34-42233 (for the New York Stock Exchange), SEC Release No. 34-42231 (for the National Association of Securities Dealers), and SEC Release No. 34-42232 (for AMEX).

[4] SEC Release No. 34-42266.

Consulting Services by External Auditor

In a number of situations, external auditors also provide tax and consulting services (or non-audit services) to audit clients. There has been much debate about whether the external auditor's independence is impaired in cases where such services are rendered. Particularly, there is concern that the external auditor will be auditing financial statements generated from accounting systems installed by their consulting department. On the other hand, the external auditor is well-qualified to provide consulting services, since the external audit firm is very familiar with the company and its operations.[5]

In 2000, the Panel on Audit Effectiveness (Panel) studied the effects on external auditor independence of non-audit services provided to audit clients.[6] The Panel's views on this issue were divided. Some Panel members believed that there is a conflict of interest when the external auditor provides non-audit services to audit clients. Other Panel members believed that the external auditor can maintain independence and objectivity while providing audit and non-audit services to the same client.

The Panel did not make a recommendation regarding an exclusionary rule that would prohibit an external auditor from providing non-audit or non-tax services. However, the Panel did make recommendations to various audit committees and others. Exhibit 12-3 summarizes these recommendations.

Exhibit 12-3
The Panel's Recommendations:
Non-Audit Services and Auditor Independence

To the Independence Standards Board:

The Panel recommends that the ISB identify factors to be considered by auditors, audit committees, and client management (1) when implementing ISB 1 and the SEC's new audit committee disclosure requirements and (2) when determining whether a specific non-audit service is appropriate. Important factors include:

---

[5] The SECPS prohibits its member firms from performing psychological testing, public opinion polls, merger and acquisition assistance for a finder's fee, executive recruitment, and actuarial services to insurance companies.

[6] As discussed in Chapter 4, "Additional Development from *Treadway* to 2001," in September 1998 at the request of the chairman of the SEC, the Public Oversight Board of the AICPA Practices Section appointed the Panel on Audit Effectiveness. The Panel issued its final report in September 2000. The report is available at www.pobauditpanel.org.

- Whether the service is being performed principally for the audit committee.
- The effects of the service, if any, on audit effectiveness or on the quality and timeliness of the entity's financial-reporting process.
- Whether the service would be performed by specialists (for example, technology specialists) who ordinarily also provide recurring audit support.
- Whether the service would be performed by audit personnel, and if so, whether it will enhance their knowledge of the entity's business and operations.
- Whether the role of those performing the service would be inconsistent with the auditor's role.
- Whether the audit firm personnel would be assuming a management role or creating a mutuality of interest with management.
- Whether the auditors, in effect, would be "auditing their own numbers."
- Whether the project must be started and completed very quickly.
- Whether the audit firm has unique expertise in the service.
- The size of the fee(s) for the non-audit service.

To Audit Committees:

- The Panel recommends that audit committees pre-approve non-audit services that exceed a threshold amount determined by the committee.
- When audit committees determine whether to approve specific non-audit services, the Panel recommends that they consider the factors listed above.

To the SEC and the Independence Standards Board:

The Panel recommends that the SEC and the ISB evaluate, on a continuing basis, the effectiveness of the disclosures made under ISB 1 and the SEC's new audit committee disclosure rules, as well as any new rules issued by the ISB or by the SEC pursuant to its rule-making initiatives.

Disclosure of Non-Audit Fees and Audit Committee Statement Regarding Non-Audit Services

In November 2000, the SEC approved final rules on auditor independence.[7] The primary motivation behind the SEC's rulemaking was the performance

---

[7] SEC Release Nos. 33-7919 and 34-43602.

of non-audit services by external auditors for their audit clients, especially services related to information technology. The new rules require registrants to disclose fees from the principal external auditor for the most recent year in their proxy and information statements. The fees must be categorized as follows:

1. Annual audit and quarterly review services applied to the company's financial statements.
2. Financial information systems design and implementation.
3. All other fees, including those for tax-related services.

In addition, the registrant must also disclose whether the audit committee considered the non-audit services performed in 2 and 3 above and whether the performance of those services was compatible with maintaining the principal auditor's independence. (The SEC does not require companies to disclose the conclusions of the audit committee deliberations.) The rationale for these disclosures, according to the SEC, is to better able investors to evaluate the independence of external auditors.

The new SEC rule also requires the company's management to acknowledge in writing to the audit committee and the external auditor their responsibility for internal controls and the adequacy of the financial reporting system. This written acknowledgement from management is required whenever the company engages the external auditor to perform non-audit services related to (1) financial information systems and (2) internal audit outsourcing (see Chapter 11, "Relationship with the Internal Auditor"). The authors believe that this is a good practice for the performance of all non-audit services by the external auditor over a designated amount, except for tax work.

Engagement Letters

The external auditor is required to establish an understanding with the client regarding the services to be performed. The purpose of the understanding is to reduce the risk that the client or the external auditor may misinterpret the needs or the expectations of the other party. The understanding should be documented. The best way to meet this documentation requirement is to use an engagement letter. Exhibit 12-4 lists matters that are normally included in the engagement letter.

The engagement letter should be presented on the external auditor's letterhead. The external auditor should acknowledge that the external auditor is ultimately accountable to the board of directors and its audit committee as representatives of the shareholders. Thus, the engagement letter should be addressed to the board of directors and the shareholders. The engagement letter should set forth the scope of the audit engagement, identifying the entities and the financial statements that are covered. If the external auditor also performs the review of the quarterly financial statements (required by the SEC), these services should be included in the engagement letter or set forth in a separate letter.

Management's responsibilities for internal control over financial reporting and the financial statements should be clearly identified. Specifically, the engagement letter should address management's responsibilities for adjusting the financial statements to correct material misstatement and for affirming that the effects of any uncorrected misstatement are immaterial. The external auditor's responsibilities for obtaining an understanding of internal control over financial reporting and expressing an opinion on the financial statements should also be described.

The engagement letter should state the estimated fee for the services to be provided by the external auditor. It is a good practice for the audit committee to review the proposed audit fee annually to be sure that it is sufficient to allow the external auditor to provide a competent audit. In addition, the audit committee should be satisfied that the fee is reasonable in relation to the amount of work involved. Appendix 13 presents an illustrative engagement letter.

Exhibit 12-4
Engagement Letter Topics

The engagement letter generally includes the following matters:

- The objective of the audit is the expression of an opinion on the financial statements.
- Management is responsible for the company's financial statements.
- Management is responsible for effective internal control over financial reporting.
- Management is responsible for ensuring that the company complies with applicable laws and regulations.
- Management is responsible for providing all financial records and related information to the auditor.
- Management is responsible for providing a written representation letter to the auditor at the end of the engagement.
- Management is responsible for adjusting the financial statements to correct material misstatements.

- Management is responsible for affirming in the management representation letter that any uncorrected misstatements are immaterial.
- The auditor is responsible for conducting the audit in accordance with GAAS.
- The auditor is responsible for obtaining an understanding of internal control sufficient to plan the audit.
- The limitations of the engagement include the fact that the auditor obtains reasonable assurance about whether the financial statements are free of material misstatements and that the auditor does not provide assurance on internal control.
- Arrangements regarding fees and billing.

An engagement letter may include other matters such as:

- Arrangements about the conduct of the engagement (for example, timing, client assistance).
- Arrangements about the involvement of specialists or internal auditors, if applicable.
- Indemnification arrangements if the client provides false information to the auditor (the SEC prohibits such arrangements).
- Conditions for access to the auditor's working papers.
- Additional services (for example, tax and other non-audit services).

Responsibility for Fraud

The external auditor provides reasonable assurance that the financial statements are free of material misstatement, whether caused by error or fraud. Fraud can be divided into two categories: (1) fraudulent financial reporting and (2) misappropriation of assets. The external auditor assesses the risk of material misstatement due to fraud and considers that assessment in designing the audit procedures to be performed. In making that assessment, the external auditor is required to consider fraud risk factors relating to fraudulent financial reporting and misappropriation of assets. Appendix 14 presents examples of risk factors relating to fraudulent financial reporting and misappropriation of assets. The external auditor also has responsibilities for communicating certain information related to fraud. These responsibilities are discussed later in this chapter as part of the external auditor's required communications.

The Panel on Audit Effectiveness studied the effectiveness of audits in detecting fraud. The Panel found that the risk assessment and the response process called for by existing auditing standards falls short in effectively deterring fraud or significantly increasing the likelihood that the external auditor will detect material fraud, largely because the standard fails to direct auditing procedures specifically toward fraud detection. Based on its findings, the Panel made recommendations to various constituents including the AICPA's Auditing Standards Board (ASB), audit firms, and audit committees. Exhibit 12-5 summarizes these recommendations.

Exhibit 12-5
The Panel's Recommendations: Fraud

The ASB should require in all audits:

- Discussion by supervisory engagement personnel with other engagement team members about the vulnerability of the entity to fraud.
- A forensic-type phase in which the auditor presumes the possibility of management dishonesty.
- Retrospective audit procedures that analyze selected opening balance sheet accounts of previously audited financial statements.

Audit firms should:

- Begin work immediately with the concepts underlying the proposed changes to the auditing standards.
- Develop or expand training programs for auditors at all levels oriented toward responsibilities and procedures for fraud detection.
- Discuss with audit committees the vulnerability of the company to fraud.

Audit committees should:

- Accept the responsibility of ascertaining that the auditors are receiving the necessary cooperation from management to carry out their duties in accordance with the strengthened audit standards to be developed by the ASB.

Responsibility for Illegal Acts

Illegal acts are violations of laws or government regulations. Some illegal acts have a direct effect on a financial statement amount. For example, violations of tax laws dealing with how a company's tax liability is measured directly affect line-item amounts in the financial statements. An external auditor provides reasonable assurance that these illegal acts will be detected and reported if they are material.

Other illegal acts have an indirect effect on the financial statements. These other illegal acts include violations of laws and regulations related to securities trading, occupational safety and health, food and drug adminis-tration, environmental protection, equal employment and antitrust. Because these laws and regulations deal primarily with the company's operations, vi-olations of these laws and regulations typically do not affect a line item in the financial statements. However, these other illegal acts often lead to dis-ciplinary and legal actions, thereby creating material contingent liabilities that should be recorded or disclosed in the financial statements.

An audit does not normally include audit procedures specifically de-signed to detect other illegal acts. However, procedures applied for the pur-pose of forming an opinion on the financial statements may bring possible illegal acts to the auditor's attention. The external auditor should be aware of the possibility that other illegal acts may have occurred. If information in-dicates that other illegal acts may have occurred, the external auditor should apply audit procedures to address the matter. The external auditor is re-quired to communicate certain matters about illegal acts as discussed later in this chapter.

As explained in Chapter 9, "The Audit Committee's Oversight of Inter-nal Control," the external auditor may be engaged to perform agreed-upon procedures to assist a company or its audit committee in evaluating the ef-fectiveness of the company's internal controls over compliance with some aspects of a rule, law, or regulation. These engagements are performed un-der Statements on Standards for Attestation Engagements (SSAE) 3, *Com-pliance Attestation.*

Responsibility for Internal Control

The external auditor performs some internal control work on every audit en-gagement (discussed in Chapter 9). The external auditor obtains an under-standing of internal control over financial reporting and assesses its effec-tiveness. The external auditor uses this understanding and assessment to plan the audit of the financial statements. The external auditor does not ex-press an opinion on internal control over financial reporting when engaged to audit financial statements. However, the external auditor may be engaged in a separate engagement to report on the effectiveness of an entity's inter-nal control over financial reporting under SSAE 2, *Reporting on an Entity's Internal Control Over Financial Reporting.*

When auditing the financial statements, the external auditor may become aware of control deficiencies (referred to as "reportable conditions"). If so, the auditor has a responsibility to communicate these deficiencies. These internal control communications are discussed along with other required communications later in this chapter.

Using the Work of the Internal Auditor

As discussed in Chapter 11, "Relationship with the Internal Auditor," the internal auditor performs a variety of assurance and consulting activities for a company. Usually, some of these activities are relevant to an audit of financial statements. Recall that the internal audit function is part of the monitoring element of internal control. Thus, the external auditor is required to obtain an understanding of that function sufficient to identify internal audit activities relevant to planning the external audit. Relevant activities include those that provide evidence about the effectiveness of controls over financial reporting and those that provide direct evidence about misstatements of financial statement amounts, such as accounts receivable confirmations.

After obtaining the required understanding, the external auditor may decide to use the work of the internal auditor, thereby reducing some of the external auditor's tests of controls over financial reporting or tests of amounts in the financial statements. Or, the external auditor may decide to use the direct assistance of the internal auditor in testing controls over financial reporting and testing the numbers in the financial statements. In either case, the external auditor should assess the competence and objectivity of the internal auditor. When using the work of the internal auditor, the external auditor should test some of the internal auditor's work. When using the direct assistance of the internal auditor, the external auditor has additional responsibilities. The external auditor should supervise, review, evaluate, and test the internal auditor's work.

Although the external auditor may use the work of the internal auditor, the external auditor does not share responsibility for reporting on the financial statements with the internal auditor. The responsibility to report on the financial statements rests solely with the external auditor.

Management Representation Letter

During the course of the audit, management makes various representations to the external auditor. At the end of the audit, the external auditor is required to obtain written representations from management about certain matters. These written representations from management are referred to as a management representation letter. The purpose of the management representation letter is to remind management about its responsibilities regarding the financial statements and to reduce the opportunity for misunderstanding by asking management to put certain oral representations in writing. Appendix 15 presents an illustrative management representation letter.

The management representation letter covers all periods addressed in the audit report. It is addressed to the external auditor, dated no earlier than the date of the external auditor's report, and signed by management (typically the chief executive officer and the chief financial officer) on client letterhead. The letter should be tailored to the entity's circumstances. Management's refusal to provide a representation to the external auditor constitutes a scope limitation that would prompt a qualified opinion or a disclaimer of an opinion on the financial statements.

Review of Interim Financial Information

The SEC requires that a company's quarterly financial statements be reviewed by an external auditor prior to filing Form 10-Q (or Form 10-QSB).[8] SAS 71, *Interim Financial Information,* provides guidance to the external auditor for conducting such reviews.

The objective of a review of the quarterly financial statements is to provide the external auditor with a reasonable basis for providing limited assurance that no material modifications should be made to the interim financial information to conform such information with GAAP. The external auditor reaches this conclusion based on the performance of inquiry and analytical procedures. Before selecting which inquiry and analytical procedures to perform, the external auditor first should gain a sufficient understanding of controls over the interim financial statements.

The external auditor is not required to issue a report to meet the requirements of the timely review. However, if the company states in Form 10-Q that the interim financial statements have been reviewed by an external auditor, the external auditor's review report must be filed with the interim financial statements.[9] Exhibit 12-6 presents an example of a report on interim financial information.

---

[8] SEC Release No. 34-42266.
[9] *Ibid.*

Exhibit 12-6
Accountant's Standard Review Report for a Public Entity

Independent Accountant's Report

Board of Directors and Shareholders of XYZ Company

We have reviewed the accompanying balance sheet, income statement, statement of retained earnings, and statement of cash flows of XYZ Company as of September 30, 20X1, and for the nine-month period then ended. These financial statements are the responsibility of the company's management.

We conducted our review in accordance with standards the American Institute of Certified Public Accountants established. A review of interim financial information consists principally of applying analytical procedures to financial data and making inquiries of persons responsible for financial and accounting matters. It is substantially less in scope than an audit conducted in accordance with generally accepted auditing standards with the objective of expressing an opinion regarding the financial statements taken as a whole. Accordingly, we do not express such an opinion.

Based on our review, we are not aware of any material modifications that should be made to the accompanying financial statements for them to conformity with generally accepted accounting principles.

Burke & Guy, CPAs
November 10, 20X1

Required Communications

During an audit of financial statements, the external auditor obtains information that may be useful for audit committees. The auditor is required to communicate certain information about the scope and results of the audit by the following authoritative pronouncements:

- SAS 61 — *Communication with Audit Committees*
- SAS 82 — *Consideration of Fraud in a Financial Statement Audit*
- SAS 54 — *Illegal Acts by Clients*

- SAS 60 — *Communication of Internal Control Related Matters Noted in an Audit*
- SAS 71 — *Interim Financial Information*
- SAS 74 — *Compliance Auditing Considerations in Audits of Governmental Entities and Recipients of Governmental Financial Assistance*

In addition, communication of certain independence matters is required by ISB 1, *Independence Discussions with Audit Committees*. Appendix 16 contains a checklist for required communications by the external auditor to the audit committee.

SAS 61 Communications. The external auditor should ensure that the audit committee receives information about:

- The auditor's level of responsibility.
- Significant accounting policies.
- Significant unusual transactions.
- Accounting estimates (and reserves).
- Audit adjustments.
- Other information in documents containing audited financial statements.
- Auditor's judgment about the quality of the entity's accounting principles.
- Disagreements with management.
- Consultation with other accountants (second opinions).
- Issued discussed prior to retention.
- Difficulties encountered during audit.

The external auditor should communicate some of this information; management may communicate some. The external auditor is not required to repeat information that management has communicated; however, he or she is not precluded from communicating the information. Exhibit 12-7 provides a brief description of the SAS 61 communication requirements.

Exhibit 12-7
SAS 61 Communications

Auditor's Level of Responsibility

The auditor should communicate the level of responsibility assumed under GAAS for internal control and the financial statements. The auditor should explain to the audit committee the concepts of materiality, audit tests and reasonable, as opposed to absolute, assurance.

Significant Accounting Policies

The auditor should determine that the audit committee is informed about the initial selection of, and changes in, significant accounting policies or their application.

Significant Unusual Transactions

The auditor should determine that the audit committee is informed about the methods used to account for significant unusual transactions. The audit committee also should be informed of the effect and implications of existing accounting policies in controversial or emerging accounting areas, such as revenue recognition, off-balance-sheet financing, and accounting for equity investments.

Accounting Estimates (and Reserves)

The auditor should determine that the audit committee is informed about (1) the process used by management in formulating particularly sensitive accounting estimates, and (2) the basis for the auditor's conclusions about the reasonableness of those estimates.

Audit Adjustments

The auditor should inform the audit committee about audit adjustments — both those recorded and those not recorded — arising from the audit that could, in his or her judgment, either individually or in the aggregate, have a significant effect on the financial reporting process. The auditor also should inform the audit committee about uncorrected misstatements aggregated by the auditor that pertain the latest period presented and were determined by management to be immaterial.

Quality of the Entity's Accounting Principles

The auditor should discuss his or her judgments about the quality, not just the acceptability, of the company's accounting principles with the audit committees of SEC clients. Management should be an active participant in the discussion.

Other Information

The auditor should discuss his or her responsibility for other information, including "Management's Discussion and Analysis of Financial Condition and Results of Operations," in documents containing audited financial statements, any procedures performed, and the results of those procedures.

Disagreements with Management

The auditor should discuss any disagreement with management, whether or not resolved, about matters that individually or in the aggregate could be significant to the financial statements or the audit report. Disagreements may arise over (1) the application of accounting principles, (2) scope of the audit, (3) financial statement disclosures, and (4) wording of the audit report.

Consultation with Other Accountants (Second Opinions)

If management consults with other accountants about auditing and accounting matters, the auditor should discuss his or her views about significant matters that were the subject of the consultations.

Issues Discussed Prior to Retention

The auditor should discuss any major issues that were discussed with management in connection with the initial or recurring retention of the auditor. Issues include, among other matters, any discussion regarding the application of accounting principles and auditing standards.

Difficulties Encountered during Audit

The auditor should inform the audit committee of any significant difficulties encountered in dealing with management related to the performance of the audit. Difficulties include, among other matters, (1) unreasonable delays by management in permitting the commencement of the audit or in providing needed information, (2) whether the timetable set by management was unreasonable under the circumstances, (3) unavailability of client personnel, and (4) failure of client personnel to complete client-prepared schedules on a timely basis.

Fraud Communications. The external auditor should communicate three items involving fraud:

- Fraud involving senior management.
- Fraud (whether caused by senior management or other employees) that causes a material misstatement of financial statements.
- Fraud risk factors having control implications that the auditor deems to be reportable conditions (see SAS 60 below).

In addition, the external auditor should reach an understanding with the audit committee about the expected nature and extent of communication involving immaterial fraud perpetrated by lower-level employees.

Illegal Acts Communications. The external auditor should assure himself or herself that the audit committee is adequately informed about illegal acts that come to the auditor's attention. The communication should describe the act, the circumstances of its occurrence, and the effect on the financial statements. If senior management is involved in the illegal act, the external auditor should communicate directly with the audit committee. The external auditor need not communicate matters that are clearly inconsequential and may reach agreement in advance with the audit committee on the nature of such matters to be communicated.

Internal Control Communications. As discussed in Chapter 9, "The Audit Committee's Oversight of Internal Control," the external auditor should communicate reportable conditions that come to his or her attention during the audit. Some reportable conditions may already be known and, in fact, may represent a conscious decision by management to accept the risk associated with the deficiency. For such reportable conditions, the auditor may decide the matter does not need to be reported provided that the audit committee has acknowledged its understanding and consideration of such deficiency and the associated risk. However, the auditor should consider whether, because of changes in management, the audit committee, or because of the passage of time, it may be appropriate to report the matter.

SAS 71 Communications. The external auditor should consider whether any of the communications described in SAS 61 above, as they relate to interim financial information, have been identified. The external auditor should communicate such matters to the audit committee or be satisfied, through discussions with the audit committee, that management has communicated these matters to the committee. Such communications with the committee, or at least its chairman and a representative of financial management, should be made prior to the filing of Form 10-Q or as soon as practicable under the circumstances.

In addition, if the external auditor becomes aware of (1) reportable conditions, (2) matters involving fraud, or (3) matters involving illegal acts, while performing the SAS 71 review, those items should be communicated to the audit committee.

Compliance Auditing Considerations in Audits of Governmental Entities and Recipients of Governmental Financial Assistance. If, during a GAAS audit, the external auditor becomes aware that the entity or company is subject to an additional audit requirement that is not encompassed by the engagement terms, the auditor should communicate this to the audit committee.

Independence Discussions with Audit Committees. As discussed earlier in this chapter, the external auditor should (at least annually):

- Disclose to the audit committee in writing all relationships between the auditor (and related entities) and the company (and related entities) that in the auditor's judgment may reasonably bear on independence.
- Confirm in the letter above that his or her firm is independent of the company within the meaning of the Securities Acts.
- Discuss independence, including the performance of any non-audit services, with the audit committee.

Responsibilities for Other Information

The annual report to shareholders is a document prepared by management. The annual report contains information (referred to as other information) in addition to the audited financial statements. This other information may include, but is not limited to, the president's letter, management's discussion and analysis, and the report of management (discussed in Chapter 9).

In an audit of financial statements, the external auditor is not required to perform any audit procedures to substantiate the other information in the annual report to shareholders. However, the external auditor is required to read the other information and consider whether such information is materially inconsistent with the information in the financial statements. For example, when reading a president's letter in the annual report, the external auditor should assess whether the president's comments about operating income are consistent with the income statement. If the external auditor does not identify any material inconsistencies, no comment whatsoever is made about the other information. However, if the other information is not consistent with the financial statements and the financial statements are correct, the external auditor would take one of the following steps:

1. Request the company to revise the information to eliminate the inconsistency.
2. Revise the audit report to include an explanatory paragraph describing the inconsistency.
3. Withhold the audit report in the document.
4. Withdraw from the engagement.

Although the external auditor's responsibility for information in the annual report is limited to the financial information identified in the audit report, the external auditor may be engaged to report on the other information. As previously discussed, the external auditor may be engaged under

SSAE 2, *Reporting on an Entity's Internal Control Over Financial Reporting*, to examine and report on management's representation found in the report of management about the effcctiveness of internal control. Similarly, the external auditor may be engaged to examine or review management's discussion and analysis (MD&A) and report on it. Such engagements are governed by SSAE 8, *Management's Discussion and Analysis*. Exhibit 12-8 presents an example of a standard examination report on MD&A.

Exhibit 12-8
Example of a Standard Examination Report
on Management's Discussion and Analysis

Independent Accountant's Report

Board of Directors and Shareholders of XYZ Company

We have examined XYZ Company's Management's Discussion and Analysis taken as a whole, included [*incorporated by reference*] in the Company's [*insert description of registration statement or document*]. Management is responsible for the preparation of the Company's Management's Discussion and Analysis pursuant to the rules and regulations adopted by the Securities and Exchange Commission. Our responsibility is to express an opinion on the presentation based on our examination. We have audited, in accordance with generally accepted auditing standards, the financial statements of XYZ Company as of December 31, 20X1 and 20X0, and for each of the years in the 3-year period ended December 31, 20X1, and in our report dated February 14, 20X2, we expressed an unqualified opinion on those financial statements.

Our examination of Management's Discussion and Analysis was made in accordance with attestation standards established by the American Institute of Certified Public Accountants and, accordingly, included examining, on a test basis, evidence supporting the historical amounts and disclosures in the presentation. An examination also includes assessing the significant determinations made by management as to the relevancy of information to be included and the estimates and assumptions that affect reported information. We believe that our examination provides a reasonable basis for our opinion.

The preparation of Management's Discussion and Analysis requires management to interpret the criteria, make determinations as to the relevancy of information to be included, and make estimates and assumptions that affect reported information. Management's Discussion and

Analysis includes information regarding the estimated future impact of transactions and events that have occurred or are expected to occur, expected sources of liquidity and capital resources, operating trends, commitments, and uncertainties. Actual results in the future may differ materially from management's present assessment of this information because events and circumstances frequently do not occur as expected.

In our opinion, the Company's presentation of Management's Discussion and Analysis includes, in all material respects, the required elements of the rules and regulations adopted by the Securities and Exchange Commission; the historical financial amounts included therein have been accurately derived, in all material respects, from the Company's financial statements; and the underlying information, determinations, estimates, and assumptions of the Company provide a reasonable basis for the disclosures contained therein.

Burke & Guy, CPAs
February 14, 20X2

Materiality

As discussed in Chapter 4, "Additional Developments from *Treadway* until 2001," on September 28, 1998, SEC Chairman Arthur Levitt delivered his "numbers game" speech about earnings management. He identified five accounting gimmicks that were contributing to the erosion of the quality of earnings and financial reporting. One of these gimmicks was immaterial misapplications of accounting principles. He noted that some companies recorded errors in their financial statements and justified not correcting such errors because the effect on the bottom line was below a specified percentage ceiling, such as five percent. According to Chairman Levitt, the concept of materiality cannot be used to excuse deliberate misstatements of performance.

Chairman Levitt instructed the SEC staff to develop guidance on materiality that emphasized both the quantitative and the qualitative aspects of earnings. The result was Staff Accounting Bulletin (SAB) 99, *Materiality,* which addresses the application of materiality thresholds to the preparation and audit of financial statements filed with the SEC. According to SAB 99:

- Registrants and auditors should evaluate misstatements in light of quantitative and qualitative factors to determine whether a misstatement is material.

- Registrants and auditors should evaluate each misstatement separately and the aggregate effect of all misstatements.
- Intentional misstatements that are not material are unlawful in certain circumstances.

The focus of SAB 99 is the evaluation of misstatements discovered in the financial reporting and auditing processes. It does not affect the external auditor's consideration of materiality in planning the audit.

As a result of Chairman Levitt's remarks and SAB 99 on materiality, the AICPA modified existing auditing standards on engagement letters, management representation letters, and communications with audit committees. The engagement letter standard now states that terms of the engagement generally should include management's responsibility for adjusting the financial statements to correct material misstatements and for affirming to the external auditor in the representation letter that the effects of any uncorrected misstatements are immaterial. The sample engagement letter in Appendix 13 includes these matters. The new management representation standard recommends that one of management's representations should be its belief that the effects of any uncorrected financial statement misstatements aggregated by the auditor are immaterial. A summary of the uncorrected misstatements should be included in or attached to the representation letter. The sample management representation letter in Appendix 15 incorporates this representation. The revised standard on communications with audit committees requires the auditor to inform the audit committee about uncorrected misstatements that were determined by management to be immaterial. This latest SAS 61 communication is included on the checklist of required communications in Appendix 16.

Oversight Responsibilities

Because of the importance of the external audit in establishing the credibility of the company's financial reporting, the audit committee and the external auditors have common goals, and a satisfactory working relationship must be established between the two groups. However, it is important to the audit committee to keep its role clearly in focus, since it performs only an oversight function regarding financial reporting and related risks and controls. The audit committee cannot become too deeply involved in either management's or the external auditor's responsibilities. In discharging its oversight responsibilities, the audit committee simply needs to be sure that these groups are performing their tasks appropriately and that necessary documentation is in place. Exhibit 12-9 identifies key functions that the audit committee typically performs in carrying out its oversight of the external auditor.

Exhibit 12-9
Oversight of the External Auditor

1. Selecting, evaluating, and replacing the external auditor.
2. Reviewing the external audit plan.
3. Evaluating the annual audited financial statements.
4. Overseeing the external audit process and audit results.
5. Monitoring the external auditor's independence.
6. Reviewing interim financial statements.

Selecting, Evaluating and Replacing the External Auditor

The audit committee should oversee the selection, evaluation, and replacement of the external auditor. Audit committee involvement helps ensure the competence and independence of the external auditor. These oversight responsibilities are discussed in Chapter 8, "The Responsibilities of an Audit Committee" and Chapter 14, "Termination of the External Auditor." Appendix 17 presents a form that the audit committee may use to evaluate the effectiveness of the external auditor.

Reviewing the External Audit Plan

The audit committee should review the external audit plan. The purpose of the review is to determine that the audit will meet the needs of the company's board of directors and its shareholders. Most audit committees hold a pre-audit meeting to discuss the audit plan with the external auditor. Appendix 18 presents a list of items typically discussed at the pre-audit planning meeting. The items included in Appendix 18 address audit scope, staffing, locations to be visited, fraud risk factors, and the use of internal and other external auditors.

Evaluating the Annual Audited Financial Statements

As discussed in Chapter 8, the audit committee chairperson should instruct the external auditor, the CFO, and the internal auditor to advise the committee of unusual items or anything else that requires the committee's attention at the completion of interim audit work, if not before. Timely notification will enable the committee to consider significant accounting and disclosure issues, if any, that will require resolution before the audit is completed and the financial statements are issued.

Upon completion of the audit, the full audit committee should meet with the CFO, the internal auditor, and the external auditor (that is, the post-audit meeting) to evaluate the annual financial statements before they are filed or distributed. The audit committee should consider the following items for discussion at the post-audit meeting:

- Accounting policies.
- Significant fluctuations.
- Unusual transactions.
- Differences in financial statement presentation format.
- Accounting estimates.
- Disagreements with management about accounting matters.
- Audit adjustments.
- Quality of accounting principles.

Appendix 19 presents a list of items related to the financial statements typically discussed with the external auditor at the post-audit meeting. The items in Appendix 19 are segregated between the financial statements and the results of the audit.

Overseeing the External Audit Process and Audit Results

At the completion of interim audit work, the audit committee chairperson should discuss any unexpected results with the external auditor. At the completion of the audit (that is, post-audit meeting), the audit committee should discuss the external audit process and the audit results with the external auditor. Given the nature of the agenda relating to the external audit process, the audit committee usually has private meetings with the external auditor and the CFO.

At the completion of the interim audit work, the audit chairperson and the external auditor should discuss any unanticipated problems and the need to expand audit scope as a result of those problems. At the post-audit meeting, the audit committee should receive a complete explanation of any audit report modifications or qualifications (that is, any changes from a standard audit report). In addition, the audit committee should consider the following items for discussion at these meetings:

- Disagreements (or differences of opinion) with management about (1) the scope of the audit or (2) the wording of the audit report.

- Discussions, if any, that the company has had with another external accountant about audit report modifications or qualifications.
- Difficulties, if any, experienced with management during the audit engagement. Difficulties include unreasonable (1) delays in starting the audit, (2) delays in providing information, (3) timetables for completing various audit tasks, and (4) delays by employees in completing needed schedules for the external auditor.
- Fraud risk factors identified by management and the external auditor and their response to those risk factors. (Appendix 14 presents examples of fraud risk factors that are grouped in two categories — risk factors relating to fraudulent financial reporting and risk factors relating to misappropriation of assets.)
- Any matter (material or otherwise) pertaining to suspected fraud, irregularities, or intentional misstatement of financial information that involves senior management of the company or any material fraud, misappropriation, or defalcation involving senior management or other employees.
- Any suspected illegal act (violation of law, rule, or regulation) involving senior management or other employees of the company.
- Departures from the initial audit plan, including significant audit fee overruns and the reasons for such overruns.

In discussing the above items, the external auditor should reach an understanding with the audit committee about the need to communicate information about immaterial fraud and inconsequential illegal acts that involve only lower-level employees. One of the primary matters that the audit committee should also discuss with the external auditor concerns significant detected deficiencies in internal control over financial reporting (that is, reportable conditions).

Appendix 19, which lists items related to audit results typically discussed at the post-audit meeting, includes the above items.

Monitoring the External Auditor's Independence

As previously stated, the audit committee is required by the SEC to indicate in its annual report whether the committee (1) received the external auditor's disclosures about independence and (2) discussed independence with the external auditor. To monitor independence, the committee, preferably before the audit has started, should discuss the external auditor's independence letter and the relationships identified therein and any other relationships of concern to the committee. In addition, the discussion should include any new or emerging independence rules or issues that have been published or are under consideration by the SEC, ISB, or the AICPA. The committee should also consider discussing with the external auditor all consulting services that the external auditor plans to perform for the company.[10] If the committee discusses the external auditor's independence before the completion of the audit, the committee should reconfirm independence at the post-audit meeting.

Appendix 20 presents an illustrative letter from the external auditor to the chairperson of the audit committee that is designed to initiate the independence discussions. The letter should foster an open channel of communication between the audit committee and the external auditor.

Finally, the audit committee should focus on the external auditor's confirmation of independence, which is included in the external auditor's annual independence letter to the audit committee. Appendix 21 presents an illustrative independence letter from the external auditor to the audit committee that is responsive to the requirements of the ISB.

Reviewing Interim Financial Statements

The SEC requires a timely review of a company's quarterly financial statements by the external auditor. Given that requirement, the audit committee or its chairperson should evaluate the interim financial statements and the external auditor's review of those statements prior to filing or distribution. The external auditor and the CFO should participate in the audit committee's discussion of the interim financial statements. In considering the interim financial statements and the external auditor's review of those statements, the audit committee should evaluate and understand the:

- Terms of the review engagement and the level of assurance provided by the external auditor on the interim financial statements.
- Company's risks related to preparing interim financial information and internal controls that pertain to those risks.
- Significant deficiencies in internal control over interim financial reporting that were identified by the external auditor during the review engagement.
- Significant changes in risks and internal controls since the most recent audit or review that could affect the interim financial information.

---

[10] The AICPA's SEC Practice Section requires the external auditor to annually communicate to the audit committee or the board of directors the nature of and the amount of fees billed for consulting services to the company.

- Changes in the company's accounting policies and business that could affect the interim financial statements.
- Reasons for fluctuations in the interim financial information as compared to the immediately preceding interim period and for the corresponding prior interim period.
- Methods used to account for significant unusual transactions and seasonal variations in revenues, costs, and expenses.
- Management's representation letter stating, among other things, that management believes the interim financial statements are presented in conformity with GAAP.
- The external auditor's review report, if issued, on the interim financial statements. (The external auditor is not usually engaged to issue a report on the review.)

In addition to the above items, the audit committee should determine if there were:

- Any disagreements with management about the scope of the review (or wording of the review report, if one is issued).
- Discussions with another external accountant about the measurements and disclosures in the interim financial statements.
- Difficulties experienced with management during the review engagement.
- Any matters involving suspected fraud or illegal acts.

The audit committee should also discuss the views of the external auditor and the CFO about the quality of the company's accounting principles that were applied in the interim financial statements. Finally, if the company records conference calls with financial analysts, the audit committee should review the audiotapes that are distributed to the committee.

Here is a summary of the key points in this chapter:

The Auditing Profession

1. The American Institute of Certified Public Accountants (AICPA) is the national professional organization of CPAs.
2. The AICPA has taken steps to ensure the quality of external audits, including: (a) establishing quality control standards, (b) creating a related peer review program, and (c) establishing authoritative standards for external audits and related engagements.

The External Auditor's Responsibilities

3. The external auditor's overall objective is to express an opinion whether the financial statements of a company are fairly presented in accordance with GAAP.
4. The external auditor's opinion is contained in the external auditor's report. The standard report issued by the external auditor has three paragraphs: (a) an introductory paragraph, (b) a scope paragraph, and (c) an opinion paragraph.
5. The best opinion that the external auditor can express is an unqualified opinion. An unqualified opinion means that the financial statements conform to GAAP in all material respects. Conditions such as significant limitations on the scope of the audit or material departures from GAAP cause the auditor to issue a qualified opinion, an adverse opinion, or a disclaimer of an opinion.
6. The external auditor must be independent to perform an audit and express an opinion on a company's financial statements. To be independent, the external auditor must comply with requirements set by the AICPA, the SEC, and the ISB.
7. There has been much debate about whether the external auditor's independence is impaired when the external auditor provides consulting services (or non-audit services) to audit clients. The SEC requires companies to disclose fees to its principal auditor categorized by (1) audit/review fees, (2) financial information system consulting fees, and (3) all other fees. The audit committee must consider items (2) and (3) and whether they are compatible with maintaining the external auditor's independence.
8. The external auditor is required to establish an understanding with the company regarding the services to be provided. An engagement letter is the best way to document this understanding.
9. The external auditor provides reasonable assurance that the financial statements are free from material misstatements. Misstatements include errors (unintentional misstatements), fraud (intentional misstatements), and illegal acts (violations of laws and governmental regulations) that directly affect line-item amounts in the financial statements.
10. The external auditor has a responsibility to assess the risk of material misstatement due to fraud and consider that assessment in planning the audit. In making that assessment, the external auditor is required to consider risk factors relating to the two categories of fraud: (a) fraudulent financial reporting and (b) misappropriation of assets.
11. Illegal acts can be divided into two categories: (a) illegal acts that have

a direct effect on a line item in the financial statements and (b) other illegal acts, such as violations of laws and regulations related to environmental protection, equal employment, and antitrust. The external auditor provides no assurance about other illegal acts.

12. The external auditor has a responsibility to obtain an understanding of internal control over financial reporting sufficient to plan the audit. The auditor does not express an opinion on internal control over financial reporting in a financial statement audit.

13. When obtaining an understanding of internal control, the external auditor obtains an understanding of the internal audit function. The internal auditor may decide to use the work of the internal auditor or use the direct assistance of the internal auditor. If so, the external auditor has certain responsibilities, including assessing the competence and the objectivity of the internal auditor.

14. At the end of the audit or review engagement, the external auditor should obtain a management representation letter.

15. The external auditor is required to communicate certain information about the scope and results of the audit by the following authoritative pronouncements:
   - SAS 61 — *Communication with Audit Committees*
   - SAS 82 — *Consideration of Fraud in a Financial Statement Audit*
   - SAS 54 — *Illegal Acts by Clients*
   - SAS 60 — *Communication of Internal Control Related Matters Noted in an Audit*
   - SAS 71 — *Interim Financial Information*
   - SAS 74 — *Compliance Auditing Considerations in Audits of Governmental Entities and Recipients of Governmental Financial Assistance*

The Relationship between the External Auditor and the Audit Committee

16. The audit committee has an oversight relationship with the external auditor.

17. To effectively carry out its oversight role of the external auditor, the audit committee should:
   a. Oversee the selection, evaluation, and replacement of the external auditor.
   b. Review the external audit plan.
   c. Evaluate the annual audited financial statements.
   d. Oversee the external audit process and audit results.
   e. Monitor the external auditor's independence.
   f. Review the interim financial statements.

CHAPTER 13
AUDIT COMMITTEE MEETINGS

This chapter discusses the frequency of audit committee meetings and who should set the agendas for those meetings. In addition, the chapter discusses who should attend the meetings, who should prepare the minutes, and where the committee should meet.

Number of Meetings

Most audit committees today have two to four scheduled meetings per year, depending on the scope of their activities and the size of the company (larger companies tend to have more meetings than smaller ones). Adequate time should be allowed at each meeting so that a detailed agenda can be covered in a professional and complete manner. Of course, the time allocated to a given meeting is dependent on the number of topics and the complexity of those matters. Because of the variation of topics and in the frequency of meeting, a rule-of-thumb on the length of meetings is probably not useful. The National Association of Corporate Directors' *Audit Committees: A Practical Guide* suggests that quarterly meetings should last a half-day.[1] Obviously, that period of time may be too long or too short depending on the agenda for the particular company. In any event, the chairperson of the audit committee must assure that each meeting allows significant time for committee members' questions and related dialogue.

In addition to regularly scheduled meetings, most audit committees have the authority to hold special meetings when needed. A properly structured audit committee should have this authority.

SEC registrants are required to have their quarterly financial statements reviewed by the external auditor under SAS 71, *Interim Financial Information,* before Form 10-Q (or Form 10-QSB) is filed. Audit committees should be involved in overseeing the quarterly financial statements and the external auditor's review of those statements. Whether an actual face-to-face meeting or a telephone conference call is held for such purpose depends on the facts and circumstances for the particular company. Adding an additional face-to-face meeting for each quarterly review will substantially increase the time commitment of committee members and may produce more costs than benefits. Accordingly, it may be appropriate to delegate to the chair-

---

[1] Report of the NACD Blue Ribbon Commission, *Audit Committees: A Practical Guide* (Washington, D.C.: National Association of Corporate Directors, 2000), p. 15.

person the responsibility for having quarterly reviews with the external auditor and financial management by telephone. When required, of course, the chairperson may involve other committee members in the telephone conference call or, when needed, call a face-to-face meeting.

Meeting Agendas

Appendix 22 presents an illustrative audit committee agenda for four quarterly meetings. Obviously, the agendas need to be tailored to the activities of the committee and the type of business in which the company is engaged. At the early stages of the creation of an audit committee, it is probably a good idea to have very broad agendas. As time progresses and the committee assumes expanded responsibilities, the chairperson of the audit committee should prepare detailed agendas to help keep the committee focused.

The audit committee should prepare its own agenda with input from management, including the chief financial officer (CFO) and general counsel; the director of internal audit; and the external auditor. In some companies, the CFO, the internal auditor, or the general counsel (or combination thereof) prepares the agenda. However, the preferred practice in such companies is to have those individuals prepare the agenda under the direction of the chairperson of the audit committee. Under no circumstances should management alone establish the agenda. Another good practice regarding the agenda to promote active and responsible audit committees is that the chairperson should circulate the proposed agenda to all committee members and solicit their input about other agenda topics that should be added.

Final agendas and related background material should be distributed in advance to audit committee members to enable them to be adequately prepared. The authors recommend that the agenda materials be distributed to committee members well in advance of the scheduled meeting.

Regardless of the number of audit committee meetings held during the year, at least two meetings should include private agenda time for (1) management, (2) the internal auditor, and (3) the external auditor. In addition, the chairperson should schedule private agenda time for the committee at each meeting.

Attendance by Committee Members

Audit committee members must demonstrate commitment to the committee. One way of doing this is to avoid being absent from scheduled committee meetings. In fact, near perfect attendance is essential. The minutes of each committee meeting should record attendance. Members who miss meetings should be asked to resign or be removed from the committee.

Attendance by Company Personnel and External Auditor

A representative of the company's financial management should attend each committee meeting. It is common for the CFO and the controller, as the chief accounting officer, to attend all meetings. However, those individuals should not be present for discussions about management with the internal auditor and the external auditor. In addition, a representative of the internal auditor should attend all meetings. Specialists, such as the director of tax, director of corporate environmental matters, and others may attend selected audit committee meetings when items on the agenda call for a report or information from them.

The chief executive officer (CEO) should attend audit committee meetings only when invited by the audit committee chairperson. In the authors' opinion, the attendance of the CEO at all meetings would impede the open and frank discussion among financial management, the internal auditor, and the external auditor. In many cases, of course, the CEO's attendance can provide a useful perspective on a number of matters relevant to the agenda. The audit committee should remember that management can provide important information relevant to its deliberations. However, the chairperson must exercise care to see that management does not control meetings and divert attention from important and perhaps sensitive areas.

The audit committee chairman normally communicates with the CFO and the director of internal auditing regarding who should attend audit committee meetings and how the agenda should be structured (topics and time allocations). The CFO, or his or her delegate, normally handles correspondence relating to planning and calling audit committee meetings. In many companies, the director of internal auditing serves as secretary to the audit committee. A representative of the external auditor should attend all meetings, especially since the external auditor reviews quarterly financial information prior to filing by the company.

Preparation of Minutes

The audit committee should keep minutes of each meeting to document the processes followed by the committee in discharging its oversight responsibilities and to capture highlights of important discussions and conclusions. Minutes should be detailed enough to indicate the matters covered and decisions reached, but should not contain exhaustive discussion of all the points that were considered at the meeting. That is, minutes should focus on documenting processes and conclusions and should not be transcripts of the discussions that took place. Exhibit 13-1 summarizes best practices regarding matters that should be captured in minutes.[2] Minutes of the meeting must reflect the integrity and fairness of the committee's decision-making process.

Some companies have various financial management personnel prepare minutes during the audit committee meeting. This is a good practice because it allows audit committee members to become acquainted with and observe members of the financial accounting staff who may be candidates for increased responsibilities in the company in the future.

Exhibit 13-1
Minutes: Best Practices

Minutes or highlights of audit committee meetings should:

1. Record time, place, and date of meeting.
2. Note attendees, members and others, along with time in attendance.
3. Document satisfaction of quorum requirements.
4. Note when advanced materials were circulated.
5. Highlight important points made in discussions and debates (pro and con), along with time spend on subject.
6. Record actions taken and conclusions reached.
7. Record dissents and abstentions, along with their rationale.
8. Summarize or append reports presented.
9. Be circulated in draft form to members for final approval.

Location of Meetings

Audit committee meetings will normally be held at the company headquarters (or the location of the company's accounting department). However, the audit committee should consider holding at least one meeting per year at an important operating division. A visit to an operating division by the audit committee not only emphasizes the interest of the board of directors in lo-

---

[2] See also Charles R. McCarthy, "The Chronicling of Corporate Minutes, Continued: A Retrospective Look at *Van Gorkom,*" Director's Monthly (September 1999), pp. 6-10.

cal operations, but also motivates employees to take their responsibilities for the integrity of financial reporting seriously.

If a company has foreign operations, the audit committee should consider visits to sites having a material effect on the company's operations to determine that appropriate internal controls are in place as required by the Foreign Corrupt Practices Act. While meetings in foreign locations may be expensive, the audit committee will normally find that a foreign venue is an appropriate expenditure of company funds because it allows the audit committee to conduct oversight over a broader scope of risks and controls over financial reporting.

Here is a summary of the important points of this chapter:

Number of Meetings Per Year

1. Most audit committees today have two to four scheduled meetings per year, depending on the scope of their activities and the size of the company.
2. Adequate time should be allowed at each meeting so that the agenda can be covered in a professional and complete manner.
3. Audit committees should be involved in overseeing the quarterly financial statements and the external auditor's review of those statements. Whether an actual face-to-face meeting or a telephone conference call is held for such purpose depends on the facts and circumstances for the particular company.
4. In addition to scheduled meetings, an audit committee must have the authority to hold special meetings as needed.
5. The CFO, or his or her delegate (for example, the internal auditor), handles audit committee correspondence relative to planning and calling meetings.

Meeting Agendas

6. The chairperson of the audit committee should prepare the meeting agenda. The chairperson, working with the CFO, the internal auditor, and general counsel, along with input from the external auditor, should prepare detailed agendas with topic and time allocations to help keep the committee focused.
7. The chairperson of the audit committee should circulate proposed audit committee agendas to all committee members to obtain their input about topics that should be added.

8. Under no circumstances should management alone prepare the audit committee agenda.
9. Meeting agendas and related background materials should be distributed to committee members in advance of scheduled meetings.

Attendance by Committee Members

10. The minutes of each meeting should record attendance by members (and others).
11. Members who miss meetings should be asked to resign or be removed from the committee.

Attendance by Company Personnel and the External Auditor

12. A representative of the company's financial management should attend each audit committee meeting, but should not be present for private discussions with the internal and external auditors.
13. A least two meeting per year should include private agenda time for (1) management, (2) the internal auditor, and (3) the external auditor.
14. The CFO and the controller usually attend all meetings.
15. A representative of internal audit, such as the director of internal auditing, should attend all meetings.
16. Specialists, such as the director of taxation, should attend selected meetings.
17. Legal counsel should participate in audit committee meetings as appropriate.
18. The CEO should attend meetings only when invited.
19. A representative of the external auditor should attend all meetings, particularly given that the external auditor reviews quarterly financial information prior to filing by the company.

Preparing Minutes of Meetings

20. Minutes of each meeting should be prepared to document the processes followed by the audit committee in discharging its oversight responsibility, and to capture highlights of important discussions and conclusions.

Location of Meetings

21. Usually the meetings are held at company headquarters or at the location of the company's accounting department.
22. Consideration should be given to holding at least one meeting per year at significant operational sites, including foreign locations.

CHAPTER 14
TERMINATION OF THE EXTERNAL AUDITOR

This chapter presents the considerations that are involved in making a decision to change auditors and the steps that are included in the audit engagement proposal process. The chapter also presents ideas on how the proposal process should be protected in the interest of fairness to the company and to the proposing CPA firms.

Considerations in Changing Auditors

Today, companies are placing more emphasis on reviewing the external audit relationship. This, in turn, is producing more frequent changes of auditors.[1] In many cases, the primary motivation for changing external auditors is the audit fee. The accounting profession, particularly the "Big Five" CPA firms, are very competitive with one another, especially in the audit fee domain.[2] In many cases, low fees are quoted simply to obtain the audit engagement in order to gain access to lucrative consulting or non-audit work. In other words, the audit engagement is treated as a loss leader or a conduit to obtaining consulting engagements.

The audit committee must be particularly sensitive to this type of activity. Audit committees should be concerned that the audit fee quoted is adequate to enable the external auditor to perform the work necessary to provide an effective audit. Aside from fee considerations, the audit committee (as discussed in Chapter 12, "Relationship with the External Auditor") should review the adequacy of the external auditor's work on an annual basis to determine that the personnel assigned to the audit engagement are qualified and compatible with company personnel. In addition, the external audit engagement personnel should demonstrate an understanding of the company's business and its industry and issues related thereto, together with the need to anticipate the effect of new accounting, audit, SEC, and tax requirements. The audit committee should also determine that the external auditor, particularly in the areas of industry and SEC expertise, is effectively and efficiently providing the professional services needed by the company.

---

[1] The SEC requires registrants to disclose a change of auditors in Form 8-K. In addition, the SEC Practice Section requires member CPA firms to notify the Chief Accountant of the SEC within five business days when the auditor-client relationship ceases.

[2] The term "audit fee" as used in this chapter includes fees associated with performing reviews of quarterly financial information.

The audit committee should inquire as to the external audit firm's quality control policies, including its independence policies and procedures. The audit committee should also understand the external auditor's policies for rotation of personnel and determine that rotation is being done as needed on the engagement.[3]

If the audit committee determines that a change of the external auditors is appropriate, the committee should be sure that it seriously intends to make a change in the relationship. If the consideration of a change is merely an exercise with no real intent to make a change, the audit committee should not undertake the effort, since it is a very expensive and time-consuming process for both the company and the proposing CPA firms. Furthermore, if there is little chance that the current external auditor will be reappointed, the audit committee should not ask the current auditor to submit a proposal.

External Auditor's Accountability to the Audit Committee— A Reminder

As discussed in Chapter 5, "The 1999 Blue Ribbon Committee on Improving the Effectiveness of Corporate Audit Committees — Another Major Milestone," the *Blue Ribbon Report* recommended that both the New York Stock Exchange (NYSE) and the National Association of Securities Dealers (NASD) should require that:

1. The audit committee charter for every listed committee specify that the external auditor is ultimately accountable to the board of directors, and
2. The audit committee, as representatives of the shareholders, has the ultimate authority and responsibility to select, evaluate, and, where appropriate, replace the external auditor (or to nominate the external auditor to be proposed for shareholder approval).

As a result of the *Blue Ribbon Report,* the NYSE, the NASD, and the American Stock Exchange (AMEX) amended their listing requirements to mandate the above requirements.

---

[3] SEC Practice Section member CPA firms are required to assign a new audit partner to be in charge of each SEC engagement that has had another engagement partner for a period of 7 consecutive years. In addition, the incumbent engagement partner is prohibited from returning as engagement partner for at least 2 years. (The rotation requirement does not apply to CPA firms that have less than 5 SEC clients and less than 10 partners.)

Requesting Audit Engagement Proposals

If the audit committee determines that proposals should be requested from other external auditors for future audit work, the committee should compile a working list of potential CPA firms. The list should include CPA firms known to be strong in the company's industry (or industries) that have a good reputation with companies in that industry. However, the audit committee should be aware of the potential conflict of interest that relationships between a CPA firm and the company's competitors could cause. Thus, the audit committee may insist that engagement personnel of the CPA firm finally selected be composed of individuals who do not have contact with competitors.

CPA firms known to have specific tax or consulting expertise in the company's industry may also be considered, depending on the company's policy on performance of non-audit services by its external auditor. Whether only the large international CPA firms are to be considered or other firms are also to be considered depends on the judgment of the company's financial management and the audit committee, and the needs and geographic dispersion of the company and its markets.

A. Statement of Qualifications

To control the preliminary proposal process, the audit committee should select a group no larger than five or six CPA firms. To make a preliminary evaluation of the CPA firms, the audit committee should request those firms to submit statements of qualifications outlining their audit philosophies, management structures, and primary areas of professional practice. The company's financial management should review the statements of qualifications that are submitted by the various CPA firms and should verify claims relating to expertise or special knowledge that are made in the submitted statements. In addition, the CPA firms should provide specific references that should be checked by the company. The initial information requested should include a five-year summary of publicly held clients won and lost, together with a summary of companies (public and private) won or lost in the company's industry during the five-year time period.

After the statements of qualifications are submitted, the CPA firms should be requested to have two or three of its personnel make a brief presentation (of no more than one hour) to the company's financial management personnel. The purpose of this meeting is to determine if the CPA firm appears to have a real interest in the potential engagement and a knowledge of the company's business and industry. Management should ask the individuals making the presentations what their roles would be in the external audit if the engagement were awarded to their firm. Many CPA firms use marketing and sales personnel to make presentations, while others do the actual work. Company management and the audit committee should insist that the persons making the presentations are the individuals who will actually work on the audit if it is awarded to their firm.

If the company is only considering two or three CPA firms, the statement of qualifications may be eliminated and the firms may be asked for a formal proposal. The proposal process starts with visits to the company and omits the initial steps leading up to the statement of qualifications.

B. The Formal Proposal

After the statements of qualifications are reviewed and the oral presentations made, the reviewing group should select the two or three most qualified CPA firms to proceed to the next step — the formal proposal. The remaining CPA firms should be advised that they are no longer under consideration.

In the next stage of the proposal process, the finalists should be given the opportunity to inspect the books and records of the company and visit key locations and key personnel. While this process requires significant time, it also allows company personnel to have a closer look at the individuals who would actually be involved in the audit engagement if that CPA firm is selected. Company personnel should be asked to prepare evaluation forms for each representative of the CPA firm with whom they come in contact. Again, the individuals representing the CPA firm should be the persons who will actually be involved in the audit engagement, not marketing or industry specialists from the CPA firm who will probably never see the company's premises again. Particular attention should be given to the quality of personnel visiting the company's foreign locations and to the recommendations from company personnel in those locations.

After the visits are completed, the company should send a letter to the CPA firms requesting that they submit a formal proposal that addresses the scope of the audit, the personnel to be assigned to the engagement and their expertise, the tax and other capabilities that would be available to the company as a result of engaging the firm, and the estimated audit fee. The request for proposal should specify that a fee for a period of three years should be submitted and the services covered by the proposed fee should be specifically identified. If there is to be any increase in fees for special services, such as SEC registrations or filings, the proposal should specifically provide that such fees would be in addition to the audit fee. The current average hourly rates for the level of personnel that would be involved in performing special services should be set forth in the proposal. The proposal should be brief and limited to a defined number of pages (for example, 25 pages). Appendix 23 presents a sample request packet for soliciting formal audit (and quarterly review) engagement proposals.

When the formal written proposals are received, financial management should prepare a comparison of the proposals to facilitate the evaluation committee's analysis. Frequently, particularly in specialized industries, the most qualified CPA firm will be obvious from the material submitted. Quite often, however, the most qualified firm will not submit the lowest proposed audit fee.

The audit committee should not be reluctant to request that the most qualified CPA firm reconsider the proposed engagement fees. Because of the competitive environment, most CPA firms will at least consider reductions of their initial bid, particularly if they are sincerely interested in obtaining the company as an audit client. However, a CPA firm that is highly qualified and does not reduce its fees should not be automatically excluded from further consideration. The audit committee must remember that an adequate fee must be paid to obtain an effective and efficient audit. As previously stated, the audit committee must carefully consider drastic fee cutting at any point in the evaluation process. Drastic fee reductions may be a clear sign that the company is buying an ineffective audit.

After the formal proposals have been reviewed and summarized by management for the audit committee, a formal meeting with each of the prospective CPA firms should be held with the appropriate representatives of management and members of the audit committee. Appendix 24 presents sample questions to be asked during a meeting with a prospective external auditor. After the formal presentation by the prospective CPA firms, the group should meet and make a final decision as quickly as possible. Each CPA firm participating in the proposal process should be formally notified as to the decision of the company at the earliest possible time.

Protecting the Proposal Process

Large CPA firms participate in the audit engagement proposal process on a daily basis and have accumulated significant expertise in making proposals. In addition, the large CPA firms usually have many contacts within public companies that are not their audit clients. As a result, when a company issues a request for a statement of qualifications or a request for a proposal, it is likely that at least one representative of every major CPA firm will have an acquaintance(s) within the company. The CPA firm may try to use such acquaintances to gain inside information about the proposal process. The audit committee must clearly set forth the rules for submitting proposals, making it clear that contacts with company personnel not designated as contacts by the company will disqualify the CPA firm. Furthermore, contacts with members of the board of directors, particularly members of the audit committee, are also grounds for disqualifying a CPA firm. Otherwise, company personnel and board members who may not be involved in the auditor selection process may waste considerable time with phone calls and other interruptions. Certainly, the audit committee does not want employees of the company, particularly personnel in financial management, to be burdened with telephone calls from CPA firms asking how the process is going and what level of fees will be required to obtain the engagement.

While it does not occur often, on occasion, a company employee will provide copies of written material submitted by one CPA firm to another CPA firm for comparison purposes. The audit committee should stress that any employee engaging in such activity will be subject to disciplinary action, including possible dismissal.

Respect the Proposal Process

The audit committee must be careful that it is not subject to improper external influences, such as contacts from accounting firms. In one instance, the chief financial officer (CFO) of a company had requested statements of qualifications from four large CPA firms. As a result, two CPA firms were invited to submit formal written proposals. At that point, the CFO advised the audit committee of the process that the company was following. The chairman of the audit committee, who had a close personal friend in the executive office of one of the large CPA firms that was not asked to submit a statement of qualifications, demanded that his friend's firm be allowed to submit a formal proposal. The audit committee chairman then guided his friend's firm through the proposal process and used his influence to cause that CPA firm to be selected as the company's external auditor, even though the CPA firm selected did not make nearly the commitment made by the other two proposing CPA firms. In fact, during the first year of the audit, the audit fee quoted in the proposal was substantially increased. The CPA firm had to bring in experts from other offices — a step not anticipated in the proposal.

In the above situation, the audit committee chairman should have respected the confidentiality of the selection process and the process being used by the company to select the most appropriate CPA firm as their external auditor. The audit committee chairman's interference and use of his position to select a CPA firm that clearly was not the best firm was a disservice to the company and its shareholders.

In another situation, the CFO became irritated with the external auditor for rather insignificant reasons. While the external auditor had significant expertise in the company's industry and otherwise performed an excellent audit, the CFO decided that proposals should be requested from three other firms as "punishment" for the incumbent. The company never really intended to change external auditors, but merely intended to use the exercise to lower the audit fee and to "punish" the incumbent. The result was that the other CPA firms spent considerable time and money preparing statements of qualification and formal proposals, visiting the company's headquarters (situated in a rather inaccessible locale), and traveling to international locations. All of their efforts were worthless, because the company never really intended to change external auditors. This approach is simply unethical and must be avoided by audit committees.

Here is a summary of some of the important points in this chapter:

General

- If the audit committee determines that a change in external auditors is appropriate, the committee should be sure that it intends to make the change before starting the proposal process.
- The audit committee should determine that the audit/review fees quoted in a proposal are adequate to enable the external auditor to perform the engagements effectively.

Steps in the Proposal Process

1. Compile a working list of potential CPA firms that could perform the company's audit.
2. Select a group of 5 or 6 of the best CPA firms on the list in Step 1.
3. Request those selected CPA firms to submit a statement of their qualifications.
4. Request the selected CPA firms to have 2 or 3 of their personnel make a brief presentation to the company's financial management. (Insist that the individuals making the presentation are the persons who will actually work on the engagement.)

5. Select 2 or 3 of the most qualified CPA firms to inspect the books and records, visit key locations, and meet key personnel of the company.
6. Have company personnel evaluate each representative of the CPA firm with whom they come into contact.
7. Request the finalist CPA firms to submit a formal proposal (limited to a defined number of pages).
8. Prepare a comparison of the proposals to facilitate the evaluation committee's analysis.
9. Hold a formal meeting among each of the prospective CPA firms and representatives of management and members of the audit committee.
10. Meet and make a final selection of the new external auditor.

Protecting the Proposal Process

- The audit committee should make it clear that contact with company personnel not designated as contacts by the company and members of the board of directors, including members of the audit committee, will disqualify the CPA firm from proposing on the engagement.
- The audit committee should stress that written materials pertaining to the proposal process submitted by one CPA firm should not be provide to another CPA firm.

CHAPTER 15
EVALUATING THE AUDIT COMMITTEE

This chapter discusses the evaluation processes that an audit committee should carry out to be effective and to maintain effectiveness. The evaluation processes require (1) a self-assessment by the audit committee as a whole, (2) assessments of each committee member's performance by the chairperson, (3) assessment of the chairperson's performance by the board of directors, and (4) a comparison of the committee's duties, responsibilities, and activities with best practices recommended by various commissions, committees, and study groups.

The Self-Assessment

The authors recommend that the audit committee should complete a self-assessment every two or three years, unless circumstances dictate a more frequent assessment. The self-assessment should cover the committee's duties and responsibilities in relation to its charter, effectiveness of its meetings, and its relationships with the board of directors, senior management, the internal auditor, and the external auditor. Appendix 25, "Audit Committee: Self-Assessment," presents a data-collection tool that the committee could use in performing an assessment.

After completing the self-assessment, the chairperson should present the results to the board of directors. The board is then in a position to approve and implement needed changes.

Individual Member and Chairperson Evaluations

Each year, the chairperson of the audit committee should assess each member of the audit committee during such member's term and recommend to the board of directors (or the appropriate committee of the board of directors) whether the member should be appointed for another term. The chairperson should be objective and candid in his or her assessment and recognize the importance of having quality members on the audit committee. In addition, the chairperson of the board of directors (or the appropriate committee of the board) should evaluate the chairperson of the audit committee and determine whether that person should continue in that position (or, in fact, should continue as a member of the audit committee).

When the audit committee chairperson assesses the performance of individual committee members, he or she should consider attributes such as each member's:

- Financial literacy.
- Independence in thought and action.
- Expertise.
- Knowledge of the company and its industry.
- Exercise of sound judgment.
- Inquiring attitude.
- Commitment to the committee's duties and responsibilities.
- Willingness to work and devote the necessary time.
- Attendance and participation at meetings.

Likewise, the board of directors should also consider the above attributes when evaluating the audit committee chairperson. In addition, the board should assess the chairperson's leadership and communication skills.

Committee Activities vs. Best Practices

The authors recommend that an audit committee hold a special meeting every two or three years to consider what other audit committees are doing and recommendations about best practices. In arranging the special meeting, the committee may find it beneficial to retain an outside facilitator to review the committee's charter and its activities and to compare those matters with recommendations made by groups such as the 1999 Blue Ribbon Committee on Improving the Effectiveness of Corporate Audit Committees (discussed in Chapter 5) and the 2000 Panel on Audit Effectiveness (discussed in Chapter 4). In addition, the facilitator should obtain input from the chairperson of the board of directors, senior management, the internal auditor, and the external auditor about the efficiency and effectiveness of the audit committee.

The main purpose of the special "best practices" meeting is to:

1. Assess the current status of the audit committee in terms of duties, responsibilities, and activities.
2. Determine where the committee should be in terms of duties and activities, including resources needed.
3. Identify obstacles in getting from point 1 to point 2.
4. Develop a proposed action plan and timetable for change.
5. Present the findings and recommendations to the board of directors.

Importance of Annual Member and Chairperson Evaluations and Committee Self-Assessment

An effective evaluation of an audit committee adds support to representations that the board of directors is using the audit committee for the proper purposes and that the board is satisfied that the audit committee is performing satisfactorily. Such evidence may be helpful in minimizing potential legal liability for both the audit committee and the board and its members.

In addition, third parties, such as insurance carriers, might be interested in using the annual evaluation process as a means of rating the effectiveness of audit committees for directors and officers insurance premium purposes. While there is no activity in this area at present, as major accounting misstatements and frauds continue to occur, insurers will eventually look more toward the audit committee function as part of the process for determining the insurability of a particular company, its officers, and directors.[1]

Here is a summary of the important points in this chapter:

1. The chairperson of the audit committee should assess the performance of each committee member at least once each year.
2. The board of directors should assess the performance of the audit committee chairperson at least once each year.
3. The audit committee should obtain input from the board of directors, senior management, the internal auditor, and the external auditor about the committee's efficiency and effectiveness. This information should be obtained as a prelude to performing a self-assessment.
4. The audit committee should perform a self-assessment every two or three years.
5. The audit committee should hold a special meeting every two or three years to compare the committee's duties, responsibilities, and activities with best practices. The committee should recommend needed changes to the board of directors for approval and implementation.

---

[1] See "D&O Woes Might Prompt Shakeout," *National Underwriter* (February 15, 1999), p. 29.

CHAPTER 16
AUDIT COMMITTEES FOR NOT-FOR-PROFIT
AND PUBLIC SECTOR ENTITIES [1]

Because of increasing pressure for accountability, many boards or governing bodies of not-for-profit and public sector entities are implementing a corporate model allowing the oversight body to focus on policy matters while the chief executive officer or top managerial professional devotes full-time to entity operations. Historically, many not-for-profit entities, particularly charities, relied heavily on volunteers to perform all or substantially all of the operational functions of the organization, and frequently the governing body also became involved in operational matters.

Donors, members, and taxpayers expect high-quality services from not-for-profit and public sector entities. Often there is a significant gap between the services expected and those delivered. Under the corporate model, greater accountability and quality of services is achieved by having, among other things, effective organizational and internal control systems over (1) financial reporting, (2) compliance, and (3) operations. The purpose of this chapter is to provide a brief discussion of the unique features of audit committees in not-for-profit and public sector entities.

Use of Audit Committees

The establishment of audit committees has become more common in not-for-profit and public sector entities. The authors believe that all not-for-profit entities that raise funds from the public, receive grants, or have membership dues, and all public sector entities that are required to be audited or are audited should have audit committees or committees with equivalent responsibilities. A not-for-profit or public sector entity may assign the audit committee duties and responsibilities to a finance, budget, or executive committee. Although the authors believe that a separate audit committee is preferable, such assignments are acceptable provided the committee has the time, resources, and independence (both in fact and appearance). Of

---

[1] Grant Thornton has published an excellent booklet, *Serving on the Audit Committee of a Not-for-Profit Organization* (Grant Thornton LLP, 1999). Their national office telephone number is (312) 856-0001. Information and publications (for example, *Understanding Nonprofit Financial Statements*) about not-for-profit entities are also available from the National Center for Nonprofit Boards at www.ncnb.org.

course, the designated committee has to perform the functions of an audit committee.

Many not-for-profit and some public sector entities have at least two oversight committees — the audit committee and the nominating committee. Also, there may be fundraising or development committees, investment committees, compensation committees, or similar committees, depending on the size and activities of the entity.

Because the audit committee is primarily responsible for the organization's financial integrity, it should be made up of directors who are independent of management of the entity, just as with a for-profit corporation. Officers and employees of the entity should not be members of the audit committee, although they should attend audit committee meetings as requested and when needed.

Similar to a for-profit corporate audit committee, the committee is primarily responsible for overseeing the entity's financial data, its internal controls over financial reporting, the external audit process, and for communication with the entity's internal auditor (if any), the external auditor, and the staff responsible for financial reporting. The responsibility and authority of an audit committee for a not-for-profit or public sector entity should be essentially the same as those for a for-profit corporation.

Internal Control in Not-for-Profit Entities

Not-for-profit organizations frequently generate funds through mailings, door-to-door solicitations, telephone pledges, dinners, and various other ways. Internal controls over funds raised at such functions can be difficult to establish and maintain. Accordingly, it is essential that a not-for-profit entity develop adequate systems of internal control to ensure that all receipts are actually received by the entity and properly recorded in its financial statements.

Because of the informal structure of many not-for-profit entities, management should document the internal control systems that apply to solicitation of funds, personnel and payroll procedures, disbursement procedures, and other important functions. The audit committee should see that internal control systems of a not-for-profit organization are appropriately documented. The audit committee should also devote special attention to the procedures and controls over sensitive and high-risk areas such as professional and consulting fees, executive compensation, and travel and entertainment. Exhibit 16-1 summarizes the special oversight issues that the board of directors or the audit committee should monitor in a not-for-profit entity.

Exhibit 16-1
Special Oversight Issues in a Not-for-Profit Entity

Need to Monitor	*Potential Problem*
1. Controls over donations	Safeguarding of assets against misappropriation requires unique controls
2. Tax-exempt status of the entity*	Losing tax exemption may devastate the entity
3. Private inurement (entity's assets are used for personal benefit of an insider)	Losing tax exemption and damaging reputation
4. Unrelated business income (income from sources that are unrelated to the entity's tax exemption)	Losing tax exemption

---

*The Internal Revenue Code of 1986 (as amended) identifies 27 types of non-profit entities. These entities range from a 501(c)1, such as a federal credit union, to 512(a), a farmer's cooperative association. Common types of nonprofit entities include 501(c)3 — charitable, educational, and scientific groups, 501(c)4 — advocacy groups, and 501(c)6 — trade and professional associations.

Internal Control in Public Sector Entities

For public sector entities, creation of effective internal control systems can provide added assurance that high quality and efficient services will be provided. Strict standards of accountability simply cannot be achieved without well-developed internal control systems over financial reporting, compliance, and operations. Therefore, as a significant component of its control system, a public sector entity should establish an audit committee as a permanent committee of its governing body. The concept can be readily used by most public sector entities governed by a legislative body, board, council, or commission. For example, a public sector entity with a six-member commission could designate three of its independent members to serve as an audit committee, or an elected official who heads a public sector entity could appoint an audit committee composed of independent individuals, knowledgeable in financial matters.

Internal Audit Function

Larger not-for-profit and public sector entities should consider establishing an internal audit function to monitor financial reporting and related risks and controls. Churches, charities, colleges, universities, public school districts, water districts, hospitals, housing authorities, and similar entities can benefit from an internal auditing function, especially when they reach a critical size.

Number of Meetings

The rule of thumb or best practices for corporate audit committee meetings of at least four meetings per year may not apply to not-for-profit and public sector entities. The need to oversee the issuance of interim or quarterly financial statements generates the need for more meetings (or telephone conferences) per year in the corporate environment. The number of meetings per year in the not-for-profit and public sector arena is dependent primarily on how frequently financial statements are issued. The audit committee of a not-for-profit or a public sector entity ordinarily should meet at least twice a year — once to review the external audit plans (that is, the pre-audit meeting) and later to discuss the results of the audit, including the required external auditor communications, and the annual financial statements (that is, the post-audit meeting).

Adopting the Corporate Model

For not-for-profit and public sector entities, the corporate model is a positive innovation that should become a part of the structure of the entity if it is to be effective in today's environment. The corporate model allows development of a level of not-for-profit or public sector management commensurate with that of some of the time more effective profit-making entities.

For example, under the corporate model, the separation of responsibility and authority assists in curing problems inherent in the traditional volunteer dominance in the not-for-profit sector. The corporate model allows the board of directors to concentrate on policy matters and provides that the chief executive officer is the entity's top manager. A guide should be developed regarding board responsibilities to clearly indicate whether management of the entity or the board is responsible for a particular issue. Clearly, the corporate model allows more flexibility, reduces costs, and provides a more efficient mechanism for making decisions. While there may be some concern about the corporate model narrowing the influence and importance of volunteer board members, this approach allows the use of board expertise in the financial and control areas, particularly with the audit committee, to improve not-for-profit accountability.

Here is a summary of the important points of this chapter:

General

1. Many governing bodies of not-for-profit and public sector entities are implementing a corporate model allowing the oversight body to focus on policy matters while the chief executive officer devotes full-time to entity operations.
2. Under the corporate model, greater accountability and quality of services is achieved by having effective controls over (a) financial reporting, (b) compliance, and (c) operations.

Use of Audit Committees

3. All not-for-profit entities that raise funds from the public, receive grants, or have membership dues should consider the need for an audit committee.
4. All public sector entities that are required to be audited or are audited should consider the need for an audit committee.
5. The audit committee should be made up of directors who are independent of management and who are financially literate. Officers and employees should not be members of the audit committee.
6. The responsibility and authority of an audit committee for a not-for-profit or public sector entity should be essentially the same as a for-profit corporation.

Internal Control in Not-for-Profit Entities

7. The audit committee should see that the internal control systems are appropriately documented.
8. The audit committee should devote special attention to controls over sensitive and high-risk areas such as professional and consulting fees, executive compensation, travel and entertainment, and donations.

Internal Control in Public Sector Entities

9. A public sector entity should establish an audit committee as a permanent committee of its governing body.

Internal Audit Function

10. Larger not-for-profit and public sector entities should consider establishing an internal audit function.

Number of Meetings

11. The number of audit committee meetings per year in not-for-profit and public sector entities is dependent primarily on how frequently financial statements are issued.

Adopting the Corporate Model

12. By using full-time management in not-for-profit and public sector entities, and by bringing the expertise of governing body members in the financial and controls areas to bear through the audit committee, improved accountability will result.

CHAPTER 17
LEGAL LIABILITY OF THE AUDIT COMMITTEE
AND ITS MEMBERS

According to state laws, directors, including audit committee members, are fiduciaries of the company and its shareholders.[1] They are fiduciaries because their relationship with the company is based on trust and confidence.[2] As fiduciaries, directors must observe (1) the duty of care, and (2) the duty of loyalty to the company and to the shareholders or owners they represent. The laws of the state or jurisdiction in which the company is incorporated define those duties.

This chapter presents a brief overview of the legal liability of an audit committee member. The chapter also discusses differential liability for audit committee members and how to minimize and protect against liability. The chapter concludes with a section on the use of legal counsel by the audit committee.

Duty of Care

According to the duty of care, a director must:

1. Act in good faith.
2. Exercise the care that an ordinary prudent person would exercise in similar circumstances.
3. Act in what he or she considers the best interest of the company.

Directors must be informed about company matters. They must do what is necessary to be informed, such as asking for information from those who have it, reading reports, and reviewing other materials. They must inform themselves of all reasonably available information and must critically evaluate such information. The duty of care obligates the directors to ask probing questions when circumstances would alert the prudent director to such need. Obviously, the very nature of the audit committee's assignment requires that it follow this admonition. As *Treadway* states (discussed in Chapter 3),

---

[1] One of the best sources for corporate statutes of state law is Cornell University's Legal Information Institute at http://fatty.law.cornell.edu/topics/state_statutes.html.

[2] Directors are sometimes inappropriately characterized as agents or trustees. They are neither since no individual director can bind the company, and unlike trustees, they do not own or hold title to assets for the benefit and use of others.

members of the audit committee must be informed, vigilant, and effective — the essence of due care. In *Caremark* (discussed in Chapter 10), the Delaware Chancery Court stated that directors may incur personal liability if they fail to attempt in good faith to determine that a company's information and reporting systems are adequate.

Duty of Loyalty

Directors are required to be faithful to their obligations and duties. The duty of loyalty requires them to subordinate their personal interest to the welfare of the company. Directors are precluded from competing with companies on whose boards they serve. Their fiduciary duty requires them to fully disclose potential conflicts of interest that might arise from company transactions. In brief, they can not exploit the company for personal gain.

Business Judgment Rule

Directors are not insurers of the success of the business. When they make mistakes of judgment or poor decisions, directors are not necessarily liable to the company for resulting damages. The business judgment rule generally immunizes directors for liability for the consequences of decisions made if directors:

1. Are informed,
2. Make decisions based on a rational basis, and
3. Do not have a conflict between their personal interest and the interest of the company.

Consequently, if there is a reasonable basis for a business decision, usually courts will not interfere with that decision, even when the company suffers a loss.

Cases involving the duty of care frequently pertain to situations when directors engage in one or more of the following activities:

- Competing with the company.
- Taking personal advantage of the company.
- Having an interest that conflicts with the interest of the company.

While the authors know of no case involving the *Caremark* approach, we believe that the *Caremark* duty of care will be extended to cases in which directors have not followed the mandate set forth therein.

Reliance on Information Furnished by Others

Directors are required to act in accordance with their own knowledge and training. However, most states and the Revised Model Business Corporation Act allow directors to rely on information provided by others in making decisions. Section 8.30(b) of the Revised Model Act states (in part):

> In discharging his [or her] duties a director is entitled to rely on information, opinion, reports, or statements, including financial statements and other financial data, if prepared or presented by:
>
> (1) one or more officers or employees of the corporation whom the director reasonably believes to be reliable and competent in the matters presented;
>
> (2) legal counsel, public accountants, or other persons as to matters the director reasonably believes are within the person's professional or expert competence; or
>
> (3) a committee of the board of directors of which he is not a member if the director reasonably believes the committee merits confidence.

According to Section 8.30(c), a director is not acting in good faith if he or she relies on information furnished by others when having knowledge that makes reliance on such information unwarranted.

Differential Liability for Audit Committee Members

At least one publication has suggested that members of a standing committee of the board of directors, such as the audit committee, may have exposure to legal liability under the standard of differential liability.[3] Under this concept, a director assuming special duties is obligated to inquire, learn, and act affirmatively upon matters within the purview of those duties. However, it is not entirely clear that audit committee members, other than those willfully ignoring their responsibilities, have a potentially greater degree of liability than other members of the board of directors.

Unless the audit committee is governed by specific statutory provisions such as the Federal Deposit Insurance Corporation Improvement Act of 1991 (FDICIA), the paucity of legislated audit committee duties suggests that no firm legal basis exists for distinguishing audit committee members

---

[3] See generally Lipman, Bono, Genkin, and Taylor, *Audit Committees,* Portfolio 49-2nd (The Bureau of National Affairs, Inc.— 1995), Sec. VI, pp. A-52-53.

from other members of the board of directors in terms of liability. With the exception of the obligation to oversee financial statements and other legislatively required activities, audit committees should be treated as a standing committee of the board of directors with functions established voluntarily by individual boards. Accordingly, the audit committee, from a state law perspective, should only be subject to the director's general fiduciary duties of care and loyalty, which, of course, are left to judicial definition and interpretation in the jurisdiction where the company is incorporated.

The National Association of Corporate Directors' *Audit Committees: A Practical Guide,* in discussing differential liability, concluded:

> A small number of courts have suggested that service on an audit committee imposes a different level of duty of care. We believe that those courts are mistaken. While it is true that particular situations presented to a board or committee will change the content of what a director should do to meet his or her duty of care, it is not appropriate, and is not good public policy, in our view, to suggest that the duty is not defined in the same way for all directors. In fact, all directors have the same duty to act in good faith with ordinary care in the circumstances and in what the director reasonably believes are the best interests of the corporations and its owners. Audit committee members should not be held to a higher standard. Rather, the usual ordinary care standard should be applied to the particular work of the audit committee.[4]

Certainly a board of directors of a public company that does not establish an audit committee could be subject to criticism for failure to exercise due care in discharging its responsibilities. Obviously, such a board would have considerable difficulty in defending itself, for example, if the company suffered significant losses because of inadequate internal controls, particularly internal controls over financial reporting. Likewise, if a company has an audit committee but the committee does not follow its charter or otherwise live up to its responsibility, the errant committee would elevate the board's liability exposure. In the latter situation, legal complaints sometimes single out audit committee members for knowingly or recklessly permitting the company to issue false financial statements and for not monitoring the com-

---

[4]National Association of Corporate Directors and The Center for Board Leadership, Report of the NACD Blue Ribbon Commission, *Audit Committees: A Practical Guide* (NACD, Washington, DC, 2000) p. 29.

pany's accounting and reporting practices. This typically occurs when the audit committee does not conduct the activities described in proxy statements, for example, by not holding meetings or performing the described oversight activities.

If an audit committee has requirements such as those mandated under the FDICIA, then the statutory requirements should be interpreted as holding all directors, not just audit committee members, accountable. In other words, unless rule, regulation, or legislation creates greater duties for the audit committee than the normal duties required of the entire board of directors, there should be no differential liability attributed to audit committees.

As discussed in Chapter 8, "The Responsibilities of an Audit Committee," the SEC requires audit committees to report certain information directly to shareholders via proxy statements. *Treadway* (Chapter 3) and the *Blue Ribbon Report* (Chapter 5) suggested that audit committees report to shareholders. Those recommendations and the SEC proposed rule generated substantial discussion that such reports would exacerbate audit committee legal liability. However, as stated in the SEC's final rule, audit committee members should be protected under state law by the business judgment rule and also by the "safe harbor" provisions of the rule. Obviously, if direct reporting to shareholders by audit committees gives rise to separate liability exposure, such exposure would be a powerful disincentive preventing qualified directors from serving on audit committees.

Federal Securities Law

Federal securities law has a different purpose than state law in the corporate area. Normally, controversies involving company mismanagement or breach of fiduciary duty by those in charge of the affairs of a company are subject to litigation in the state courts. Federal securities laws are not designed to bring fiduciary controversies into the federal courts. Hence, the wisdom or fairness of corporate acts is not usually within the purview of federal securities law.

Federal securities laws are designed to impose a duty to disclose and inform investors of material facts related to a decision to purchase or sell securities. Consequently, such laws are generally aimed at enhancing the disclosure process and are normally not a source of liability for officers or directors unless there has been a breach of a disclosure duty or other duty specified in the law (see Exhibit 17-1). Hence, nondisclosure of material facts in connection with a breach of fiduciary duty may fall within the scope of federal securities law even though the breach of duty itself is not covered by federal law.

Exhibit 17-1
Director Liability under the Securities Acts

Securities Act of 1933 imposes obligations on directors when the company issues securities. Any purchaser of securities issued under a registration statement containing a materially false statement, or a material omission, may bring an action against the company and its directors for damages.

Securities Exchange Act of 1934 indicates that directors can be liable for making or for participating in a company's distribution of materially false and misleading information.

Minimizing Legal Liability

A number of suggestions have been made as to steps that might be taken to protect the audit committee (and the board of directors) from liability. Simply stated, the exercise of proper diligence by directors generally, and the audit committee specifically, should make the business judgment rule available to protect them from liability.

Obviously, the audit committee must understand the qualifications of the external audit firm, its independence, and the results of the peer review of its attest practice. The audit committee should also review the audit engagement letter. The audit committee should carefully document that there has been proper oversight of the external audit. Review of the audit plan in advance of the audit clearly is the first step in achieving this goal. Also, the audit committee must have a clear understanding of any disagreements between management and the external auditor that arise during the audit.

In overseeing the financial statements and annual report of the company, the audit committee should be satisfied that there is a fair and meaningful presentation of the financial information and other related information. Further, there must be full disclosure of all material changes in accounting principles or policies that occurred during the year. Obviously, all material information regarding litigation, claims. assessments, and other contingencies should be disclosed. In addition, the audit committee should review the recommendations made by the external auditor in its reportable conditions or management letter and should ask management and the external auditor if those recommendations were implemented.

The audit committee should be generally familiar with all significant legal changes regarding the status of the company and its compliance with relevant laws such as antitrust, tax, securities, labor, and other regulatory fiats. Also, transactions with related parties and employees should be fully understood by the audit committee.

All of the suggestions regarding oversight of the internal audit function as discussed in Chapter 11, "Relationship with the Internal Auditor," should be carried out by the audit committee. The audit committee should be thoroughly familiar with the activities of the internal auditor. In particular, the audit committee should be satisfied that the internal auditor's recommendations have been implemented, or the reasons for management's failure to implement those recommendations are appropriate.

If delegated by the board of directors, the audit committee should review all relevant regulatory areas such as tax, environmental, and other areas subject to significant government regulation and in which the company has significant legal exposure. Also, the quality and effectiveness of the company's financial personnel should be reviewed regularly to be satisfied that the company is adequately staffed to produce accurate, reliable, and timely financial information.

If the audit committee diligently works in all of the above areas and documents its work through audit committee meeting minutes and other documents, the work of the audit committee should reasonably ensure that no unforeseen liabilities will result from audit committee activities.

Protection Against Liability

All directors, not just members of the audit committee, must be concerned with protection from liability for actions taken in good faith on behalf of the company. Despite a thoroughly considered decision by the board of directors, a controversial decision or poor financial performance by the company may result in litigation naming the directors as defendants. While the directors may ultimately be subject to protection under the business judgment rule, in anticipation of the possibility of such disputes, legal counsel and directors should determine that certain steps are taken to fully protect innocent directors.

Even if directors avoid personal liability for a particular board action because of the business judgment rule, there should nevertheless be indemnification and directors and officers (D&O) liability insurance to assure directors that expenses resulting from claims relating to their services will be advanced (or reimbursed) by the company or an insurance company. Indemnification (see Exhibit 17-2) is defined as the reimbursement by the company to officers and directors for liabilities (for example, judgments, settlements, expenses, and legal fees) incurred by such individuals in connection with their work for the company. D&O insurance generally provides for both reimbursement to the company for indemnification payments made to directors and officers and coverage for directors and officers in circumstances when indemnification is not available. Directors should determine if the company is providing sufficient indemnification and D&O insurance to protect the director's personal wealth from frivolous, but expensive, legal claims. Unless a company provides adequate indemnification and D&O insurance, qualified individuals will not serve as directors because of the liability potential.

Exhibit 17-2
Indemnification

Indemnification is reimbursement by the company to its directors for judgments, settlements, expenses and attorney's fees incurred by the directors in the course of their service to the company.

State statutes allowing director indemnification are intended to protect directors from pecuniary liability only if the court finds that the directors exercised sufficient care in the decision-making process. Typically, the indemnification provision in a company's charter follows applicable state law or provides for elimination of director liability to the fullest extent permitted under state law.

As indicated above, a comprehensive indemnification provision should be accompanied by appropriate D&O insurance to cover directors in circumstances where indemnification from the company is not available or is not adequate. D&O insurance is also needed to reimburse the company for indemnification payments made to directors. It may also be appropriate to have other insurance, such as securities act liability insurance and individual director insurance, to cover exclusions in the D&O policy.

Directors should insist that legal counsel provide a periodic review of the company's indemnification provisions and the coverage of its D&O insurance (and supplemental policies, if any). Counsel should cover at least the following points regarding D&O insurance:

- Define the insured.
- Define covered acts.
- Define type of policy (claims-made policy or a more comprehensive occurrence policy).
- Define exclusions and deductible.
- Define coverage.
- Review annual cost including recent premium history.

If a company and its legal counsel develop a sound indemnification and D&O insurance program and keep directors continually informed about the coverage available, these factors should assist the company in attracting quality directors and audit committee members.

Use of Counsel by Audit Committee

In addition to providing audit committee members comfort regarding potential legal liability arising from their roles as audit committee members, the availability of legal counsel is essential since a number of things the committee is called upon to monitor or consider have legal and financial implications. In fact, having legal counsel available is critical to the audit committee in demonstrating adherence to its fiduciary duty of care.

Presence of legal counsel during significant parts of audit committee meetings and the consultation with legal counsel during the course of the committee's activities should clearly demonstrate the committee's dedication to performing its functions properly. Also, when the audit committee is directing or supervising special investigations (for example, investigations involving allegations of financial statement fraud), legal counsel is absolutely essential.

For most legal needs, the audit committee can use in-house counsel. However, in-house counsel is part of the company's management and therefore conflicts may exist. Also, in-house counsel may lack knowledge or experience in a particular area of importance to the committee. In cases when a conflict or a lack of objectivity may exist or the necessary expertise is not available, the committee will find outside counsel more acceptable.

At a minimum, the audit committee should have legal counsel continually providing oversight as to (1) the legal obligations of the committee and its members and (2) the legal and regulatory requirements under which the company operates. Further, legal counsel, probably in-house counsel, should keep the committee advised of significant litigation matters involving the company and its officers and directors.

An audit committee would be ill-advised not to have substantial involvement of in-house counsel in its ongoing activities and have access to outside counsel, when appropriate. If using outside counsel, the committee will have to determine when it is best to use the company's outside counsel or to use counsel with no pre-existing relationship with the company. Use of the latter is important when outside counsel has less objectivity relative to the matter or does not have the special knowledge that is needed.

Exhibit 17-3 summarizes the advantages and disadvantages of using in-house counsel, outside counsel, or counsel with no pre-existing relationship with the company.

Exhibit 17-3
Advantages and Disadvantages of Using Legal Counsel Having Various Relationships with the Company

In-House Counsel

Advantages are:
1. Familiarity with the company.
2. May be more accessible.
3. Less costly.

Disadvantages are:
1. May not have expertise needed.
2. May be less objective.

Outside Counsel

Advantages are:
1. More objectivity.
2. General understanding of the company.
3. Specialized knowledge usually available.
4. Higher costs.

Disadvantages are:
1. May have provided advice to the company about the matter and be less objective.
2. May be on the board of directors.

Counsel with no Pre-existing Relations with Company

Advantages are:
1. Very independent and objective.
2. Specialized knowledge of matter.
3. Enhances shareholder confidence.

Disadvantages are:
1. No familiarity with the company.

Here is a summary of the important points of this chapter:

Fiduciary Responsibilities

1. Directors, including audit committee members, are fiduciaries of the company and its shareholders.
2. As fiduciaries, they must observe (1) the *duty of care* and (2) the *duty of loyalty.*
3. The *duty of care* requires directors to (1) act in good faith, (2) use prudent judgment, and (3) act in the company's best interest.
4. The *duty of loyalty* requires directors to subordinate their personal interest to the welfare of the company.
5. Directors are required by the *duty of loyalty* to fully disclose potential conflict of interest to the company.

The Business Judgment Rule

6. The business judgment rule generally immunizes directors for liability for the consequences of decisions made if directors (a) are informed, (b) make decisions based on a rational basis, and (c) do not have a conflict between their personal interest and the company's interest.

Reliance on Information Provided by Others

7. Directors are entitled to rely on information provided by officers, employees, legal counsel, external auditors, or others if the director reasonably believes the information is within the person's professional or expert competence. In addition, directors are entitled to rely on other committees of the board if the director reasonably believes that the other committee merits confidence.

Differential Liability

8. Unless rule, regulation, or legislation creates expanded duties for the audit committee beyond the normal duties required of the entire board, there should be no differential liability for audit committees.

Minimizing Liability

9. If the audit committee diligently works at its duties and records evidence of its work through minutes and other documents, the committee should be reasonably certain that the business judgment rule is available to protect the committee from legal liability.

Protection Against Liability

10. Although directors may ultimately be protected under the business judgment rule, the company should provide adequate protection to directors, particularly from frivolous and expensive legal disputes.
11. The company should provide indemnity to directors to the fullest extent available under applicable state law.
12. The company should also provide appropriate D&O insurance for directors and officers (including supplemental policies as needed).
13. Legal counsel should periodically review with the entire board of directors the company's indemnification and D&O insurance coverage.

Seeking Legal Advice

14. The availability of legal counsel is essential to the audit committee since a number of matters that the committee is called upon to monitor have legal as well as financial implications.
15. The audit committee should seek legal advice on (a) legal obligations of the audit committee and its members, (b) legal obligations of the company, (c) litigation involving the company or its officers and directors, and (d) special investigations of company matters.
16. The audit committee should decide, depending on the matter under consideration, whether in-house counsel, outside counsel, or counsel with no pre-existing relations with the company should be consulted.

CHAPTER 18
AUDIT COMMITTEES AND EXPANDED
RESPONSIBILITIES

In looking at the future responsibilities of audit committees, the authors believe that the committee should discuss a number of issues. This chapter presents those issues that the committee should consider. The chapter discusses environmental risks and controls, industry expertise on the committee, oversight responsibility of systems for compliance with laws and ethical conduct, risks and controls related to new financial information system installation, assurances on management's representations about internal controls and on management's discussion and analysis, continuous or real-time reporting of financial information, the need for an internal audit function, financial risks and controls related to international operations, and the need for independent consultants.

Mandated New Responsibilities

As additional rules and regulations mandate new responsibilities for audit committees, companies will have difficulty in attracting qualified committee members **if those obligations create differential liability for members.** The authors recommend that when new rules and requirements are established for audit committees, the requirements should clearly specify that the audit committee is discharging a part of the responsibilities of the overall board of directors. In addition, the requirements should indicate that the liability of the committee members is not increased because of their oversight of a new activity and that the liability of other board members is not decreased.

Environmental Exposures

As pressures increase on companies in all businesses to be sensitive to environmental matters, audit committees need to be familiar with the environmental exposures of the company. Such exposures easily translate in many cases into significant financial statement impacts. Unless the responsibility to oversee environmental matters is delegated to another committee, the board of directors should consider having the audit committee meet periodically with the officer responsible for environmental matters in the company and determine that an on-going program of monitoring environmental risks and controls is in place.

Specialized Industry Expertise

As business becomes more complex, more emphasis should be placed on specialized industry expertise for audit committee members. That is, not only will members with broad general business experience be needed, but also individuals having particular knowledge of the intricacies of financial accounting and related risks and controls in the particular industry (or industries) in which the company operates will be needed on the audit committee. Certainly, if the company is involved in a specialized industry, audit committee members should be able to probe financial management, the internal auditor, and the external auditor about specifics relating to financial statement risks and controls in that industry.

The *Caremark* Decision

Caremark (discussed in Chapter 10) may impose responsibilities on boards of directors for monitoring all operating systems, not just accounting systems, to ensure that proper internal controls exist. Informed boards will consider whether the audit committee (or another committee) should oversee all systems for compliance with law and regulations to which the company is subject and the system related to ethical conduct (if that is not already delegated to the audit committee). While *Caremark* may not be considered the authority requiring the monitoring functions described in that case, well-informed boards should review the *Caremark* doctrine carefully and create necessary oversight processes and procedures to deal with the apparent requirements of the decision.

New Information Systems

Significant changes and upgrades occur in information systems that affect financial information with increasing frequency in companies of all size. While the new systems provide a high degree of integration, which can significantly increase efficiency and improve the quality of information available, the implementation of new and improved systems have a significant effect on the risks and controls of existing systems. When systems are replaced, the existing financial and operational processes and procedures are also replaced, sometimes with generic processes and procedures provided by the vendor of the new information technology. Such issues affect the company's risks and controls, its financial reporting, and its audit processes. The audit committee should determine that adequate oversight is being done within the company to be sure that new systems that affect financial information are functional and are meeting the needs of the company and preparing it for the continuous reporting which will undoubtedly be part of financial reporting in the not-too-distant future.

Management's Report on Internal Controls

The management report on internal controls recommended by *Treadway* (discussed in Chapter 9, "The Audit Committee's Oversight of Internal Control") is being used by an increasing number of companies as a good corporate governance practice.[1] However, only a small percentage of those reports are examined (or audited) by the company's external auditor. As discussed in Chapter 9, an external auditor may be engaged to express an opinion on the effectiveness of a company's internal control over financial reporting (discussed in Appendix 11, "Example of External Auditor's Attest Report on Internal Control Over Financial Reporting").

As public attention increasingly focuses on fraud resulting from weak and nonexistent internal controls over financial reporting, the authors believe that demand for attest reports on internal control will increase. The authors also believe that legislation, similar to the Federal Deposit Insurance Corporation Improvement Act (FDICIA) (discussed in Chapter 4, "Additional Developments from *Treadway* to 2001"), requiring examination of management's representations about internal control over financial reporting, will be forthcoming for other industries, or perhaps eventually for all public companies, in the next few years. An informed audit committee should seriously consider the cost and benefits of engaging the external auditor to examine management's representations about internal control over financial reporting.

Continuous Financial Reporting

As capital suppliers gain real-time access to a company's financial accounting data, the importance of annual and quarterly financial statements with attestation by the external auditor will be of decreasing importance.[2] Accordingly, an informed audit committee should become familiar with the steps necessary to provide continuous assurance from the external auditor that the information in the company's financial databases is reliable or that

---

[1] David M. Willis and Susan Lightle, "Management Reports on Internal Control," *Journal of Accountancy* (October 2000), pp. 57-64.

[2] Dan Seligman, "24–7 Accounting," *Forbes* (October 30, 2000), pp. 146 & 148. (Note: The 24–7 refers to the availability of accounting data 24 hours a day, 7 days a week.)

the system itself is highly likely to produce reliable data. In today's sophisticated technological world, more complete and better financial data is available much faster than ever before. Accordingly, the traditional annual audit function will ultimately become outdated. The primary function of the external auditor will become attesting to systems rather than auditing the information or data produced by such systems. Audit committees should, at an early date, place continuous assurance on the audit committee agenda so that the company will be prepared to meet the needs of its lenders, shareholders, and other third-party users of financial information.

Management's Discussion and Analysis (MD&A)

The SEC adopted requirements for MD&A in 1974 to have management provide a narrative explanation of the financial statements. The idea was to allow shareholders to see the company's financial statements through management's eyes. As discussed in Chapter 12, "Relationship with the External Auditor," the board of directors and its audit committee may engage an external auditor to attest to MD&A. Two levels of service are available — an examination (that is, an audit) or a review. A review report is restricted as to use and cannot be circulated to shareholders and other third parties. In contrast, an examination report is intended for general use. Exhibit 12-8 presents an example of an external auditor's examination report on MD&A. The audit committee should be aware of the assurance levels that the external auditor may be engaged to perform on MD&A and should consider whether it is cost beneficial to engage the external auditor to examine or review MD&A.

Requirement for an Internal Audit Function

As suggested by *Treadway* (discussed in Chapter 11, "Relationship with the Internal Auditor"), all public companies should have an internal audit function. Despite the recommendation of *Treadway* in 1987, a number of public companies have not considered this recommendation. While it is possible that there will ultimately be requirements for an internal audit function in all public companies, at least public companies of certain sizes, those companies not having an internal auditor should seriously consider establishing an internal audit function. A board of directors and its audit committee may decide for cost benefit reasons not to create an internal audit function. However, the discussion leading to such decision should be documented, and from time to time the decision should be revisited. In any event, the board, the audit committee, and management should periodically address the need to establish an internal audit function. The discussion in Chapter 11, especially Exhibit 11-3, "Checklist: When to Establish an Internal Auditing Function," may be helpful in framing the issues that should be considered.

International Operations

As more and more companies become involved in international operations, the audit committee should be attentive to the risks and controls involved in those operations. Significant changes in economic conditions and currency valuations can occur quickly in the world economy in which companies operate. Further, because of the Foreign Corrupt Practices Act (FCPA) (discussed in Chapter 2, "Early History of the Audit Committee Concept — 1939 to 1987"), the audit committee may have oversight responsibility to monitor a company's compliance with the requirements of U.S. law in foreign operations, not only for illegal payments, but also for the maintenance of adequate internal controls and accounting records in foreign locations as required by the FCPA.

Independent Consultants for Audit Committees

As provided in FDICIA and typically in the audit committee charter, there is increasing discussion of the ability of audit committees to retain independent outside or expert consultants or advisors, other than the company's external auditor, to assist them as needed. Thus, the audit committee should consider retaining independent outside consultants to, among other things, review the effectiveness of the audit committee on a periodic basis and to conduct educational sessions on topics relevant to the committee's charter.

Here is a summary of the important points of this chapter:

Mandated New Responsibilities

1. To avoid differential liability for audit committees, rules and regulations that mandate new responsibilities should clearly specify that the committee is discharging a part of the responsibilities of the board of directors.

Environmental Exposures

2. Unless the responsibility to oversee environmental matters is delegated to another committee, the board of directors should consider having the

audit committee meet periodically with the officer responsible for environmental matters and determine that an on-going program of monitoring environmental risks and controls is in place.

Specialized Industry Expertise

3. The audit committee should consider the need to appoint members having industry expertise.

The Caremark Decision

4. The board of directors should consider whether the audit committee should oversee all systems (a) for compliance with law and regulations and (b) related to the company's ethical conduct.

New Information Systems

5. The audit committee should determine that adequate oversight is being done within the company when new financial systems and upgrades to existing systems are in process.

Management's Report on Internal Controls

6. The audit committee should consider the cost and benefits of engaging the external auditor to examine management's representations about internal control over financial reporting.

Continuous Financial Reporting

7. The audit committee should place continuous assurance on the committee agenda so that the company will be prepared to meet the needs of shareholders and others as those third parties demand access to financial information on a real-time basis.

Management's Discussion and Analysis

8. The audit committee should be aware of the assurance levels that the external auditor may be engaged to perform on MD&A and should consider whether it is cost beneficial to engage the external auditor to examine or review MD&A.

Requirement for an Internal Audit Function

9. If the company does not have an internal auditor, the audit committee should periodically address whether an internal audit function should be established.

International Operations

10. The audit committee should be attentive to the financial risks and controls related to international operations and may have oversight responsibility to monitor a company's compliance with the requirements of U.S. law in foreign locations.

Independent Consultants

11. The audit committee should consider retaining independent outside consultants to review the effectiveness of the committee on a periodic basis, to conduct educational sessions, and to perform other needed tasks.

APPENDIX 1
SENIOR MANAGEMENT ASSESSMENT
BY AUDIT COMMITTEE

Rate senior management in each area (5 = Excellent to 1 = Very Poor).
If the rating is not acceptable, state what steps are necessary
to improve the rating.

Area	Rating (1-5)	Comments
Sets an appropriate tone at the top regarding ethics, accuracy, and truthfulness in reporting financial information.		
Understands and supports the oversight role of the audit committee and fully cooperates with the committee's efforts.		
Understands the audit committee's expectations and seeks to meet such expectations.		
Maintains regular contact with the audit committee chairperson.		
Maintains open dialogue and works well with the company's internal and external auditors and audit committee.		
Is involved (to the extent necessary) with the internal and external auditors and the audit committee in planning meeting agendas.		
Identifies important risks relevant to financial information and other audit committee responsibilities for timely committee review and provides relevant information about such risks.		
Participates in audit committee discussions about key business risks that may affect financial information.		
Willingly participates in analyzing recommendations for change made by the audit committee and the internal and external auditors.		

Area	Rating (1-5)	Comments
Provides frank, annual reviews of the performance of the internal auditor and the external auditor.		
Provides the audit committee with well-prepared (but brief) materials well in advance (e.g., two weeks) of each audit committee meeting.		
Makes carefully planned presentations (with adequate time for questions and discussions) about subjects appropriate for audit committee consideration.		
Has clear and candid discussions with the audit committee on qualitative aspects of risks, internal controls, reporting, personnel, and other important matters relevant to financial reporting matters.		
Consults with the audit committee chairman on a timely basis about important financial reporting issues (including changes in accounting policies and principles, estimates, judgments, uncertainties, unusual transactions, and regulatory matters) and other significant issues that may affect the quality of the company's accounting principles.		
Always consults with the audit committee chairman before seeking a second opinion (from an external accountant who is not the company's external auditor) on a GAAP or GAAS matter.		
Assists the audit committee in its educational efforts to stay current on the company's industry, its business, and regulatory requirements (including changes in GAAP and GAAS).		

APPENDIX 2
SAMPLE RESOLUTION CREATING AUDIT COMMITTEE

WHEREAS, in accordance with the Company's Bylaws, the Board of Directors established an Audit Committee;

WHEREAS, the Board has reviewed and discussed the adoption of an Audit Committee Charter;

IT IS THEREFORE RESOLVED, that the adoption of an Audit Committee Charter is determined to be in the best interests of the Company and its shareholders.

FURTHER RESOLVED, the Audit Committee Charter is approved and the Audit Committee of the Board of Directors shall have the authority, powers and responsibilities as set forth in the Audit Committee Charter attached to these resolutions [*not included*];

FURTHER RESOLVED, that the following persons shall serve as all of the members of the Audit Committee until their successors shall be duly nominated and selected or until their removal by the Board of Directors in accordance with the Company's Bylaws:

K. Tatum, Chairperson
F. Burke
D. Guy

FURTHER RESOLVED, that for purposes of applicable [*identify applicable stock exchange listing requirements*], Tatum, Burke, and Guy are deemed to be independent and free from any relationship that, in the opinion of this Board, would interfere with the exercise of independent judgment as a member of the Audit Committee;

FURTHER RESOLVED, that the members shall exercise their authority, powers and responsibilities in full compliance with the terms of the Audit Committee Charter attached to these resolutions.

FURTHER RESOLVED, that a majority of the members of the Audit Committee constitutes a quorum for the transaction of business, and the vote of a majority of the members present at a meeting at which a quorum is present at the beginning of the meeting constitutes the action of the Audit Committee, unless the vote of a larger number is required by statute, the Company's Articles of Incorporation, or its Bylaws;

FURTHER RESOLVED, that any action required to be taken under authorization voted at a meeting of the Audit Committee may be taken without a meeting if, before or after the action, all members of the Audit Committee consent to the action in writing, and such consent shall have the same effect as a vote of the Audit Committee for all purposes; and

FURTHER RESOLVED, that the Board of Directors be, and each individual director hereby is, authorized to execute and deliver any and all such further documents, instruments and resolutions, and to take further actions as may be deemed necessary or advisable to carry out the intent and purposes of the foregoing resolutions.

APPENDIX 3
SAMPLE BASIC AUDIT COMMITTEE CHARTER*

Purpose

The primary purpose of the Audit Committee (the "Committee") is to assist the Board of Directors (the "Board") in fulfilling its responsibility to oversee management's conduct of the Company's financial reporting process, including by overviewing the financial reports and other financial information provided by the Company to any governmental or regulatory body, the public or other users thereof, the Company's systems of internal accounting and financial controls, [*and*] the annual independent audit of the Company's financial statements [*and the Company's legal compliance and ethics programs as established by management and the Board*].

In discharging its oversight role, the Committee is empowered to investigate any matter brought to its attention with full access to all books, records, facilities and personnel of the Company and the power to retain outside counsel, auditors or other experts for this purpose. The Board and the Committee are in place to represent the Company's shareholders; accordingly, the outside auditor is ultimately accountable to the Board and the Committee.

The Committee shall review the adequacy of the Charter on an annual basis.

Membership

The Committee shall be comprised of not less than three members of the Board, and the Committee's composition will meet the requirements of the Audit Committee Policy of the [*New York Stock Exchange*] [*NASD*].

Accordingly, all of the members will be directors:

1. Who have no relationship to the Company that may interfere with the exercise of their independence from management and the Company; and
2. Who are financially literate or who become financially literate within a reasonable period of time after appointment to the Committee. In

---

* This charter is reproduced from a special edition of *The Corporate Charter,* which is published by the Corporate Department of Weil, Gotshal & Manges LLP. It is a basic or bare bones charter that should be tailored by each audit committee with the aid of counsel. It is reproduced with permission.

addition, at least one member of the Committee will have accounting or related financial management expertise.

Key Responsibilities

The Committee's job is one of oversight and it recognizes that the Company's management is responsible for preparing the Company's financial statements and that the outside auditors are responsible for auditing those financial statements. Additionally, the Committee recognizes that financial management [*including the internal audit staff*], as well as the outside auditors, have more time, knowledge and more detailed information on the Company than do Committee members; consequently, in carrying out its oversight responsibilities, the Committee is not providing any expert or special assurances as to the Company's financial statements or any professional certification as to the outside auditor's work.

The following functions shall be the common recurring activities of the Committee in carrying out its oversight function. These functions are set forth as a guide with the understanding that the Committee may diverge from this guide as appropriate given the circumstances.

- The Committee shall review with management and the outside auditors the audited financial statements to be included in the Company's Annual Report on Form 10-K (or the Annual Report to Shareholders if distributed prior to the filing of Form 10-K) and review and consider with the outside auditors the matters required to be discussed by Statement on Auditing Standards ("SAS") No. 61.
- As a whole, or through the Committee chair, the Committee shall review with the outside auditors the Company's interim financial results to be included in the Company's quarterly reports to be filed with Securities and Exchange Commission and the matters required to be discussed by SAS No. 61; this review will occur prior to the Company's filing of the Form 10-Q.
- The Committee shall discuss with management and the outside auditors the quality and adequacy of the Company's internal controls.
- The Committee shall:

  — Request from the outside auditors annually a formal written statement delineating all relationships between the auditor and the Company consistent with Independence Standards Board Standard Number 1;
  — Discuss with the outsider auditors any such disclosed relationship and the impact on the outside auditor's independence; and

— Recommend that the Board take appropriate action [*to oversee the independence of the outside auditor*]** [*in response to the outside auditor's report to satisfy itself of the auditor's independence*].***

• The Committee, subject to any action that may be taken by the full Board, shall have the ultimate authority and responsibility to select (or nominate for shareholder approval), evaluate and, where appropriate, replace the outside auditor.

** NASD language.
*** NYSE language.

APPENDIX 4
ILLUSTRATIVE DETAILED
AUDIT COMMITTEE CHARTER

Purpose

The audit committee is a committee of the board of directors. Its primary function is to assist the board in fulfilling its fiduciary responsibilities by overseeing the **financial information** that will be provided to the shareholders and others, the **systems of internal control over financial reporting** and over compliance with laws and regulations and the company's ethics programs, and **the internal and external audit processes.** In carrying out the responsibilities set forth below, the policies and procedures of the committee shall be flexible in order to react to changing conditions.

Size of the Audit Committee

The membership of the audit committee shall consist of at least **three members of the board of directors** who are financially literate (or who will become so within a reasonable period of time), including at least one member with accounting or related financial management expertise. Each member shall be independent as defined by [*identify applicable stock exchange*] and free of any relationship that, in the opinion of the board of directors, would interfere with his or her exercise of independent judgment. Members of the committee are elected for a three-year term by the full board of directors based on the recommendation of the nominating committee and serve at the pleasure of the board.

Duties and Responsibilities

1. Provide **open lines of communication** among the internal auditor, the external auditor, and the board of directors.
2. Review and **update the committee's charter** annually. Publish the charter in the company's proxy statement at least every three years.
3. **Meet at least four times per year** or more frequently as circumstances require. Ask members of management and others to attend the meetings to provide pertinent information as necessary.
4. Recommend to the board of directors **the external auditor to be selected,** approve the audit and review engagement fees, evaluate and approve the termination of the external auditor when circumstances warrant.

5. Inform the external auditor that the **board of directors and the audit committee,** as the representatives of the shareholders, **are the auditor's client.**
6. Review and approve all **consulting** (non-audit) **services** and related fees to be provided by the external auditor, and consider the impact of such services on the independence of the auditor.
7. Discuss with management and the external auditor the **rationale for employing external auditors other than the principal external auditor.**
8. Review the **appointment, replacement, reassignment, or dismissal of the internal auditor.**
9. Inquire of management, the internal auditor, and the external auditor about **significant financial risks and exposures** and assess the steps management has taken to monitor and control such risks.
10. Consider, in consultation with the external auditor and the internal auditor, the **planned external and internal audit scopes.**
11. Discuss the **coordination of audit effort** with the internal auditor and the external auditor to assure completeness of coverage, reduction of redundant work, and the effective use of audit resources.
12. Discuss with management and the external auditor the company's **interim financial statements** (Form 10-Q) before they are filed with the SEC and consider the matters communicated by the external auditor based on the external auditor's review of those statements.
13. Consider and **discuss with management and the internal auditor:**
    a. The internal audit **charter, budget, and staffing.**
    b. **Significant internal audit findings** during the year, including management's responses thereto.
    c. **Any difficulties encountered** in the course of internal audits, including any restrictions on the scope of work or access to information.
    d. **Significant changes in the scope** of the internal audit plans.
14. Consider and **discuss with the external auditor and the internal auditor:**
    a. The **adequacy of the company's internal controls over financial reporting** and over compliance with laws and regulations.
    b. **Any significant findings** (reportable conditions) **and recommendations** about internal control from the external auditor and the internal auditor.
15. Discuss **legal and regulatory matters,** including reports received

from regulators, that may have a material affect on the financial statements.

16. Discuss **legal and regulatory compliance systems** with the company counsel.

17. At the completion of the annual audit, **discuss with management and the external auditor** (prior to issuance of earnings announcements and the financial statements):

    a. The company's **annual financial statements.**

    b. The **audit of the financial statements** and related audit report.

    c. **Significant changes in the external audit plan.**

    d. Any **significant difficulties,** including any restrictions on the scope of work or access to information, **or disputes with management.**

    e. The **quality and appropriateness of the company's accounting principles,** as applied in its financial statements.

    f. **Other matters related to the audit that are required to be communicated** to the committee by Statements on Auditing Standards.

18. Receive, in writing, from the external auditor a **disclosure of all relationships** between the external auditor and the company **that bear on independence and objectivity.**

19. Receive, in writing, a **confirmation from the external auditor that the audit firm is independent** within the meaning of the Securities Acts.

20. **Discuss independence with the external auditor** and recommend that the board of directors take appropriate action regarding any independence issues.

21. Review policies and procedures on **executive expense accounts and perquisites,** including the use of company assets, and consider the results of any work in these areas by the internal or the external auditor.

22. Discuss with the internal auditor and the external auditor the results of their work, if any, on the company's system of **compliance with its code of conduct.**

23. **Meet with the internal auditor, the external auditor, and management in separate private sessions** to consider any matters that the committee or these individuals believe should be discussed with the committee.

24. **Report committee activities/actions to the board of directors** at each meeting of the board.

25. Prepare **a report for inclusion in the company's proxy statement** that states that the committee has:
    a. Reviewed and discussed the **audited financial statements** with management.
    b. Discussed the **matters that are required to be communicated by Statement on Auditing Standards No. 61, "Communication with Audit Committees"** with the external auditor.
    c. Received the **written disclosures and the letter from the external auditor on independence matters** as required by ISB Standard No. 1, "Independence Discussions with Audit Committees."
    d. Discussed **independence issues** with the external auditor.
    e. Recommended to the board of directors that **the audited financial statements be filed with the SEC.**
26. Conduct or authorize **special investigations** into any matters within the committee's scope of responsibilities. Retain, when necessary, independent counsel, accountants, or other experts to assist in the conduct of any investigation.
27. Perform such **other functions** as assigned by law, the company's by-laws, or the board of directors.
28. Annually **evaluate (by the chairperson) each committee member's performance.**
29. Periodically **perform a self-assessment of the committee** as a whole.

APPENDIX 5
STOCK EXCHANGES' INDEPENDENCE REQUIREMENTS FOR AUDIT COMMITTEE MEMBERS OF U.S. COMPANIES [1]

Membership Requirements [2]	NYSE	NASD/AMEX [3]
1. Are all members required to be independent (with the exception in 7 below)?	Yes	Yes
2. How long is a director/former employee disqualified from serving on the committee?	3 years from termination of employment from the company/affiliate (Co. A)	3 years from termination of employment from the company/affiliate (Co. A)
3. How long is an immediate family member [4] of an executive of Co. A disqualified from serving on the committee?	3 years	3 years
4. What is the maximum compensation (excluding pension plans and nondiscretionary compensation) for nonboard service that is permitted?	No rule, but a direct business relationship may cause the board to disqualify director	Disqualified if over $60,000 per year

---

[1] Companies that are not listed on an exchange and are not quoted on Nasdaq, including small business issuers, are required to disclose whether members of the committee, if a committee exists, are independent based on the NYSE, NASD, or AMEX listing standard, whichever they adopt.

[2] Each NYSE-listed company is required to confirm its independence decisions with the Exchange approximately once each year and whenever there is a change in the committee composition. Each NASD and AMEX company is also required to certify that they have independent audit committee members, but the rules are silent on the frequency of the confirmation.

[3] Requirements apply to all companies except for small businesses that file under Regulation S-B (generally a U.S. or Canadian issuer with less that $25 million of revenues and less than $25 million of public float, or a majority owned subsidiary of such company). Small businesses, as defined, must have an audit committee of at least two members.

[4] Immediate family includes a spouse, parents, children, siblings, fathers- and mothers-in-law, sons- and daughters-in-law, brothers- and sisters-in-law, and anyone (other than employees) who shares such person's home.

Membership Requirements	NYSE	NASD/AMEX
5. Are business relationships[5] with Co. B acceptable when director is a partner, controlling shareholder, or executive of Co. B?	After considering materiality, disqualified if board concludes that judgment may be impaired	Disqualified if Co. B makes or receives payments to or from Co. A that exceed 5% of Co. A's or Co. B's gross revenues or $200,000 (whichever is higher) in any of the past 3 years
6. Is a director/executive of another company (Co. B) independent when any of the company's executives (Co. A) serve on the other company's compensation committee?	No	No
7. Are waivers[6] allowed for one committee member in rare circumstances?	Only for Rules 2 or 3 above when the lack of independence is caused by the 3-year restriction in 2. above	Yes, under exceptional and limited circumstances for all rules, except for current employee and immediate family member of the employee

---

[5]Business relationships include commercial, industrial, banking, consulting, legal, accounting, and other relationships.

[6]The SEC requires companies to disclose waivers in its next annual proxy statement subsequent to the company's decision to add a member to the audit committee that does not meet the independence requirements. The disclosure must include (a) the nature of the relationship that causes the independence problem and (b) why the appointment to the audit committee is in the best interests of the company and its shareholders.

APPENDIX 6
FINANCIAL LITERACY REQUIREMENTS
FOR AUDIT COMMITTEE MEMBERS

Requirements	NYSE	NASD/AMEX
1. Are all members required to be financially literate (or to become so within reasonable period of time after becoming a member)?	Yes	Yes*
2. Definition of financial literacy?	Defined by board using its business judgment	Being able to read and understand financial statements
3. Is one member required to have accounting/financial expertise?	Yes	Yes
4. Definition of accounting/financial expertise?	Determined by board using its business judgment	Past employment experience in finance or accounting, professional certification or other comparable experience or background (e.g., CEO or CFO)
5. Is the company required to confirm 1 and 3 above with the stock exchange?	Yes, approximately once each year and whenever there is a change in the committee composition	Yes, but rules are silent on frequency of confirmation

---

* NASD and AMEX provide an exception from the financial literacy requirements for small business filers.

APPENDIX 7
ITEMS TO CONSIDER IN A CORPORATE
CODE OF ETHICAL CONDUCT

A company should tailor its code of ethical conduct to fit its unique circumstances and needs and its particular operations. The more common topics included in codes of ethical conduct are:

- Financial, political, and other conflicts of interest.*
- Procedure for reviewing and approving situations that may create a conflict of interest.
- Use of propriety and confidential information.
- Holding outside employment.
- Using corporate assets, including computers, for personal purposes.
- Receipt of loans, trips, entertainment, and gifts from outsiders or suppliers.
- Participation in political and community activities.
- Racial, sexual, and national origin harassment policies.
- Adherence to internal controls.
- Security for corporate assets, including financial and other records.
- Improper/sensitive payments and transactions, including adherence to the Foreign Corrupt Practice Act.
- Fiduciary responsibilities.
- Acceptable standards for services and products.
- Use of drugs, including alcohol.
- Means of communicating with management regarding possible violations of the code of ethical conduct, including follow-up mechanisms.
- Communicating with employees regarding the code of ethical conduct and their responsibilities thereunder.
- Monitoring and updating the code of conduct.
- Employee acknowledgement that he or she has received and read the code of ethical conduct.

---

*Among other things, a company's conflicts of interest policies should (1) require key personnel to disclose relevant outside interests and relationships and (2) regulate employee investments.

APPENDIX 8
EXAMPLE OF REPORT OF MANAGEMENT: MANAGEMENT'S RESPONSIBILITIES FOR FINANCIAL STATEMENTS AND THE INTERNAL CONTROL SYSTEM

[*XYZ Company Letterhead*]

Financial Statements

The financial statements of the XYZ Company were prepared by management, which is responsible for their reliability and objectivity. The statements have been prepared in conformity with generally accepted accounting principles and, as such, include amounts based on informed estimates and judgments of management. Financial information elsewhere in this annual report is consistent with that in the financial statements.

The Board of Directors, operating through its Audit Committee, which is composed entirely of independent directors, provides oversight of the financial reporting process and safeguarding of assets against unauthorized acquisition, use, or disposition. The Audit Committee annually recommends the appointment of independent public accountants and submits its recommendation to the Board of Directors, and then to the shareholders, for approval.

The Audit Committee meets with management, the independent public accountants and the internal auditor; approves the overall scope of audit work and related fee arrangements; and reviews audit reports and findings. In addition, the independent public accountants and the internal auditor meet separately with the Audit Committee, without management representatives present, to discuss the results of their audits, the adequacy of the Institute's internal control system, the quality of its financial reporting, and the safeguarding of assets against unauthorized acquisition, use, or disposition.

The financial statements have been audited by an independent public accounting firm, Burke & Guy, CPAs, which was given unrestricted access to all financial records and related data, including minutes of all meetings of the Board of Directors and committees of the Board. XYZ Company believes that all representations made to the independent public accountants during their audits were valid and appropriate. The report of the independent public accountants follows this statement [*not included herein*].

Internal Control System

XYZ Company maintains an internal control system over financial reporting and over safeguarding of assets against unauthorized acquisition, use or disposition which is designed to provide reasonable assurance to XYZ's management and Board of Directors regarding the preparation of reliable financial statements and the safeguarding of assets. The system includes a documented organizational structure, a division of responsibility, and established policies and procedures, including a code of conduct, to foster a strong ethical climate.

Established policies are communicated throughout the Company and enhanced through the careful selection, training, and development of its staff. Internal auditors monitor the operation of the internal control system and report findings and recommendations to management and the Board of Directors or the Audit Committee. Corrective actions are taken, as required, to address control deficiencies and implement improvements in the system.

There are inherent limitations in the effectiveness of any system of internal control, including the possibility of human error and the circumvention or overriding of controls. Accordingly, even the most effective internal control system can provide only reasonable assurance with respect to financial statement preparation and the safeguarding of assets. Furthermore, the effectiveness of an internal control system can change with circumstances.

XYZ Company has assessed its internal control system over financial reporting in relation to criteria described in *Internal Control — Integrated Framework* issued by the Committee of Sponsoring Organizations of the Treadway Commission. Based on this assessment, the Company believes that, as of December 31, 20X1, its system of internal control over financial reporting and over safeguarding of assets against unauthorized acquisition, use, or disposition met those criteria.

Burke & Guy, CPAs, also was engaged to report separately on the Company's assessment of its internal control system over financial reporting and over safeguarding of assets against unauthorized acquisition, use, or disposition. The report of the independent public accountants follows this statement [*not included herein*].

Chief Executive Officer

Chief Financial Officer

Date

APPENDIX 9
EXCERPT FROM MANAGEMENT REPRESENTATION
LETTER TO THE AUDIT COMMITTEE

Controls

To assure that financial information is reliable and assets are safeguarded, management maintains an effective system of internal controls and procedures. The company's internal control system is designed to provide reasonable assurance regarding the achievement of objectives in the following categories: (a) reliability of financial reporting, (b) effectiveness and efficiency of operations and (c) compliance with applicable laws and regulations.

Important elements of the company's system of internal controls and procedures include: careful selection, training and development of operating and financial managers; an organization that provides appropriate division of responsibility; and communications aimed at assuring that company policies and procedures are understood throughout the organization. In establishing internal controls, management weighs the cost of such systems against the benefits it believes such systems will provide.

A staff of internal auditors regularly monitors the adequacy and application of the company's internal controls and procedures. In our opinion, the internal audit function is adequately and appropriately staffed. Management has not taken any steps to discourage or prohibit the internal auditors from reporting any matters to you.

Recommendations of the internal auditors and independent auditors relating to the company's accounting systems, procedures, and internal controls are reviewed by management. Control procedures have been implemented or revised as and if appropriate to respond to these recommendations. No material control weaknesses have been brought to the attention of management.

In management's opinion, for the year ended December 31, 20X1, appropriate internal controls and procedures were in place and functioning effectively.

Source: Report of the NACD Blue Ribbon Commission, *Audit Committees: A Practical Guide* (Washington, D.C.: The National Association of Corporate Directors, 2000), p. 54.

APPENDIX 10
EXAMPLE OF SAS 60 LETTER

To the Audit Committee of XYZ Company:

In planning and performing our audit of the financial statements of XYZ Company for the year ended December 31, 20X1, we considered its internal control over financial reporting in order to determine our auditing procedures for the purpose of expressing our opinion on the financial statements and not to provide assurance on internal control. However, we noted certain matters involving internal control and its operation that we consider to be reportable conditions under standards established by the American Institute of Certified Public Accountants. Reportable conditions involve matters coming to our attention relating to significant deficiencies in the design or operation of internal control that, in our judgment, could adversely affect the organization's ability to record, process, summarize, and report financial data consistent with the assertions of management in the financial statements.

General

A standard accounting manual should be prepared that describes in detail all accounting policies and procedures of the Company. This manual would be useful in controlling operations of the various reporting units and would be a significant help in training new employees. This manual should include the following:

1. A description and a chart of the accounting organization.
2. A description of duties and responsibilities.
3. A description and an explanation of methods and procedures to be followed.
4. A chart of accounts.
5. Reporting deadlines.
6. Other documents, forms, or instructions for which uniformity is desired.

Sales

We noted that several bills of lading were not dated by the carrier. To provide adequate proof of delivery and to safeguard the Company's assets, all bills of lading should be dated by the carrier.

A number of credit memos were not approved and were not supported with adequate documentation. To reduce the possibility of unauthorized credits, all credit memos should be reviewed for proper authorization and documentation before being processed.

[*Include additional paragraphs to describe other reportable conditions noted.*]

Conclusion

This report is intended solely for the information and use of the audit committee, board of directors, management, and others within the company [*or specified regulatory agency*] and is not intended to be and should not be used by anyone other than these specified parties.

Burke & Guy, CPAs
February 20, 20X2

APPENDIX 11
EXAMPLE OF EXTERNAL AUDITOR'S ATTEST REPORT ON INTERNAL CONTROL OVER FINANCIAL REPORTING

<u>Independent Accountant's Report</u>

We have examined management's assertion included in the accompanying report [*see Appendix 8*], "Management's Responsibilities for Financial Statements and the Internal Control System," that XYZ Company maintained effective internal control over financial reporting as of December 31, 20X1, based on the criteria established in *Internal Control — Integrated Framework* issued by the Committee of Sponsoring Organizations of the Treadway Commission. Management is responsible for maintaining effective internal control over financial reporting. Our responsibility is to express an opinion on the effectiveness of internal control based on our examination.

Our examination was made in accordance with attestation standards established by the American Institute of Certified Public Accountants and, accordingly, included obtaining an understanding of the internal control over financial reporting, testing, and evaluating the design and operating effectiveness of the internal control, and such other procedures as we considered necessary in the circumstances. We believe that our examination provides a reasonable basis for our opinion.

Because of inherent limitations in any internal control, misstatement due to error or fraud may occur and not be detected. Also, projections of any evaluation of internal control over financial reporting to future periods are subject to the risk that internal control may become inadequate because of changes in conditions, or that the degree of compliance with the policies or procedures may deteriorate.

In our opinion, XYZ Company maintained, in all material respects, effective internal control over financial reporting as of December 31, 20X1, based upon the criteria established in *Internal Control — Integrated Framework.*

Burke & Guy, CPAs
February 20, 20X2

APPENDIX 12
INTERNAL AUDITOR
ASSESSMENT BY AUDIT COMMITTEE

Independence

- Does the company have a charter for internal auditing?
- What is the organizational reporting position of the internal auditor?
- Is the internal auditor objective, given the organizational reporting position?
- Does the internal auditor audit any activity that he or she has operating authority or responsibility for?
- What is the level of respect internally for the internal auditor?
- Does the internal auditor have adequate contact with management and the audit committee to ensure that appropriate responses are made to its recommendations and comments?

Resources

- Is the internal audit staff sufficient in terms of size, experience, and budgetary resources to meet the objectives of the company?
- Are members of the internal audit staff professionally certified, such as CPA or CIA?
- Is the technical knowledge of the internal audit staff adequate to ensure that duties are performed correctly?
- Does the internal audit staff have sufficient information technology expertise to adequately handle the systems used by the company?
- Does the internal auditor have a continuing education program?

Proficiency and Scope of Work

- Does the internal audit staff use its time and resources efficiently and effectively?
- Do internal audit procedures encompass operational and compliance risks and controls, as well as financial risks and controls?
- What should be done to improve the effectiveness and efficiency of the internal audit function?
- Was the scope of work planned by the internal auditor limited by management in any way?
- To what extent can the planned scope of internal audit be relied on to detect significant error and fraud in financial information, and material weaknesses in control over financial reporting?

Plans and Reports

- Is there a written annual internal audit plan for the year?
- What is the general process for prioritizing the work of the internal auditor?
- Are there areas of high priority where internal audit work has been deferred due to budget or other resource limitations?
- Is the internal audit work aimed primarily at areas of high financial, business, and regulatory risks?
- Does the internal auditor always issue written reports?
- What is the distribution of internal audit reports?
- Are internal audit reports issued on a timely basis and in sufficient detail to allow for effective action by management?
- How does management respond to recommendations and comments made by the internal auditors?

Involvement in External Auditing

- Was the internal auditor's involvement in the annual audit effective and beneficial to the external auditor?
- Does the internal audit staff appear to have rapport with the external auditors?
- Was the work of the internal and external auditor properly coordinated?
- What is the internal auditor's assessment of the effectiveness of the external auditor?

Best Practices

- Does the internal auditor follow the *Standards for the Professional Practice of Internal Auditing* and the *Code of Ethics* developed by the Institute of Internal Auditors?
- Does the internal auditor make the audit committee aware of matters that are not discussed or on the committee's agenda that the committee should know about?

APPENDIX 13
EXAMPLE OF ENGAGEMENT LETTER

Burke & Guy, CPAs

July 15, 20X1

XYZ Company
Main Street
City, State xxxxx

To the Board of Directors and Shareholders:

This letter will confirm our understanding of the arrangements covering our audit of the financial statements of XYZ Company for the period ending December 31, 20X1. We acknowledge that we are accountable to XYZ Company's Board of Directors (including its audit committee), as representatives of the shareholders.

We will audit the company's balance sheet as of December 31, 20X1, and the related statements of income, retained earnings, and cash flows for the year then ended. Our audit will be made in accordance with generally accepted auditing standards and will include obtaining an understanding of your internal control over financial reporting sufficient to plan the audit and making such tests of the accounting records and such other auditing procedures as we consider necessary in the circumstances. The objective of our audit is to express an unqualified opinion on the financial statements, although it is possible that facts or circumstances encountered may require us to express a less than unqualified opinion. If for any reason, we are not able to complete the audit, we will not issue a report.

Our procedures will include tests of documentary evidence supporting the transactions recorded in the accounts, tests of the physical existence of inventories, and direct confirmation of receivables and certain other assets and liabilities by correspondence with selected customers, creditors, legal counsel, and banks. At the conclusion of our audit, we will request certain written representations from you about the financial statements and related matters.

The fair presentation of financial position and results of operations in conformity with generally accepted accounting principles is management's responsibility. Management is responsible for the development, implementation, and maintenance of an adequate internal control system, compliance with laws and regulations, and for the accuracy of the financial statements.

Management is responsible for adjusting the financial statements to correct material misstatements and for affirming to us in the representation letter that the effects of any uncorrected misstatements are immaterial.

We plan and perform our audit to obtain reasonable assurance about whether the financial statements are free of material misstatements. Because of the concept of reasonable assurance and because we do not perform a detailed examination of all transactions, there is a risk that material errors and fraud may exist and not be detected by us. However, we will inform you of any material errors that come to our attention and any fraud that comes to our attention. We will also inform you of any illegal acts that come to our attention, unless clearly inconsequential.

During the course of our audit we may observe opportunities for economy in, or improved controls over, your operations. We will bring such matters to the attention of the appropriate level of management either orally or in writing. However, our audit is not designed and cannot be relied on to detect significant deficiencies in the design or operation of internal controls.

Fees for our services are based on our regular per diem rates plus travel and other out-of-pocket expenses. Invoices will be rendered every 2 weeks and are payable upon presentation. We estimate that our fee for this audit will be between $XXX and $YYY. Should any situation arise that would materially increase this estimate we will, of course, advise you.

Whenever possible, we will attempt to use your company's personnel. This effort could substantially reduce our time requirements and help you hold down audit fees.

We will also prepare federal and state tax returns for the year ended December 31, 20X1. The fee for tax return preparation should be approximately $XX.

[*Include understanding about review of quarterly financial statements or obtain a separate engagement letter.*]

Please indicate your agreement to these arrangements by signing the attached copy of this letter and returning it to us.

We appreciate your confidence in retaining us as your certified public accountants and look forward to working with you and your staff.

Sincerely,

Burke & Guy, CPAs

Approved

By

Title

XYZ Company

Date

APPENDIX 14
ILLUSTRATIVE FRAUD RISK FACTORS*

These fraud risk factors are not listed in any particular order. Their relevance depends on the circumstances of each company. The audit committee should assess these risks at least annually.

A. Risk Factors Relating to Fraudulent Financial Reporting

Management's Characteristics and Influence Over the Control Environment

- Motivation for management to engage in fraudulent financial reporting. For example:
  - A significant portion of management's compensation represented by bonuses, stock options, or other incentives, the value of which is contingent upon the company achieving unduly aggressive targets for operating results, financial position, or cash flow.
  - An excessive interest in maintaining or increasing the company's stock price or earnings trend through the use of unusually aggressive accounting practices.
  - A practice of committing to analysts, creditors, and other third parties to achieve what appear to be unduly aggressive or clearly unrealistic forecasts.
  - An interest in pursuing inappropriate means to minimize reported earnings for tax-motivated reasons.
- Failure by management to display and communicate an appropriate attitude regarding internal control and the financial reporting process. Specific indicators might include:
  - Ineffective means of communicating and supporting the company's values or ethics, or communication of inappropriate values or ethics.
  - Domination of management by a single person or small group without compensating controls such as effective oversight by the board of directors or audit committee.
  - Inadequate monitoring of significant internal controls.

---

*Adapted from Statement on Auditing Standards 82, "Consideration of Fraud in a Financial Statement Audit" February 1997 (AICPA, New York). Reprinted with permission of the AICPA.

—Management failing to correct known reportable conditions on a timely basis.

—Management setting unduly aggressive financial targets and expectations for operating personnel.

—Management displaying a significant disregard for regulatory authorities.

—Management continuing to employ an ineffective accounting, information technology, or internal auditing staff.

• Nonfinancial management's excessive participation in, or preoccupation with, the selection of accounting principles or the determination of significant estimates.

• High turnover of senior management, counsel, or board members, including audit committee members.

• Strained relationship between management and the current or predecessor auditor. For example:

—Frequent disputes with the current or predecessor auditor on accounting, auditing, or reporting matters.

—Unreasonable demands on the auditor including unreasonable time constraints regarding the completion of the audit or the issuance of the auditor's reports.

—Formal or informal restrictions on the auditor that inappropriately limit his or her access to people or information or his or her ability to communicate effectively with the board of directors or the audit committee.

—Domineering management behavior in dealing with the auditor, especially involving attempts to influence the scope of the auditor's work.

• Known history of securities law violations or claims against the company or its senior management alleging fraud or violations of securities laws.

Industry Conditions

• New accounting, statutory, or regulatory requirements that could impair the financial stability or profitability of the entity.

- High degree of competition or market saturation, accompanied by declining margins.

- Declining industry with increasing business failures and significant declines in customer demand.

- Rapid changes in the industry, such as high vulnerability to rapidly changing technology or rapid product obsolescence.

Operating Characteristics and Financial Stability

- Inability to generate cash flows from operations while reporting earnings and earnings growth.

- Significant pressure to obtain additional capital necessary to stay competitive considering the financial position of the company — including need for funds to finance major research and development or capital expenditures.

- Assets, liabilities, revenues, or expenses based on significant estimates that involve unusually subjective judgments or uncertainties, or that are subject to potential significant change in the near term in a manner that may have a financially disruptive effect on the company — such as ultimate collectibility of receivables, timing of revenue recognition, realizability of financial instruments based on the highly subjective valuation of collateral or difficult-to-assess repayment sources, or significant deferral of costs.

- Significant related-party transactions not in the ordinary course of business or with related entities not audited or audited by another firm.

- Significant, unusual, or highly complex transactions, especially those close to year end, that pose difficult "substance over form" questions.

- Significant bank accounts or subsidiary or branch operations in tax-haven jurisdictions for which there appears to be no clear business justification.

- Overly complex organizational structure involving numerous or unusual legal entities, managerial lines of authority, or contractual arrangements without apparent business purpose.

- Difficulty in determining the organization or individual(s) that controls(s) the entity.

- Unusually rapidly growth or profitability, especially compared with that of other companies in the same industry.

- Especially high vulnerability to changes in interest rates.

- Unusually high dependence on debt or marginal ability to meet debt repayment requirements; debt covenants that are difficult to maintain.

- Unrealistically aggressive sales or profitability incentive programs.

- Threat of imminent bankruptcy or foreclosure, or hostile takeover.

- Adverse consequences on significant pending transactions, such as a business combination or contract award, if poor financial results are reported.

- Poor or deteriorating financial position when management has personally guaranteed significant debts of the entity.

B. Misappropriation of Assets

Susceptibility of Assets to Misappropriation

- Large amounts of cash on hand or high volume of cash transactions.

- Inventory characteristics, such as small size, high value, or high demand.

- Easily convertible assets, such as bearer bonds, diamonds, or computer chips.

- Fixed asset characteristics, such as small size, marketability, or lack of ownership identification.

Internal Controls

- Lack of appropriate management oversight (e.g., inadequate supervision or monitoring of remote locations).

- Lack of job applicant screening procedures relating to employees with access to assets susceptible to misappropriation.

- Inadequate recordkeeping for assets susceptible to misappropriation.

- Lack of appropriate segregation of duties or independent checks.

- Lack of appropriate system of authorization and approval of transactions (e.g., in purchasing).

- Poor physical safeguards over cash, investments, inventory, or fixed assets.

- Lack of timely and appropriate documentation for transactions (e.g., credits for merchandise returns).

- Lack of mandatory vacations for employees performing key control functions.

APPENDIX 15
EXAMPLE OF MANAGEMENT
REPRESENTATION LETTER

XYZ Company
Main Street
City, State xxxxx

[*Date*]

Dear Burke & Guy, CPAs:

We are providing this letter in connection with your audits of the balance sheets, income statements, statement of retained earnings and statement of cash flows of XYZ Company as of December 31, 20X1, and December 31, 20X0, and for the years then ended for the purpose of expressing an opinion as to whether the financial statements present fairly, in all material respects, the financial position, results of operations, and cash flows of XYZ Company in conformity with generally accepted accounting principles. We confirm that we are responsible for the fair presentation in the financial statements of financial position, results of operations, and cash flows in conformity with generally accepted accounting principles.

Certain representations in this letter are described as being limited to matters that are material. Items are considered material if they exceed [*dollar amount*] or if they, regardless of size, involve an omission or misstatement of accounting information that, in the light of surrounding circumstance, makes it probable that the judgment of a reasonable person relying on the information would be changed or influenced by the omission or misstatements.

We confirm, to the best of our knowledge and belief as of February 14, 20X1, the following representations made to you during your audits.

1. The financial statements referred to above are fairly presented in conformity with generally accepted accounting principles.
2. We have made available to you all
   a. Financial records and related data.
   b. Minutes of the meetings of stockholders, directors, and committees of directors, or summaries of actions of recent meetings for which minutes have not yet been prepared.
3. There have been no communications from regulatory agencies concerning noncompliance with, or deficiencies in, financial reporting practices.

4. There are no material transactions that have not been properly recorded in the accounting records underlying the financial statements.

5. We believe that the uncorrected financial statement misstatements summarized in the accompanying schedule [*not included*] are immaterial, both individually and in the aggregate.

6. There has been no
   a. Fraud involving management or employees who have significant roles in internal control.
   b. Fraud involving others that could have a material effect on the financial statements.

7. The entity has no plans or intentions that may materially affect the carrying value or classification of assets and liabilities.

8. The following have been properly recorded or disclosed in the financial statements:
   a. Related-party transactions, including sales, purchases, loans, transfers, leasing arrangements, and guarantees, and amounts receivable from or payable to related parties.
   b. Guarantees, whether written or oral, under which the entity is contingently liable.
   c. Significant estimates and material concentrations known to management that are required to be disclosed in accordance with the AICPA's Statement of Position 94-6, *Disclosures of Certain Significant Risks and Uncertainties.* (Significant estimates are estimates at the balance sheet date that could change materially within the next year. Concentrations refer to volumes of business, revenues, available sources of supply, or markets or geographic areas for which events could occur that would significantly disrupt normal finances within the next year.)

9. There are no
   a. Violations or possible violations of laws or regulations whose effects should be considered for disclosure in the financial statements or as a basis for recording a loss contingency.
   b. Unasserted claims or assessments that our lawyer has advised us are probable of assertion and must be disclosed in accordance with Financial Accounting Standards Board (FASB) Statement 5, *Accounting for Contingencies.*

10. The entity has satisfactory title to all owned assets, and there are no liens or encumbrances on such assets nor has any asset been pledged as collateral.

11. The entity has complied with all aspects of contractual agreements that would have a material effect on the financial statements in the event of noncompliance.

[Add additional representations that are unique to the entity's business or industry.]

To the best of our knowledge and belief, no events have occurred subsequent to the balance sheet date and through the date of this letter that would require adjustment to or disclosure in the aforementioned financial statements.

_____

Chief Executive Officer

_____

Chief Financial Officer

_____

Date

APPENDIX 16
CHECKLIST FOR REQUIRED COMMUNICATIONS
BY THE EXTERNAL AUDITOR
TO THE AUDIT COMMITTEE

A. COMMUNICATIONS THAT MAY BE MADE BY MANAGEMENT
   OR THE AUDITOR

   Was the audit committee informed about:

   1. The initial selection of, and changes in, significant accounting policies?
   2. Methods used to account for unusual or controversial transactions?
   3. The process used by the company in formulating sensitive accounting estimates?
   4. The basis for the auditor's conclusions about the reasonableness of accounting estimates?
   5. Uncorrected misstatements (presented via a summary) that were considered immaterial?
   6. Illegal acts that the auditor detected?

B. COMMUNICATIONS THAT SHOULD BE MADE BY THE
   AUDITOR

   Did the auditor communicate and discuss:

   1. The level of responsibility assumed under GAAS for (communications may be in audit engagement letter):
      a. Internal control?
      b. The financial statements?
      c. Other information (for example, MD&A)?
   2. Information about significant audit adjustments — both those recorded and those not recorded (see A.5)?
   3. Any significant disagreements with management, whether or not resolved, about:
      a. Application of GAAP?
      b. Financial statement disclosures?
      c. Scope of the audit?
      d. Wording of the audit report?
      e. Other matters?

4. His or her views about significant auditing and accounting matters involving management's consultation with other accountants, if any?
5. Any major issues that were discussed with management in connection with:
   a. The initial retention of the auditor?
   b. Recurring retention of the auditor?
6. Any significant difficulties encountered in dealing with management related to the audit including:
   a. Unreasonable delays by management in the commencement of the audit or in providing needed information?
   b. Reasonableness of the timetable set by management for the audit?
   c. Unavailability of client personnel?
   d. Failure of client personnel to complete client-prepared schedules on a timely basis?
   e. Other matters?
7. Any fraud:
   a. Involving senior management?
   b. That is material (not involving senior management)?
8. Any fraud risk factors having internal control implications?
9. Any illegal act involving senior management (see A.6)?
10. Significant deficiencies in the design or operation of the internal controls (reportable conditions)?
11. His or her judgments about the quality of the company's accounting principles?

C. INDEPENDENCE DISCUSSIONS WITH THE AUDITOR

Did the auditor:

1. Discuss independence (including the performance of non-audit services) with the audit committee?
2. Disclose to the audit committee in writing all relationships between the auditor (and related entities) and the company (and related entities) that bear on independence?
3. Confirm in 2. that his or her firm is independent of the company within the meaning of the Securities Acts?

D. COMMUNICATIONS RELATED TO A REVIEW OF INTERIM FINANCIAL INFORMATION

1. Did the auditor or management inform the audit committee about items A.1 thru A.6 that relate to the interim review?

2. Did the auditor communicate and discuss matters in B.1 thru B.11 that relate to the interim review?
3. Were the matters above communicated prior to filing the interim financial information with the SEC and prior to any interim earnings announcement?

APPENDIX 17
EXTERNAL AUDITOR
ASSESSMENT BY AUDIT COMMITTEE

Rate the external auditor in each area (5 = Excellent to 1 = Very Poor).
If the rating is not acceptable, state what steps are necessary
to improve the rating.

Area	Rating (1-5)	Comments
Recognizes the board of directors and its audit committee (as representatives of the shareholders) as the client.		
Understands the responsibilities and operation of the committee.		
Understands the expectations of the committee and its chairperson and responds on a timely basis.		
Maintains candid and open dialogue with the committee and its chairperson.		
Participates in planning committee meetings.		
Has open and frank discussions with the committee on a regular basis about independence and financial reporting matters.		
Promptly advises the committee about significant issues and new developments regarding financial accounting and related risks and controls.		
Presents relevant, organized, and focused information to the committee as required.		
Prepares material to be discussed at committee meetings and distributes material in advance of meeting.		
Includes the concurring partner and others from the CPA firm in committee meetings when needed.		
Discusses disagreements (if any) with management before committee meetings (avoids surprises to the company).		
Coordinates the external audit with the internal audit work.		

Area	Rating (1-5)	Comments
Uses the work of the internal auditor when appropriate.		
Maintains independence and an attitude of professional skepticism.		
Has a strong knowledge of the company and its industry.		

APPENDIX 18
ITEMS TYPICALLY DISCUSSED
WITH THE EXTERNAL AUDITOR
AT THE PRE-AUDIT (PLANNING) MEETING

- The external auditor's responsibility under generally accepted auditing standards for (1) internal control and the financial statements and (2) other information that will surround the financial statements (such as management's discussion and analysis of financial condition and results of operations).
- Any major issues discussed with management in connection with initially engaging the external auditor or retaining the external auditor for the current audit.
- Issues that may bear on the external auditor's independence, including consulting and non-audit services that the external auditor plans to perform for the company over the next year.
- Qualifications/experience levels of principal supervisory external audit personnel assigned to audit engagement.
- Locations, divisions, subsidiaries, account balances and significant transactions to be selected for extensive audit coverage.
- Locations, divisions, etc., that will be subjected to limited audit coverage and the external auditor's plans to rotate visits to such locations/ subsidiaries, etc., in future audits.
- Known fraud risk factors and the auditor's plans to address such risks. (Appendix 14 presents a list of fraud risk factors.)
- Degree of planned reliance on internal controls over financial reporting.
- Coordination of audit work with internal auditor.
- Reliance on other auditors, if any, and plans to refer to such auditors(s) in the audit report.
- Use of experts, in any.
- Significant changes in audit plans as compared to prior year.
- Significant accounting and auditing problems that exist this year.
- Recent developments in GAAP, regulatory requirements, and generally accepted auditing standards, and how they will affect the audit.
- Changes in company activities and operations likely to affect the audit.
- Timetables and expected completion dates, including audit report deadlines.
- Expected modifications in the audit report, if any.
- Special reporting requirements, if any, in addition to the audit report.

- Discussion of audit committee's desire to expand audit scope to address special concerns.
- Other areas to be covered in the audit, such as the company's code of conduct, officer and director expense accounts, and perquisites, etc.
- Estimated audit fee and other matters covered in the audit engagement letter that are not listed above.

APPENDIX 19
ITEMS TYPICALLY DISCUSSED AT THE POST-AUDIT MEETING WITH THE CFO, INTERNAL AUDITOR, AND EXTERNAL AUDITOR

Evaluating the Annual Audited Financial Statements

- New accounting policies and new methods of applying existing accounting policies.
- Effect/implications of existing accounting policies in controversial or emerging areas.
- Reasons for major fluctuations in financial statements items.
- Unusual transactions.
- Significant audit adjustments proposed by the external auditor — both recorded and those not recorded, including the external auditor's summary of uncorrected adjustments that management considers immaterial.
- Significant differences in presentation of information in the financial statements and in other reports, including differences in format or disclosures from prior year(s) or from financial statements of other companies in the industry.
- Processes used by the company to formulate significant accounting estimates, and the audit approaches used by the external auditor to evaluate those estimates.
- Nature and resolution of any accounting or disclosure disagreements between the external auditor and the company, including matters when the company obtained a second opinion from another accountant on these matters.
- Quality of the company's accounting principles as applied in the financial statements.
- Procedures applied by the external auditor to other information in the annual report surrounding the financial statements to determine if such information is factually presented and consistent with the financial statements.

Overseeing the Audit Process.

- Reconfirmation of the external auditor's independence.
- Qualifications or other modifications in the external auditor's report.
- Management's discussions, if any, with another external accountant about the wording of the audit report.

- Disagreements with management about (1) the scope of the audit or (2) the wording of the audit report.
- Difficulties encountered during the audit, if any, that the external auditor had with management.
- Fraud risk factors (see Appendix 14) identified by management and the external auditor and their response to those risks.
- Matters pertaining to suspected fraud, irregularities, or intentional misstatement of financial information.
- Matters involving suspected illegal acts.
- Departures from the initial audit plan, including significant audit fee overruns.
- Reportable conditions identified by the external auditor and whether such deficiencies in internal control constitute material weakness in control (and potential violations of the Foreign Corrupt Practices Act).

APPENDIX 20
ILLUSTRATIVE LETTER FROM THE EXTERNAL AUDITOR TO THE AUDIT COMMITTEE CHAIR RE: REQUIRED INDEPENDENCE DISCUSSIONS

July 20, 20X1

Mr. [or Ms.] J. Smith
Audit Committee Chairperson
XYZ Company
Main Street
City, State xxxxx

Dear Mr. [or Ms.] Smith:

Independence Standard No. 1, *Independence Discussions with Audit Committees,* issued by the Independence Standards Board, requires annual written and oral communications between our Firm and the Audit Committee of XYZ Company (the Company) about relationships that in our professional judgment may reasonably be thought to bear on independence. Similarly, the Company's audit committee charter specifies that the Audit Committee is responsible for ensuring receipt of the communication required by the Independence Standards Board. The Company's charter also specifies that the Audit Committee is responsible for actively engaging in a dialogue with the auditors about the disclosure of any relationships or services, including non-audit services, that may reasonably be thought by the auditor to bear on independence and should take appropriate action, if necessary, to ensure the continued independence of the auditor. In addition, the SEC requires audit committees to indicate in their annual report whether (1) they received disclosures about independence from external auditors, (2) they discussed independence with external auditors, and (3) they considered the impact of the performance of non-audit services on auditor independence.

To facilitate our independence discussions with the Audit Committee, I would like to meet with you to obtain an understanding of your expectations about matters and relationships between our Firm and the Company that you believe may bear on independence. These may include specific areas of interest to you and the Audit Committee, and matters that the Audit Committee and management believe should be considered because they may be of interest to the Audit Committee as a representative of the Company's sharcholders.

I look forward to meeting you to discuss your views on auditor independence and related matters.

Sincerely,
Burke & Guy, CPAs

APPENDIX 21
ILLUSTRATIVE ANNUAL LETTER (REQUIRED) FROM THE EXTERNAL AUDITOR TO THE AUDIT COMMITTEE CONFIRMING INDEPENDENCE

September 15, 20X1

The Audit Committee
XYZ Company
Main Street
City, State xxxxx

Dear Audit Committee Member:

We have been engaged to audit the consolidated financial statements of XYZ Company (the Company) for the year end December 31, 20X1.

Our professional standards and your charter require that we communicate annually with you regarding all relationships between our Firm and the Company that, in our professional judgment, may reasonably be thought to bear on our independence. We have previously communicated with Mr. [or Ms.] J. Smith, Chairperson of the Audit Committee, to obtain his [or her] views about independence matters that should be reported to you.

We have prepared the following comments to facilitate our discussion with you about independence matters arising since September 20, 20X0, the date of our last independence letter. [Or the Firm would indicate that they are not aware of any independence matters.]

[Significant relationships or matters bearing on the Firm's independence would appear here.]

We hereby confirm that as of September 15, 20X1, we are independent accountants with respect to the Company within the meaning of the Securities Acts administered by the Securities and Exchange Commission and the requirements of the Independence Standards Board and the American Institute of Certified Public Accountants.

This report is intended solely for the use of the Audit Committee, the Board of Directors, management, and others within the company and should not be used for any other purpose.

We look forward to discussing independence matters with you at your upcoming meeting on September 30, 20X1.

Sincerely,
Burke & Guy, CPAs

SAMPLE AUDIT COMMITTEE AGENDAS FOR COMMITTEE YEAR*

Activity	1st Quarter	2nd Quarter	3rd Quarter	4th Quarter
A. *Year End Audit Finding*				
Review year end financial statements	X			
Review audit report	X			
Review management representation letter	X			
Discuss SAS No. 60 letter (management report)	X			
Discuss SAS No. 61 and other required communications	X			
Review regulatory reports	X			
B. *Audit Committee Actions Re: Annual Audit*				
Recommend to board of directors that audited financial statements be included in Form 10-K	X			
Review report of audit committee for inclusion in proxy statement	X			
C. *Quarterly Financial Statements*				
Review interim financial statements	X	X	X	X
Discuss external auditor's finding on controls and other communications related to the SAS 71 review	X	X	X	X
D. *External Auditor Independence Matters*				
Receive external auditor's independence letter	X			
Discuss independence letter and independence concerns with external auditor	X			
Approve all significant non-audit services that are to be performed by the external auditor	X	X	X	X
E. *Internal Audit Work*				
Review results of completed internal audit work	X	X	X	X

*For a calendar-year company having quarterly meetings, meetings may be held in January or February, April or May, July or August, and October or November.

Activity	1st Quarter	2nd Quarter	3rd Quarter	4th Quarter
Review internal auditor's planned scope of work for next year			X	
F. *Plans for Next Annual Audit*				
Recommend appointment of external auditor		X		
Approve proposed audit/review fees for next year		X		
Review and comment on external auditor's audit plan/scope			X	
G. *Private Meetings*				
Hold closed meeting with external auditor		X		X
Hold closed meeting with internal auditor	X		X	
Hold closed meeting with management		X		X
Hold closed meeting with committee	X	X	X	X
H. *Performance Assessments*				
Assess management		X		
Assess internal auditor				X
Assess external auditor		X		
I. *Committee Charter*				
Assess the adequacy of the charter for publication in proxy statement		X		
J. *Educational Sessions*				
Orientation of new members (when needed)				
Discuss new GAAP/GAAS matters	X	X	X	X
Discuss new regulatory and industry developments	X	X	X	X
Discuss business risks/controls (including fraud risks) related to committee's charge	X	X	X	X
Visit operating divisions (as appropriate)				

Note: In addition to the above activities, the audit committee should schedule other matters (for example, compliance with code of conduct) delegated to it. The committee should also schedule a special meeting every two or three years to discuss (1) where the committee is, (2) where the committee wants to be based on best practices, and (3) what obstacles must be overcome to move from (1) to (2). The committee should also perform a self-assessment for the special meeting.

APPENDIX 23
SAMPLE REQUEST FOR PROPOSAL —
AUDIT SERVICES

[*XYZ COMPANY LETTERHEAD*]

July 1, 20X2

Mr. Auditor, CPA
Burke & Guy
Certified Public Accountants
[*1234 Main Street*]
[*Any Town, Any State*]

Dear Mr. Auditor:

The management of XYZ Company is requesting a written proposal from your firm concerning the audit of our annual consolidated financial statements and the review of our quarterly financial statements. Your proposal should include fee arrangements for the next three years, beginning with the year ending December 31, 20X2.

To be considered, your firm must demonstrate the ability to, among other criteria, (1) meet our worldwide audit services needs and deadlines in a coordinated and efficient manner, (2) work as team members with our officers, managers and staff, and (3) provide services at a very cost-effective rate. Additionally, your firm must be able to meet our earnings release deadlines, which for the year ending December 31, 20X2, will fall on February 17, 20X3.

Ten (10) copies of your written proposal should be submitted to me in our [*Any Town, Any State*] offices by no later than 8:00 a.m. on Monday, July 26, 20X2. Your written proposal should be no longer than 25 pages. A representative from your firm should contact me at (123) 456-7890 to arrange a question-and-answer session with Company management sometime during the weeks of July 5 or July 12, 20X2.

Background information and proposal criteria are attached. Based on the written submissions, XYZ Company plans to invite at least two CPA firms to appear before our audit committee and our financial management team by September 1, 20X2.

During this proposal process, please do not contact any member of our board of directors, other officers, or employees of XYX Company. If you have any further questions concerning the proposal or the process, please contact me.

Sincerely,

John Doe
Chief Financial Officer
Enclosure

Note: Tax services, if any, should also be included in the proposal letter. Such services should be specified in detail and the proposed fee should be segregated from the audit/review services. In addition, the proposal letter should state that the bids for audit/review and tax services will be reviewed separately, as well as combined, and XYZ Company may chose to engage different CPA firms for each service.

Request for Proposal
To Serve as Auditor
July 1, 20X2

BACKGROUND ON XYZ COMPANY

XYX Company and its subsidiaries have approximately 1,400 employees worldwide with 20X2 revenues expected to exceed $260 million. The Company is based in [*Any Town, Any State*] and is listed on the [*Stock Exchange*]. The Company conducts its principal businesses in two industry segments: (1) oil field services and (2) grain storage facilities.

The Company operates its oil field services business through a wholly-owned subsidiary Company (M). M provides oil field services to the petroleum industry in the United States, Europe, and Southeast Asia.

Through its wholly-owned subsidiary, H Storage Co. (H), the Company operates grain storage facilities throughout the United States.

The most recent Annual Reports, Forms 10-K and Quarterly Reports, Forms 10-Q, for XYZ Company, separate audited financial statements of M and H, as well as corporate organizational charts, are enclosed to provide more detailed information on the various business operations [*documents not provided herein*].

ESTIMATED 20X2 REVENUES

	Million $
M Company	$ 150
H Company	90
Total consolidated revenues	$ 260

TIMETABLE

Below are the key dates in our selection process:

Date	*Event*
July 1, 20X2	Requests for Proposal (RFP) mailed
July 5-16, 20X2	Question-and-answer session*
July 26, 20X2	Written proposals are due 8:00 a.m.
August 28-29, 20X2	Oral presentations of selected firms to audit committee and management, and selection of auditors

---

* The question-and-answer session will be a private session between your firm and Company management. With advance notice, we can also arrange for visits to significant operating units during the week ending July 16, 20X2.

SCOPE OF SERVICES

A general listing of the auditing and review services covered by this request for proposal is presented below:

Company	Primary Location
Audited/Reviewed U.S. GAAP Financial Statements:	
M Company(**)	[*Any Town, Any State*]
H Company(**)	[*Any Town, Any State*]

Other services that are a part of the RFP:

- Annual letters of no default to banks.
- Quarterly letter on the review of computation of X's Preferred Stock dividend.
- Routine meetings and telephone conversations on accounting and auditing issues.
- Annual letter to the audit committee on significant internal control weaknesses (reportable conditions letter).
- Attendance at audit committee and annual shareholders' meetings.

Although not included as a part of this RFP, the selected firm would be provided the opportunity to contract with local operating units for statutory audit requirements, including the following:

XYZ Europe Co.	London, U.K.
XYZ Southeast Asia Co.	Singapore

STRUCTURE OF PROPOSAL

Your proposal should address the following items in a clear and concise manner. Your proposal should be as specific to XYZ Company as possible. Also, avoid generalizing and highlight, when possible, unique features of your audit/review approach as compared to other firms.

- State the reasons your firm should be selected to conduct the audit and review engagements. Describe what you see as the most important issues to be addressed. Describe why your firm can offer the Company the finest professional services for the fee proposed.

(**) To be included in Annual Reports and Forms 10-K and Forms 10-Q.

- Give an overview of the resources and organization of your firm, both audit and otherwise, including a description of your international organization structure. Provide a schedule of your firm's offices to be involved in servicing the Company. Specify to what extent, if any, the audits will require correspondents or others that are not an integral part of your organization.
- Describe your audit approach and how you will coordinate our worldwide audits to ensure the timely and efficient completion of the necessary work. Describe how your firm minimizes the costs and maximizes the effectiveness of the services performed.
- Describe your firm's decision-making procedures for reviewing accounting and reporting matters affecting the Company.
- Describe how you will ensure effective communication with corporate and operating management, our Audit Committee, and firm personnel at foreign and other locations.
- Describe how your firm will effect a smooth transition of auditor responsibilities for this engagement. Outline your approach to the transition process.
- Describe how you will coordinate your work with our internal auditors.
- Provide the qualifications of personnel designated for this engagement, including the primary audit partner, lead manager, and other key personnel.
- Provide a fee proposal for the next three years, for the scope of services included in this RFP, detailed by location.
- For services not contemplated herein, provide a schedule outlining the hourly rate, by level of personnel, that you would bill for such services.
- Provide a draft of the engagement letter required by your firm for the services referred to in this RFP.
- Attach your most recent peer review report (including the related letter of comment) to your proposal.
- Describe any known relationships that exist between your partners and staff and our officers or key employees.

EVALUATION CRITERIA

XYZ Company will use the following criteria to evaluate the firms participating in the selection process:

- *Expertise* — Does the firm have the U.S. and international resources required to service our needs?
- *Resource Dedication* — Is the firm dedicated to providing the continuity of qualified personnel required to service our needs?

- *Responsiveness*—Does the firm demonstrate accessibility, responsiveness, and flexibility to meet the Company's worldwide needs?
- *Creativity/Problem-Solving*—Does the firm and engagement management demonstrate creativity in approach and problem-solving techniques?
- *Culture/Fit*—Do we feel comfortable with all levels of firm personnel? Will firm personnel be well-received by operating management?
- *Fee*—Is the firm committed to provide services at a very cost-effective fee?

APPENDIX 24
SAMPLE QUESTIONS TO BE ASKED DURING INTERVIEW OF POTENTIAL EXTERNAL AUDITOR

FEES

- What services does your fee proposal include and exclude?
- Are you committed to maintaining your fee proposal for a period of three years?
- If not, how will fee increases be determined?

EXPERTISE

- What is your firm's national and international expertise in the industries in which XYZ Company is involved?
- How will you bring your firm-wide industry expertise to bear on the audit of XYZ Company?

LITIGATION

- Is your firm involved in any pending local, national, or international litigation that could adversely impact your firm and its reputation?
- Are any litigation or other matters pending that could detract from the attention of the proposed engagement team for the XYZ Company audit?

EMPLOYEE TURNOVER

- How do you plan to compensate for the expected turnover that occurs in public accounting firms, and how will such turnover affect the audit of XYZ Company?

CONSULTING SERVICES (If Any)

- Does your firm anticipate that it will be performing any non-audit services for XYZ Company?
- If so, what type or types do you anticipate performing?
- Do you believe that providing non-audit services to XYZ Company will impede your independence with respect to the audit of XYZ Company?

APPENDIX 25
AUDIT COMMITTEE SELF-ASSESSMENT [1]

Rate the audit committee in each area listed below (5 = Excellent to 1 = Poor). If the practice is not being followed or the rating is not acceptable, state what steps are necessary to implement the practice, if needed, and to improve the rating.

Practice	Practice Is Followed (Yes/No/NA)?	Effectiveness Rating (1-5)	Comments
Charter and Committee Membership			
Has a written charter that is approved by the board of directors, reviewed annually, and amended as necessary.			
All members are independent.			
All members are appointed by the board or its nominating committee.			
All members are financially literate, with at least one member having accounting or related financial management expertise.			
Has an appropriate number of members, given its delegated duties.			
Members serve at the pleasure of the board with terms of service determined by the board, giving consideration to the needs of continuity and fresh perspective.			
Training and Resources			
Has sufficient training and receives relevant information to discharge its duties and responsibilities.			
Receives training and information on a continuous basis, especially new information about the company and its business.			
Has the opportunity to attend seminars for continuing education purposes.			

---

[1] This form was adapted, after substantial revision and update, from The Institute of Internal Auditors Research Foundation, *Improving Audit Committee Performance: What Works Best* (1993), pp. 77-86.

Practice	Practice Is Followed (Yes/No/NA)?	Effectiveness Rating (1-5)	Comments
Has adequate expertise and resources to handle its duties and responsibilities.			

Meetings

Meets regularly, preferably at least quarterly for public companies, with special meetings called when needed.			
Obtains meeting agendas and related background information prior to meetings.			
Limits attendance at meetings to invited members of management who have reports to make or information to provide.			
Has sufficient time at meetings for questions and discussions.			
Meets privately with management, the internal auditor, and the external auditor at least once or twice a year.			
Meets periodically in private to assess management's effectiveness, the internal auditor's effectiveness, and the external auditor's effectiveness.			
Holds a special meeting every two or three years to discuss best practices and reports the results to the board.			

Activities

Reviews and approves the internal auditing charter.			
Reviews factors impinging on the objectivity of the internal auditor.			
Reviews and concurs with the appointment, replacement, reassignment, or dismissal of the director of internal auditing.			
Reviews the staffing and budget of the internal auditing function to determine if their resources are adequate.			

Practice	Practice Is Followed (Yes/No/NA)?	Effectiveness Rating (1-5)	Comments
Instructs both the external auditor and the internal auditor that the committee should receive timely notification if there are any areas that require special attention.			
Inquires about the coordination of work between the external auditor and the internal auditor.			
Reviews the internal auditing plan to ensure that internal auditing's involvement in control systems and the financial reporting process is appropriate. Subsequent changes to the plan are also reviewed.			
Reviews significant findings from completed internal audits and management responses to those findings.			
Ascertains whether the internal auditor follows the *Standards for the Professional Practice of Internal Auditing* promulgated by The Institute of Internal Auditors.			
Inquires as to the results of external auditor's last peer review, the status of significant litigation problems, or disciplinary actions by the SEC or others.			
Approves the selection, reappointment, or termination of the external auditor.			
Reviews the engagement letter and audit plan of the external auditor. Also reviews changes to the audit plan.			
Inquires as to the extent to which external auditors other than the principal external auditor are to be used in the audit.			
Reviews and approves management's plans for engaging the external auditor to perform significant non-audit services during the year.			

Practice	Practice Is Followed (Yes/No/NA)?	Effectiveness Rating (1-5)	Comments
Reviews the external auditor's independence letter and discusses independence matters with the external auditor at least once a year.			
Reviews with management the company's process of assessing the risk that the financial statements may be materially misstated by fraud or error, and related controls to mitigate this risk.			
Inquires as to the extent to which the planned audit scope of the internal auditor and the external auditor can be relied on to detect material misstatements, including fraud, and significant control deficiencies.			
Reviews with the internal auditor and the external auditor their assessment of weaknesses in controls and the effectiveness of controls over financial reporting.			
Obtains from management explanations for all significant variances in the financial statements from prior year and from budgeted results.			
Inquires about the existence and substance of significant accounting accruals, reserves, or other estimates made by management having a material effect on the financial statements. Also reviews charges made against reserves established in prior periods.			
Meets periodically with general counsel, and outside counsel when appropriate, to discuss legal matters that may significantly affect the financial statements.			
Discusses with management and the external auditor the substance of any significant issues raised by counsel concerning litigation, claims, assessments, and contingencies and understands how such matters are presented in the financial statements.			

Practice	Practice Is Followed (Yes/No/NA)?	Effectiveness Rating (1-5)	Comments
Reviews the income tax status of the company and makes inquiries about the status of related tax accruals.			
Makes inquiries of management and the external auditor about the appropriateness of accounting principles, changes in accounting principles, and the reasons for changes not mandated by standards setters or regulators and their effect on the financial statements.			
Makes inquiries of management and the external auditor about significant accounting and reporting issues during the period and how they were resolved.			
Reviews the management representation letter to the external auditor and asks the external auditor whether any difficulties were encountered in obtaining the letter or any specific representations therein.			
Is always advised of the circumstances causing management to seek a second opinion on an accounting or auditing issue.			
Assesses whether the financial statements are complete and consistent with information known to the committee.			
Asks the external auditor whether the information included in "Management's Discussion and Analysis" and other information in documents containing financial statements is consistent with the information in the financial statements.			
Receives and discusses the information required to be communicated under auditing standards (about fraud, illegal acts, reportable conditions, and SAS No. 61 matters).			
Recommends publication of the annual financial statements in the company's 10-K.			

Practice	Practice Is Followed (Yes/No/NA)?	Effectiveness Rating (1-5)	Comments
Oversees the quarterly reporting process, including the external auditor's review of the quarterly financial reports before they are filed with regulators.			

Reports

Reports its activities to the full board after each meeting.			
Includes a report to stockholders in the company's proxy statement as required by law for public companies.			
Chairman annually assesses performance of individual members and reports results to board.			
Performs a self-assessment every 2 or 3 years and reports results to board.			

Additional Responsibilities (If Delegated by Board)

Reviews risks and controls related to compliance with the company's code of conduct.			
Monitors the company's systems over compliance with laws and regulations in areas in which it has oversight responsibility.			
Reviews policies and procedures for the review of officers' expenses and perquisites, including the use of corporate assets, makes inquiries about the results of the review and, if appropriate, reviews a summary of the expenses and perquisites for the period.			

Future Issues

Considers whether there are emerging issues that will need attention at future meetings.			

Practice	Practice Is Followed (Yes/No/NA)?	Effectiveness Rating (1-5)	Comments
Asks management, the internal auditor, and the external auditor about his or her greatest concerns about the well-being of the company.			

WHERE TO FIND MORE INFORMATION

America Accounting Association
5717 Bessie Drive
Sarasota, FL 34233-2399
Phone: 941-921-7747
Fax: 941-923-4093
http://www.rutgers.edu/Accounting/raw/aaa

Audit Committee Institute
Phone: 877-576-4224
www.us.kpmg.com/auditcommittee

American Institute of Certified Public Accountants
1211 Avenue of the Americas
New York, NY 10036-8775
Phone: 212-596-6200
Fax: 212-596-6213
www.aicpa.org

American Stock Exchange
86 Trinity Place
New York, NY 10006
Phone: 212-306-1000
www.amex.com

The Canadian Institute of Chartered Accountants
277 Wellington Street West
Toronto, ON, M5V 3H2 Canada
Phone: 416-977-3222
Fax: 416-977-8585
www.cica.ca

The Committee of Sponsoring Organizations of the Treadway Commission
www.coso.org

Financial Accounting Standards Board
401 Merritt 7
P.O. Box 5116
Norwalk, CT 06856-5116
Phone: 203-847-0700
Fax: 203-849-9714
www.fasb.org

Financial Executives International
10 Madison Avenue
P.O. Box 1938
Morristown, NJ 07962
Phone: 973-898-4600
Fax: 973-898-4649
www.fei.org

Independence Standards Board
1211 Avenue of the Americas — 6th Floor
New York, NY 10036-8775
Phone: 212-596-6133
Fax: 212-596-6137
www.cpaindependence.org

Institute of Internal Auditors
249 Maitland Ave.
Altamonte Springs, FL 32701-4201
Phone: 407-830-7600
Fax: 407-831-5171
www.theiia.org

National Association of Corporate Directors
1707 L Street NW
Suite 560
Washington, DC 20036
Phone: 202-775-0509
Fax: 202-775-4857
www.nacdonline.org

National Association of Securities Dealers
(NASD/NASD Regulation/Nasdaq)
1735 K Street, NW   and 33 Whitehall Street
Washington, DC 20006-1500   New York, NY 10004-2193
Phone: 202-728-8000   Phone: 212-858-4000
Inquiries: 301-590-6500   Fax: 212-858-3980
Fax: 202-293-6260
www.nasd.com

National Center for Nonprofit Boards
Suite 900
1828 L Street, NW
Washington, DC 20036-5104
Phone: 202-452-6262 or 800-883-6262
Fax: 202-452-6299
www.ncnb.org

The New York Stock Exchange
11 Wall Street
New York, NY 10005
Phone: 212-656-3000
www.nyse.com

The Public Oversight Board
One Station Place
Stamford, CT 06902
Phone: 203-353-5305
Fax: 203-353-5311
For information on the Panel on Audit Effectiveness:
www.pobauditpanel.org

The Securities and Exchange Commission
SEC Headquarters
450 Fifth Street, NW
Washington, DC 20549
Office of Investor Education and Assistance:
Phone: 202-942-7040
www.sec.gov

GLOSSARY

Accounting estimate— An approximation of a financial statement element, item, or account. Accounting estimates are presented in financial statements because (a) the measurement of some amounts is uncertain, pending the outcome of future events, and (b) data needed for events that have already occurred cannot be obtained on a timely, cost-effective basis.

Adverse opinion— An opinion in an auditor's report that states that the financial statements are not fairly presented in conformity with GAAP. An adverse opinion is issued when there is a very material GAAP departure or when there are multiple GAAP departures and, as a result, the overall financial statements are not reliable.

Agreed-upon procedures engagement— An engagement in which the external auditor agrees to perform specific procedures for certain defined parties. The auditor's report is restricted to the defined parties.

American Institute of Certified Public Accountants (AICPA)— The national professional organization for certified public accountants. Its mission is to provide members with the resources, information, and leadership that enable them to provide valuable services in the highest professional manner to benefit the public as well as employers and clients. In fulfilling its mission, the AICPA works with state CPA organizations and gives priority to those areas where public reliance on CPA skills is most significant. The AICPA has over 340,000 members.

Attest engagement— A term that covers audits, reviews, examinations, and agreed-upon procedures engagements related to financial statements and other kinds of information (for example, effectiveness of internal control).

Audit committee— A standing committee of the board of directors that is charged with overseeing the integrity of the company's financial reporting processes. The audit committee oversight responsibility typically includes (1) internal and external financial reporting, (2) risks and controls related to financial reporting, and (3) the internal and external audit processes.

Audit committee charter— The formal written document that serves as a guide to the audit committee in carrying out the responsibilities delegated to it by the board of directors and the responsibilities required by the stock exchanges. The charter should be developed at the same time that the board creates an audit committee.

Audit engagement— An engagement in which the external auditor examines a company's financial statements to determine if they are in conformity with GAAP.

Audit opinion — See *Auditor's report.*

Auditing Standards Board — The AICPA body responsible for the promulgation of auditing and attestation standards and procedures to be observed by members of the AICPA in accordance with its Bylaws and *Code of Professional Conduct.* The board is composed of 15 members, including representatives from the Big Five, regional, and local CPA firms, as well as a representative from education.

Auditor's report — The report containing the auditor's opinion. This opinion as to whether the financial statements are presented fairly, in all material respects, in accordance with GAAP is the external auditor's primary responsibility. Because the external auditor's opinion (a paragraph in the report) is the most significant element of the external auditor's report, the terms "auditor's report" and "auditor's opinion" are often used interchangeably.

Blue Ribbon Report — The report issued on February 8, 1999, by the Blue Ribbon Committee on Improving the Effectiveness of Corporate Audit Committees. The full title of the report is the *Report and Recommendations of the Blue Ribbon Committee on Improving the Effectiveness of Corporate Audit Committees.* The New York Stock Exchange and the National Association of Securities Dealers sponsored the committee at the request of Arthur Levitt, SEC Chairman. The recommendations were directed to regulators and standard setting bodies — the NYSE, NASD, AMEX, SEC and AICPA — that have the authority to mandate the suggested practices.

Board of directors — The ultimate governance body for a company. A board of directors has several basic responsibilities. The board: (1) must provide the policies, oversight, and general direction for the company's activities, (2) is responsible for selecting, monitoring, and changing management of the company when appropriate, and (3) must set the business and ethical standards of the company (usually referred to as the tone at the top). Accordingly, the board must have appropriate mechanisms in place to assure that such standards are communicated, complied with, and properly administered by the company.

Business judgment rule — A rule that generally immunizes directors from liability for the consequences of decisions made if directors (1) are informed, (2) make decisions based on a rational basis, and (3) do not have a conflict between their personal interest and the interest of the company. Consequently, if there is a reasonable basis for a business decision, courts will not usually interfere with that decision, even when the company suffers loss.

Business risk audit approach — In a business risk audit approach, the auditor strives to obtain an understanding of the company's overall business strategy and objectives, attempts to identify risks that would prevent the company from achieving its objectives, and obtains an understanding of how management controls these risks. The business risk audit approach is similar to the approach based on reliance on controls. It differs from the reliance on controls in that the auditor attempts to obtain an understanding of all significant business risks, not just risks associated with financial reporting.

Business Roundtable — An association of chief executive officers of leading U.S. corporations with a combined workforce of more than 10 million employees in the United States. The chief executives are committed to advocating public policies that foster vigorous economic growth, a dynamic global economy, and a well-trained and productive U.S. workforce essential for future competitiveness. Established in 1972, the Business Roundtable was founded in the belief that chief executives of major corporations should take an increased role in the continuing debates about public policy.

Cadbury Committee — The United Kingdom's Committee on the Financial Aspects of Corporate Governance. In December 1992, this committee, which was sponsored by the Financial Reporting Council, the London Stock Exchange, and the accounting profession, issued a report regarding the financial aspects of corporate governance. The Cadbury Committee established a Code of Best Practice that has been adopted by the London Stock Exchange. The Code describes the conduct of boards of directors and requires UK-listed companies to state in their reports whether they complied with the Code and to identify and give reasons for any areas of non-compliance. The external auditor is required to review the company's statement of compliance before publication. The Code of Best Practice requires companies to establish an audit committee of at least three non-executive directors (a majority should be independent of the company) with written terms of reference. The audit committee should normally meet at least twice a year. The membership of the committee should be disclosed in the annual report and the chairperson of the committee should be available at the annual meeting to answer questions.

Canadian Institute of Chartered Accountants (CICA) — The organization which, together with the provincial and territorial institutes of chartered accountants, represents a membership of over 66,000 professional accountants in Canada. The CICA conducts research into current business issues and sets accounting and auditing standards for business, not-for-profit organizations and government. It issues guidance on control and governance, publishes professional literature, develops education programs, and represents the profession nationally and internationally.

Code of Best Practice — See *Cadbury Committee.*

Committee of Sponsoring Organizations of the Treadway Commission (COSO) — A voluntary private sector organization dedicated to improving the quality of financial reporting through business ethics, effective internal controls, and corporate governance. COSO was formed in 1985 to sponsor the National Commission on Fraudulent Financial Reporting, an independent private sector initiative which studied the causal factors that can lead to fraudulent financial reporting and developed recommendations for public companies and their independent auditors, for the SEC and other regulators, and for educational institutions. COSO was jointly sponsored by the five major financial professional associations in the United States: the American Accounting Association, the American Institute of Certified Public Accountants, the Financial Executives Institute, the Institute of Internal Auditors, and the National Association of Accountants (now the Institute of Management Accountants).

Consulting services — Services defined in the AICPA's *Statement on Standards for Consulting Services: Consulting Services: Definitions and Standards* as professional services that employ the practitioner's technical skills, education, observations, experiences and knowledge of the consulting process. Examples of consulting services include analysis of an accounting system, providing computer system installation, and valuation services. (See also non-audit services.)

Control activities — One of the five interrelated components of internal control defined in the COSO Report, control activities are the policies and procedures that help ensure that the necessary actions are taken to address risks related to achieving the company's objectives. Control activities have various objectives and occur throughout the company, at all levels and in all functions. Control activities that are relevant to the achievement of the objective of reliable financial reporting include: performance reviews, general controls over data center operations and system software, applications controls over transactions, security of assets, and segregation of duties.

Control environment — One of the five interrelated components of internal control defined in the COSO Report, the control environment is the foundation for all of the other components. It sets the tone of the company and influences the control consciousness of its employees. Control environment factors include the attention and direction provided by the company's board of directors and its audit committee, the integrity and ethical values of management, management's commitment to competence, management's philosophy and operating style, the company's organizational structure, the way management assigns authority and responsibility, and human resource policies and practices.

Corporate governance — A term used to describe the responsibility for the supervision, control, and direction of a company by its board of directors.

Corporation — A corporation is an association of individuals, or other business entities, formed to carry on a joint enterprise having the capacity to act as an entity or person under the law. A corporation is technically an artificial person composed of natural persons or other business entities, and has interests distinguishable from the interests of its individual members. Traditionally, corporate attributes include: (1) the power to sue and be sued in the company name; (2) the power to hold, own, and convey property in the company name; (3) free transferability of company stock; (4) perpetual succession; (5) limited liability; and (6) centralization of management in a board of directors.

COSO Report — A 1992 publication, *Internal Control — Integrated Framework*, issued by the Committee of Sponsoring Organizations of the Treadway Commission (COSO) to provide a common framework for internal control.

Derivative action — A suit brought by a shareholder on the company's behalf to redress some perceived violations of the law, including a breach of fiduciary duty, or because of a corporation's failure to take action against a third party.

Differential liability — Liability attributed solely to members of the audit committee as differentiated from the board of directors.

Director — A person who manages the affairs of a company and sits on the company's board of directors.

Directors and officers insurance (D&O insurance) — Insurance that assures directors that expenses resulting from claims relating to their services will be advanced (or reimbursed) by the company or an insurance company. D&O insurance generally provides for both (1) reimbursement to the company for indemnification payments made to directors and officers and

(2) coverage for directors and officers in circumstances not covered by indemnification.

Disclaimer of opinion — A statement in the auditor's report that the external auditor does not express an opinion on the financial statements. The external auditor issues a disclaimer when a very significant scope limitation exists. The external auditor is also required to issue a disclaimer if the auditor is not independent.

Duty of care — The requirement that a director must (1) act in good faith, (2) use prudent judgment and exercise the care that an ordinary prudent person would exercise in similar circumstances, and (3) act in the company's best interest. This duty requires that directors be informed about company matters.

Duty of loyalty — The requirement that directors subordinate their personal interest to the welfare of the company. It precludes directors from competing with companies on whose boards they serve. Directors cannot exploit the company for personal gain.

Earnings management — A pattern that may occur when companies try to meet or beat Wall Street earnings projections to grow market capitalization and maintain or increase the value of its stock. Such earnings management practices erode the quality of financial statements.

Engagement letter — A way to document the requirement that an external auditor establish an understanding with the client regarding the services to be performed. (The purpose of the understanding is to reduce the risk that the client or the external auditor may misinterpret the needs or the expectations of the other party.) Exhibit 12-4 lists matters that are normally included in the engagement letter.

External auditor — A CPA or firm of CPAs that audits and reports on the financial statements of a company in accordance with generally accepted auditing standards (GAAS).

Fiduciary — A person who has a special relationship of trust and obligation to others, such as a director. According to state laws, directors, including audit committee members, are fiduciaries of the company and its shareholders. They are fiduciaries because their relationship with the company is based on trust and confidence. As fiduciaries, directors must observe (1) the duty of care, and (2) the duty of loyalty to the company and to the shareholders or owners they represent.

Financial Accounting Standards Board (FASB) — An organization in the U.S. that has the primary responsibility to establish and improve GAAP.

Federal Deposit Insurance Corporation Improvement Act (FDICIA) — The first U.S. federal legislation to mandate audit committees. This Act became law in 1991. The Act's implementing regulations require certain banks and other depositories to have audit committees consisting of outside directors. For large depositories, the audit committee is required to include members with banking or financial management expertise.

Financial Executives Institute (FEI) — A professional association for senior financial executives representing over 15,000 individuals. FEI provides peer networking opportunities, emerging issue alerts, personal and professional development, and advocacy services to chief financial officers, controllers, treasurers, tax executives, and finance and accounting educators.

Financial literacy — A requirement for audit committee members. (NASD and AMEX provide an exception from the financial literacy requirements for small business filers.) The meaning of financial literacy and accounting/ financial expertise varies between the NYSE, NASD, and AMEX. The NYSE leaves the decision about whether an individual has financial literacy and accounting/financial expertise up to the board of directors and its judgment. In contrast, NASD and AMEX define financial literacy to mean a member who is able to read and understand basic financial statements, including a balance sheet, income statement, and cash flow statement. NASD and AMEX define accounting/financial expertise as past experience in finance or accounting or other comparable experience or background that results in financial sophistication. The latter, according to NASD and AMEX, would include being or having been a CEO, CFO, or other senior officer with financial oversight responsibilities. The meaning of financial literacy, even as defined by NASD and AMEX, is vague. At a minimum, the authors believe that each audit committee member should have a general knowledge of GAAP. This knowledge is essential if committee members are to ask probing questions about financial information and are able to analyze responses to those questions.

Foreign Corrupt Practices Act (FCPA) — This Act, which amended the Securities Exchange Act of 1934, has two parts: one deals with specific acts and penalties associated with certain corrupt practices such as bribery; the second, with requirements relating to internal accounting controls (that is, internal controls over financial reporting).

Form 10-K — A company's annual report to the SEC. (Form 10-KSB may be used for a company that qualifies as a small business filer.)

Form 10-Q — A company's quarterly report to the SEC. (Form 10-QSB may be filed by a company that qualifies as a small business filer.)

Generally accepted accounting principles (GAAP) — GAAP is a technical accounting term that encompasses the conventions, rules, and procedures necessary to define accepted accounting practice at a particular time. It includes not only broad guidelines but also detailed practices and procedures. Those conventions, rules and procedures define the standard for measuring financial statement presentations.

Generally accepted auditing standards (GAAS) — The broad authoritative rules and guidelines set down by the AICPA's Auditing Standards Board. GAAS is composed of:

(1) Ten broad standards adopted and approved by the AICPA membership. Of the ten standards, three are general standards that address qualities that the auditor should possess. Three are fieldwork standards that deal with the conduct of an audit. Four are reporting standards that deal with the form and content of the auditor's report.

(2) Statements on Auditing Standards and related interpretations.

High level controls — Those controls associated with the control environment (for example, the role of the audit committee) and monitoring (for example, reviews of actual performance versus budgets) as opposed to specific/detailed control activities (for example, inspection of sales transaction documents such as customer orders, shipping documents, and sales invoices for evidence that control procedures related to the sales transaction were performed).

Immediate family member — For the purpose of applying the NYSE, NASD, and AMEX independence requirements for audit committee members of U.S. companies, an immediate family member of an executive of a company is defined as a person's spouse, parents, children, siblings, mothers- and fathers-in-law, daughters- and sons-in-law, sisters- and brothers-in-law, and anyone other than an employee who shares such person's home.

Indemnification — Reimbursement by the company to its directors for judgments, settlements, expenses and attorney's fees, incurred by the directors in the course of their service to the company.

Independence (for audit committee members)—Members of the audit committee are considered independent if they have no relationship with management and the company that may interfere with the exercise of their objective judgment. Examples of relationships that impair independence include:

- Current employees.
- Former employees during the last three years.
- Immediate family members of an executive of the company.
- Directors of other companies when there are cross-compensation committee links.
- Partners, controlling shareholders, or executives of companies that have business relationships with the company.
- Directors who have direct business relationships with the company.

Independence (for external auditors)—An ethical and legal requirement that obligates the external auditor to have integrity, objectivity, and the appearance of integrity and objectivity from the perspective of a reasonable investor.

Independence Standards Board (ISB)—An independent body, funded by the AICPA's SECPS, that has the authority from the AICPA and SEC to establish independence requirements for external auditors of public companies. The ISB has eight members. Four (including the chairperson) are public members, three are senior partners of SECPS member firms, and one is the president of the AICPA. (The Panel on Audit Effectiveness has recommended that a majority of the members of the ISB be made up of public members.)

Information and communication— One of the five interrelated components of internal control defined in the COSO Report, information and communication involves timely identification, capture, and communication of internal and external information that enable the company's personnel to carry out their responsibilities. Information systems should produce reports containing financial, compliance, and operational information that make it possible to run and control the company. All personnel should receive a clear message from top management that control responsibilities must be taken seriously at all levels. Each employee should understand his or her role in the internal control system, as well as how individual activities relate to the work of others. A mechanism must be provided for communicating significant information upstream, as well as to external parties such as suppliers, customers, regulators, and shareholders.

Institute of Internal Auditors (IIA) — An organization that serves over 70,000 members in internal auditing, governance and internal control, information technology audit, education, and security from more than 100 countries. The IIA's activities include presenting conferences and seminars for professional development, producing educational products, certifying qualified auditing professionals, providing quality assurance reviews and benchmarking, and conducting research projects through the IIA Research Foundation. The IIA also provides internal auditing practitioners, executive management, boards of directors and audit committees with standards, guidance, and information on internal auditing best practices.

Internal auditing — An independent, objective assurance and consulting activity designed to add value and improve an organization's operations. It helps an organization accomplish its objectives by bringing a systematic, disciplined approach to evaluating and improving the effectiveness of risk management, control, and governance processes.

Internal control — Defined in the COSO Report as a process, effected by the company's board of directors and its audit committee, management, internal auditors, and other company personnel, designed to provide reasonable assurance about the achievement of the company's: (1) reliability of financial reporting, (2) compliance with applicable laws and regulations, and (3) effectiveness and efficiency of operations.

Internal Control Letter — See *SAS 60 letter.*

Macdonald Commission — Canada's Commission to Study the Public's Expectation of Audits. In 1988, the Commission issued its final report, which included several recommendations relating to corporate accountability and strengthening the audit environment and audit committees.

Management advisory services — See *consulting services.*

Management letter — See *SAS 60 letter.*

Management representation letter — Required written representations obtained from management by the external auditor as part of an audit of financial statements performed in accordance with generally accepted auditing standards.

Management's Discussion and Analysis — A narrative explanation of a company's financial condition and results of operations. The SEC requires management's discussion and analysis in various reports filed with the SEC.

Management's report on internal control — A report, included in the company's annual report, in which management may acknowledge its responsibility for internal control over financial reporting and comment on the effectiveness of internal control. The management report may be based on (1) management's best knowledge and belief or (2) an evaluation made by the company using control criteria set forth in the COSO Report.

Material control weakness — A reportable condition in internal control that produces a risk of misstatement in the financial statements that is not low.

Materiality — A matter is "material" if there is a substantial likelihood that a reasonable investor would consider it important. In its Statement of Financial Accounting Concepts No. 2, the Financial Accounting Standards Board stated the essence of the concept of materiality as follows:

> The omission or misstatement of an item in a financial report is material if, in the light of surrounding circumstances, the magnitude of the item is such that it is probable that the judgment of a reasonable person relying upon the report would have been changed or influenced by the inclusion or correction of the item.

This formulation in the accounting literature is in substance identical to the formulation used by the courts in interpreting the federal securities laws. The Supreme Court has held that a fact is material if there is "a substantial likelihood that the . . . fact would have been viewed by the reasonable investor as having significantly altered the 'total mix' of information made available."

Monitoring — One of the five interrelated components of internal control defined in the COSO Report, monitoring is a process that assesses the quality of internal control over time. This process is accomplished through ongoing monitoring activities and separate evaluations. Ongoing monitoring activities occur in the course of operations and include regular management and supervisory activities.

National Association of Corporate Directors (NACD) — An educational, publishing and consulting organization in board leadership and the membership association for boards, directors, director-candidates and board advisors. NACD promotes high professional board standards, creates forums for peer interaction, enhances director effectiveness, asserts the policy interests of directors, conducts research, and educates boards and directors about various issues.

National Association of Securities Dealers (NASD) — The largest securities-industry self-regulatory organization in the United States. Through its subsidiaries, NASD Regulation, Inc., The Nasdaq Stock Market, Inc., and NASD Dispute Resolution, Inc., the NASD develops rules and regulations, conducts regulatory reviews of members' business activities, disciplines violators, and designs, operates, and regulates securities markets and services for the benefit and protection of the investor.

Non-audit services — A term used by the SEC to include all services performed by an external auditor for a company other than audit and review services.

Panel on Audit Effectiveness — A panel established in October 1998 by the Public Oversight Board in response to a request by the SEC. The Panel conducted a comprehensive review and evaluation of the way independent audits of financial statements of publicly traded companies are performed and assessed the effects of recent trends in auditing on the quality of audits and on the public interest. The final report of the Panel was issued on August 31, 2000.

Peer review — An examination of a CPA firm's accounting and auditing quality control procedures by another CPA firm or group of CPAs. A CPA firm with an accounting and auditing practice and one or more AICPA members is required to enroll in a peer review program (either the AICPA peer review program or the SECPS peer review program) and undergo a peer review at least once every three years.

Proxy — A means by which a shareholder authorizes another to act as a substitute for the shareholder and to vote according to the shareholder's instructions.

Proxy statement — A document that accompanies a proxy solicitation and provides information on a company's proposed action.

Public Oversight Board (POB) — An independent private sector body that oversees the self-regulatory programs of the SEC Practice Section of the AICPA.

Qualified opinion — An opinion in an auditor's report which states that the financial statements conform with GAAP, in all material respects, except for the effects of the matters to which the qualification relates. Matters that cause the external auditor to issue a qualified opinion include a significant limitation on the scope of the external auditor's work or a material departure in the financial statements from GAAP.

Quality control—Policies and procedures that auditing firms are required to establish to provide reasonable assurance of conforming with generally accepted auditing standards. The five elements of quality control are (1) independence, integrity, and objectivity, (2) personnel management, (3) acceptance and continuation of clients and engagements, (4) engagement performance, and (5) monitoring.

Reasonable assurance — The concept in the standard audit report that means that the auditor provides a high level of assurance, not an absolute guarantee, that the financial statements are fairly presented in accordance with GAAP.

Report of the National Commission on Fraudulent Financial Reporting— The report issued in October 1987 by The National Commission on Fraudulent Financial Reporting, a private-sector initiative jointly sponsored by the American Institute of CPAs, the American Accounting Association, the Financial Executives Institute, the Institute of Internal Auditors, and the National Association of Accountants, now known as the Institute of Management Accountants. Better known as the *Treadway Commission*, the working group had three major objectives: (1) to determine the causes of fraudulent financial reporting, (2) to examine the external auditor's role in preventing, detecting, and reporting fraud, and (3) to identify corporate structural attributes contributing to fraudulent financial reporting.

Reportable condition—A reportable condition is a significant deficiency in the design or operation of internal control that comes to the external auditor's attention that could cause the financial statements to be materially misstated.

Reportable conditions letter— See *SAS 60 letter.*

Risk assessment— One of the five interrelated components of internal control defined in the COSO Report, risk assessment is management's process of identifying, analyzing, and managing risks (including fraud risks as presented in Appendix 14, "Illustrative Fraud Risk Factors") that are relevant to the achievement of objectives. Once risks are identified, management considers their significance, the likelihood of their occurrence, and how they should be controlled.

SAS 60 letter—A communication, usually in writing, identifying reportable conditions. This letter may be called (1) an SAS 60 letter, (2) a reportable conditions letter, (3) an internal control letter, or (4) a management letter. Some of these letters, especially the management letter, may be more inclusive than a SAS 60 letter because they contain items other than reportable conditions related to financial reporting. For example, a management letter may identify problems noted in operational and administrative areas such as the need to develop better strategic plans. Appendix 10, "Example of SAS 60 Letter," contains a sample reportable conditions letter.

SAS 71 review — A required review of interim or quarterly financial information that enables the external auditor to provide limited assurance that no material modifications need to be made to the information to conform such information to GAAP. The external auditor reaches this conclusion by performing inquiry and analytical procedures.

Securities and Exchange Commission (SEC) — The federal agency with the primary mission of protecting investors and maintaining the integrity of the U.S. securities markets. Congress established the SEC in 1934 to enforce the Securities Act of 1933 and the Securities Exchange Act of 1934.

The SEC Practice Section (SECPS) — A division of the AICPA that was founded in 1977 as a voluntary organization of CPA firms striving for professional excellence in the auditing and attest services they provide to SEC registrants. In January 1990, AICPA members adopted a bylaw change requiring members that engage in the practice of public accounting with a firm auditing one or more SEC clients to practice in a firm that is a member of SECPS. Membership in the Section and participation in its Peer Review program complement the self-regulatory activities of the AICPA and the POB to ensure a quality practice before the SEC. There are approximately 1,300 CPA firms that are members of SECPS.

Sentencing Guidelines — The Federal Sentencing Guidelines for Organizations are issued by the U.S. Federal Sentencing Commission for judges to use in sentencing organizations convicted of crimes. The Sentencing Guidelines, which apply to virtually every type of organization (such as corporations and partnerships) and every type of business crime (such as antitrust, securities violations, wire and mail fraud, commercial bribery, money laundering, and kickbacks), provide specific rules for sentences of organizational defendants. Penalties under the guidelines range from heavy fines that can reach hundreds of millions of dollars to a possible "death penalty" for a company. In addition to paying fines, companies can be ordered to make restitution to victims and may be subject to supervised probation.

Small business filer — An issuer that (1) has revenue of less than $25 million and public float (the aggregate market value of voting common stock held by nonaffiliates) of less than $25 million, (2) is a U.S. or Canadian issuer, and

(3) if the entity is a majority-owned subsidiary, has a parent company that is a small business issuer, and (4) is not an investment company. Small business filers are exempt from certain NASD and AMEX requirements, as discussed in Chapter 5.

Statements on Auditing Standards (SASs) — Statements issued by the AICPA's Auditing Standards Board to provide CPAs with authoritative guidance regarding application of generally accepted auditing standards to the audit of historical financial statements.

Statements on Standards for Attestation Engagements (SSAEs) — Statements issued by the AICPA's Auditing Standards Board to provide authoritative guidance to CPAs engaged to perform attest services on information other than historical financial statements.

Substantive tests — Audit tests to determine if material dollar or disclosure misstatements exist in financial statements amounts.

Tests of controls — Audit tests to determine the effectiveness of the design and operation of internal controls.

Tone at the top — The tone set by top management, including the board of directors and its audit committee, that influences the corporate environment within which financial reporting occurs. To set the right tone, top management must identify and assess the factors that could lead to fraudulent financial reporting.

Treadway Commission — See *Report of the National Commission on Fraudulent Financial Reporting.*

Unqualified opinion — An opinion in an auditor's report which states that the financial statements conform with GAAP, in all material respects.

LIST OF ACRONYMS

AICPA — American Institute of Certified Public Accountants

ALI — American Law Institute

AMEX — American Stock Exchange

ASB — Auditing Standards Board

CEO — Chief executive officer

CFO — Chief financial officer

CIA — Certified internal auditor

CICA — Canadian Institute of Chartered Accountants

CMA — Certified Management Accountant

COSO — Committee of Sponsoring Organizations of the Treadway Commission

CPA — Certified Public Accountant

D&O Insurance — Directors and Officers Insurance

FCPA — Foreign Corrupt Practices Act

FDICIA — Federal Deposit Insurance Corporation Improvement Act

GAAP — Generally accepted accounting principles

GAAS — Generally accepted auditing standards

IIA — Institute of Internal Auditors

ISB — Independence Standards Board

MD&A — Management's Discussion and Analysis

NACD — National Association of Corporate Directors

NASD — National Association of Securities Dealers

NASDAQ — National Association of Securities Dealers Automated Quotation System.

NYSE — New York Stock Exchange

POB — Public Oversight Board of the AICPA's SEC Practice Section

SAS — Statement on Auditing Standards

SEC — Securities and Exchange Commission

SECPS — SEC Practice Section of the AICPA

SIAS — Statement on Internal Auditing Standards

SSAE — Statement on Standards for Attestation Engagements

INDEX